# THE BACKGROUND

OF

# ENGLISH LITERATURE

# THE BACKGROUND
## OF
# ENGLISH LITERATURE

# CLASSICAL & ROMANTIC

AND OTHER COLLECTED ESSAYS
& ADDRESSES

*By*

Sir HERBERT GRIERSON
LL.D., LITT.D., LITT. ET PHIL.D., F.B.A.

CHATTO AND WINDUS
LONDON
1970

PUBLISHED BY
CHATTO AND WINDUS LTD
LONDON

★

CLARKE, IRWIN AND CO LTD
TORONTO


ISBN 0 7011 0724 3


FIRST PUBLISHED, 1925
SECOND EDITION, 1934
REPRINTED 1950, 1960, 1962 & 1970

Printed in Great Britain by
Lewis Reprints Limited, Port Talbot,
Glamorgan

TO

M. L. G.

# PREFACE

ALL of the essays here brought together have been printed in separate brochures. The first was my opening lecture in the English classroom at Edinburgh University. I have dropped some paragraphs dealing with the work of my predecessor, Professor Saintsbury, as being of occasional and local interest. Professor Saintsbury needs no eulogy of mine. It was a piece of good fortune for me personally that at the time I returned to Scotland a comparatively young and very inexperienced professor, he also came thither, young as a professor but already mature in his knowledge of literature, classical and modern. The second address was written for the Edinburgh centre of the English Association in the year of Cervantes' centenary. It was read in London the following year, and printed by the English Association in 1921. *Lord Byron : Arnold and Swinburne* was delivered as the Warton Lecture at the British Academy in 1920. *The Metaphysical Poets* is an introduction to a selection from these poets, reprinted here with the kind permission of the Oxford University Press. *Byron and English Society* was the Byron Lecture given at Nottingham University College in 1922. *Blake and Gray* is the introduction to the Oxford University Press reproduction of the designs by Blake to Gray's poems, discovered at Hamilton Palace after they had disappeared for a hundred years. For permission to reprint this I am also indebted to the Oxford University Press. *Classical and Romantic* was the Leslie Stephen Lecture at Cambridge University in 1923, and was

PREFACE

printed separately by the Cambridge University Press.
All of the lectures—except that on *Don Quixote*—have
been retouched here and there when I thought I could
express my meaning more clearly or illustrate it more
aptly. Some paragraphs have been added to that on
*Blake and Gray*.

H. J. C. GRIERSON

1925

# CONTENTS

# THE BACKGROUND
## OF
# ENGLISH LITERATURE

To succeed to any portion of the work of so great a
scholar as Professor Saintsbury and, in doing so, to cast
the eye back over his multifarious activities is to be
reminded of the vastness and complexity of the field to
be surveyed by a professor of English Literature. Instead of selecting, by way of introduction to our work
together, some single author or fragment of the subject, I
am tempted to dwell to-day upon an aspect of English
Literature taken as an historic whole and to endeavour
to define and consider it apart, its character and its changing manifestations. Every writer, be he poet or plain
prose chronicler or expounder, writes or speaks to be understood; and of them all the poet is most concerned to be
rightly understood. "Oratory is heard; poetry is overheard." The orator speaks to Tom, Dick, and Harry,
content to sway them to his will even if he despise them
for being swayed; and he is not seldom most successful
when least understood. But the poet writes for those
who have ears to hear; you must love him or leave him
alone; you must appreciate the colour of every word he
uses, the value of every cadence. To say, indeed, as
some have, Keble for example, that the poet contemplates
no audience at all, writes only for his own ear, is surely
a mistake. Why all this toil to tell himself what he
already knows. The desire to express oneself is the
desire to communicate. The poet does not really wish

to cry his sorrows to the desert air; to give them " to be
blown about at every breaking-up of the monsoon over
a remote and unhearing ocean ". His words may be
arrows φωνᾶντα συνετοῖσιν· ἐς δὲ τὸ πᾶν ἑρμηνέων
χατίζει, with a voice for the wise, but for the multitude
needing interpreters. But it is for those wise ones he
writes, to their ears that he attunes his words. His audience may be ideal, but he lives and works in the hope
of its realising, and no one is more unhappy than the poet
whose words awaken no echo in the heart of his fellows.
It is then that he turns to Nature to seek the illusion
of sympathy:

> Away, away, from men and towns,
> To the wild wood and the downs—
> To the silent wilderness
> Where the soul need not repress
> Its music lest it should not find
> An echo in another's mind.

Now the most ordinary speaker or penny-a-liner and
the greatest poet are alike linked to their audience by
certain media of which the first is the language they use.
English journalist and English poet use the English
language because they are writing for English-speaking
people, though there may be all the difference in the
world in the degree of precision and delicacy with which
they use that language. The definable meaning of words,
the plain rules of grammar may be enough for the one;
for the other these may be quite subordinate to subtle
shades of colour or association, the rightly ordered flow.
It will be our business to consider throughout the years,
how the English language may be used, and how by
different writers it has been used. But what I wish to

insist on to-day is that this is not all, that the speaker and writer is connected with his audience by other links as well as that of a common language,—by a body of common knowledge and feeling to which he may make direct or indirect allusion confident that he will be understood, and not only this, but more or less accurately aware of the effect which the allusion will produce. He knows roughly what his audience knows, and what are their prejudices. A people is made one, less by community of blood than by a common tradition. From whatever sources they may draw their blood an American audience will respond to the words " Washington ", " Lincoln ", in a fashion as definitely American as the response of a Scottish audience to the names of " Wallace ", " Bannockburn ", " Burns " will be Scottish; or, to widen the circle, an educated Japanese or Chinese reader of our literature will never quite feel, as a Western European reader can, the effect of an allusion to classical mythology, Bible story, or Church history. To follow all the implications of this, or trace the circles within circles of common sympathies and therefore intelligible and effective allusion, would be an impossible task. What I wish to draw your attention to to-day is some of the main features in the complex background of English Literature and the changes which these have undergone in the course of the centuries since, say, Chaucer; what were and are some of the chief historical, philosophic, and scientific, but especially the literary, allusions which an English or Scottish writer could assume that his audience would understand, and on the right response to which his words would largely depend for their effect.

Of these vistas in the background of our literature

there is one which has always arrested the attention of those who approach the study of literature in an *a priori* fashion.   It is a very common assumption that a knowledge of political history is essential to a right understanding of literature.   It was this assumption which induced the Commissioners of 1889 to link the Honours study of English to the study of British History.   It was not a happy move, and the intimate connection of the two subjects has been abandoned.   Professor Saintsbury stated the truth wittily when he declared, in a lecture on the subject, that if the Honours English candidate went to the door of the history classroom and took off his hat politely, he might be considered as having discharged his obligations.   For in truth the connection of English literature with British political history is either of the slightest, or of a very indirect kind.   Chaucer lived through a great portion of the French wars of Edward III., but his poetry does not contain a single allusion to them, and but for other sources we should never have known that he had served and been made prisoner.   The connection of his work with political history is indirect. He was sent as an ambassador to Italy, and there became acquainted with the poetry of Dante, and Petrarch, and Boccaccio.   Our literary histories dilate upon the spacious times of Queen Elizabeth, and link the defeat of the Armada with the triumphs of Marlowe and Shakespeare, and the beauties of the *Faerie Queene*.   But when we look into the matter we find that, with the notable exception of Shakespeare's " Histories ", the great poetry directly inspired by patriotic or imperial feeling is small in amount.   Raleigh and Sidney, when they were not engaged in deeds " of derring do " by land or sea, were piping to their ladies in pastoral strains, or weaving end-less romances in silken phrases. The temper of the civil wars and the character of the Cromwellian captains are doubtless reflected in *Paradise Lost* and the infernal angels; but how little the civil wars count for directly in that great work compared with the Bible and the poetry of Greece and Rome! But for the accident that Burke's oratory is also literature, there would be no record in English literature of our eighteenth-century wars but Collins's lovely lyric, " How sleep the brave who sink to rest ", and that could have been written at any time.

The French Revolution and the Napoleonic wars have doubtless left a deeper mark on our literature. Yet here again it is not either the incidents or the politics which are of importance, Trafalgar or Waterloo, or the Congress of Vienna. What is the record of Trafalgar in our literature? The battle of the Baltic and our naval triumphs inspired two fine songs by Campbell. Waterloo is recorded in some magnificent rhetorical stanzas of Byron. There are two things that did leave their impress on our poetry, the ideas behind the events— liberty and nationality—and the dazzling personality of Napoleon. To the former the poetry of Burns and Coleridge and Wordsworth and Byron and Shelley reacted in complex and thrilling tones. The latter produced one fine lyric by Shelley. But perhaps the greatest poet of the period, Keats, went his way, like the Elizabethans, careless of political and martial turmoil, intent on the quest of beauty. To Jane Austen the naval wars of England were important only as a means of supplying her heroes with prize-money, and so enabling them to marry her quick-witted, satirical heroines.

B

The same fact might be illustrated by two converse arguments. The poetry that does concern itself with political events is generally of small worth. The events which bulk largely in literature are frequently of little importance to the historian. The border frays of Scots and English, the Jacobite rebellions, are of more interest to the poet than importance to the historian. Langland and Gower and Minot cannot rank as poets with Chaucer. Spenser's *Faerie Queene* only suffered by his determination to contaminate romantic legend with contemporary history, and to suggest that his paladins were politicians in disguise. Didactic and Satire, the dreariest and most ephemeral kinds of poetry, have been the offspring of the marriage of history and literature. There seem to be two main ways in which historical events can directly inspire great poetry: when the events are read as the comment on some great spiritual, religious or moral, truth, as the Jewish prophets read the history of their people, Dante the history of Florence; or when time has elapsed, when events are seen in an ennobling perspective, when the passion of the moment has subsided yielding place to emotion recollected in tranquillity.

A more important and luminous vista in the background of our literature is constituted by the philosophic and scientific conceptions current in the age in which this or that poet lived. All great poetry is in some measure metaphysical. It was a strange misconception of Macaulay's that science and poetry are necessarily antagonistic. Wordsworth came nearer to the truth when he spoke of poetry as " the impassioned expression which is in the countenance of all science ". How could it well be otherwise? For what is science but the attempt of the human mind to pierce the surface of things that presents itself to the senses, and to form a coherent conception of the framework of the universe in which we live, of the relation of its parts to each other and to the mind of man? And the greatest instrument at the disposal of the investigator is the imagination. The imagination creates the hypotheses which experiment must test; and the history of science from Empedocles and Pythagoras to Lord Kelvin and Herbert Spencer bears witness to the impatience of the imagination, its unwillingness to accept the limitations of tested and assured knowledge. What are all our philosophies, Greek or German, but the creations of the imagination, overleaping the bounds of ascertained truth, and building for its own satisfaction an ordered universe of atoms or ideas or categories. But the poet's imagination differs from the philosopher's only in its love for the concrete, and in that it works at the dictation of feeling, seeking the satisfaction not of the intellect alone but of the heart and of the sense of beauty. And so it has always been that, if the poet is little interested in the weary process of testing and rejecting, which forms so large a part of scientific investigation, he is deeply interested in scientific discovery if it touch human interests; [1] and not only so

[1] " Poetry is the first and last of all knowledge—it is as immortal as the heart of man. If the labours of men of science should ever create any material revolution, direct or indirect, in our condition, and in the impressions which we habitually receive, the poet will sleep then no more than at present: he will be ready to follow the steps of the man of science, not only in those general and indirect effects, but he will be at his side, carrying sensation into the midst of the objects of science itself. The remotest discoveries of the Chemist, the Botanist, the Mineralogist, will be as proper objects of the poet's

but in scientific hypotheses, whether of atoms or electrons, of humours or bacilli, of cataclysm or evolution, of a geocentric or a heliocentric system, on condition that these have become familiar to the popular mind or charm the imagination by their simplicity and sweep.

Turn where you will in our older poets, and you will find that to appreciate their imagery you must know something of that old physiology which, derived from the ancients, was transmitted with little modification through the Middle Ages, to disappear—if so much can be said—only as the seventeenth century drew to a close. What does Shakespeare mean when he writes:

> His life was gentle ; and the elements
> So mix'd in him, that Nature might stand up
> And say to all the world, " This was a Man! "

or,

> His two chamberlains
> Will I with wine and wassail so convince
> That memory, the warder of the brain,
> Shall be a fume, and the receipt of reason
> A limbeck only;

or another poet when he writes:

---

art as any upon which it can be employed, if the time should ever come when these shall be familiar to us, and the relations under which they are contemplated by the followers of these respective sciences shall be manifestly and palpably material to us as enjoying and suffering beings. If the time should ever come when what is now called science, thus familiarised to men, shall be ready to put on, as it were, a form of flesh and blood, the poet will lend his divine spirit to aid the transfiguration, and will welcome the being thus produced as a dear and genuine inmate of the household of man."—WORDS-WORTH, Preface to *Lyrical Ballads.*

> As our blood labours to beget
>> Spirits as like souls as it can,
> Because such fingers need to knit
>> The subtle soul that makes us man!

What are the scientific conceptions behind a passage such as this from Milton?

> For know whatever was created needs
> To be sustained and fed; of elements
> The grosser feeds the purer: earth the sea,
> Earth and the sea feed air, the air those fires
> Ethereal, and as lowest first the moon;
> Whence in her visage round those spots, unpurged
> Vapours not yet into her substance turned.
> Nor doth the moon no nourishment exhale
> From her moist continent to higher orbs.
> The sun that light imparts to all receives
> From all his alimental recompense
> In humid exhalations, and at even
> Sups with the ocean.

Shakespeare uses the same doctrine in a homelier fashion:

> The sun's a thief, and with his great attraction
> Robs the vast sea: the moon's an arrant thief,
> And her pale fire she snatches from the sun:
> The sea's a thief, whose liquid surge resolves
> The moon into salt tears: the earth's a thief,
> That feeds and breeds from a composture stolen
> From general excrement: each thing's a thief.

Modern science is no such body of stereotyped doctrines with which every one becomes more or less familiar. Yet there are few great discoveries or hypotheses which have arrested the general mind that have not become

part of the background of our literature.   The blood,
for example, was a common metaphor for passion in our
older poets:

> Bless'd are those
> Whose blood and judgment are so well commingled,
> That they are not a pipe for Fortune's finger
> To sound what stop she pleases.

It is in Dryden that we first hear of its circulation:

> Alas! the stream that circles through my heart
> Is, less than love, essential to my being.

Only poets of the last three centuries could have written:

> From my wings are shaken the dews that waken
>   The sweet buds every one,
> When rocked to rest on their mother's breast,
>   As she dances about the sun;

or:

> She saw the snowy poles and moons of Mars,
> That mystic field of drifted light
> In mid Orion and the married stars;

and:

> Still as, while Saturn whirls, his stedfast shade
> Sleeps on his luminous ring;

or:

> To-day I saw the dragon-fly
> Come from the wells where he did lie.
>
> An inner impulse rent the veil
> Of his old husk: from head to tail
> Came out clear plates of sapphire mail.
>
> He dried his wings: like gauze they grew:
> Through crofts and pastures wet with dew
> A living flash of light he flew;

or, finally:

Will my tiny spark of being wholly vanish in your deeps and
heights;
Must my day be dark by reason, O ye Heavens, of your boundless
nights,
Rush of suns; and roll of systems, and your fiery clash of meteor-
ites?

But the great poets are not content with scientific
details. "Of high poetry", Maeterlinck says, "the
constituents are threefold: beauty of language; the
passionate portrayal of what is real around us and in us,
nature and our own feelings; and, enveloping the whole,
creating its peculiar atmosphere, the idea that the poet
forms to himself of the unknown, in which float the
beings he invokes, the mystery which dominates and
judges them, which presides over and assigns their
destinies." But the ideal framework which the poet
forms for his dreams is generally derived from the current
philosophy and science of his own day, for that links his
mind to others, and the end of poetry is the communication of impassioned thought. In the science of Epicurus
Lucretius found that deliverance from the fear of death
which is the theme of his great poem. Chaucer was
by creed an orthodox Catholic; his articulate thought
on fate and free-will is derived from Boethius. Spenser
is an Italian Platonist or Neo-Platonist. Milton was no
metaphysician, but he hammered out of the text of the
Bible and his own lofty soul a creed as hard and knotty
as those of Westminster or Trent, of which *Paradise
Lost* was to be the exposition. Fortunately, the poet
ran away with the preacher and gave us Hell and Chaos,

Satan and the debating devils, Sin and Death, and Eden with all its "bowery loveliness". Shelley gave wings and a soul to the political philosophy of Godwin; and his metaphysics are those of Berkeley and Plato. Tennyson, Browning, Arnold, Swinburne are all, in different ways, the poets of nineteenth-century science, and its disintegrating or constructive implications.

But if, after nature, life and experience, science and philosophy form perhaps the most important vista in the background of literature in every era, another, and that the most shaping and colouring, is formed by literature itself; and the literary background of English, as of every Western European, literature is a singularly complex one. The student of Greek literature is not called upon to study any other literature. Behind the masterpieces of Greek literature lies an ample background of mythology and legend with which the poet presumes his audience to be familiar, which formed a vital link between him and his audience. Greek poetry, too, from Hesiod and Pindar to Aeschylus and Euripides, had its philosophical and scientific background. But no one is conscious to-day, in reading the masterpieces of Greek literature, of the shaping influence of any non-Greek literature. It is otherwise of course with Latin literature. Behind all the great poetry of Lucretius, Horace, Catullus, Virgil, lie the masterpieces of Greek literature. Not only had Greek mythology and legend and Greek science and philosophy become so completely a Roman inheritance that the poets assumed their references to these would be immediately understood, but Greek literature created all the forms taken by Latin literature and determined its metrical and rhetorical texture.

The relation of English to other literatures is not dissimilar to that of Rome to Greece, but it is a less rigid and a more complex relation. That relation will become clear if I take one or two crucial instances. Every one is familiar with Milton's great invocation to Light at the beginning of the third book of *Paradise Lost*:

> Hail, holy light, etc.

The sublimity, the pathos, the music of these wonderful lines perhaps every reader of taste will appreciate at once. But no reader can appreciate them fully unless he is familiar—the more familiar the better—with the Bible and with the Greek and Latin classics. How else shall he understand the lines:

> Blind Thamyris and blind Maeonides,
> And Tiresias and Phineus, prophets old.

But it is not a question of a few allusions. The whole construction of Milton's poem is classical, as its contents, incidents, and persons are mainly Biblical. And classical or Biblical phraseology is woven into every line. The poet's words waken a succession of echoes in the ear of the scholar:—" Bright effluence of bright essence increate ", echoes the Book of Wisdom: "Wisdom is a pure influence flowing from the glory of the Almighty— she is the brightness of the everlasting light." "Whose fountain who shall tell? " is suggested by the Book of Job. "Where is the way to the dwelling of light? " And when the poet goes on to speak of his " obscure sojourn " while he " sung of Chaos and Eternal Night ",

> Taught by the heav'nly Muse to venture down
> The dark descent, and up to reascend,
> Though hard and rare,

the classical reader recalls many things, especially Virgil's

> Sed revocare gradum superasque evadere ad auras
> Hoc opus, hic labor est;

and when Milton adds "smit with the love of sacred song", the same reader recalls—

> Dulces ante omnia Musae,
> Quarum sacra fero ingenti percussus amore.

The two vistas which thus open themselves to the reader of *Paradise Lost* are the two most important in all our literature to the present day—the Classical and the Biblical.    They displaced an older Teutonic background so completely that it is now hardly to be recovered. From the Old English poem *Widsith* we can learn that there once was such a background familiar to all the Teutonic peoples—stories of monsters and kings and leaders of migrating tribes, of the invasion of Attila, and the hoard of the Nibelungs, stories some of which have been preserved more fully in Icelandic sagas and fragments of German poetry.    The Celtic peoples too had their legendary tradition, and a poet like Barbour just lets us see for a moment that he and his readers were familiar with the story of Finn.    But with one important exception to which I shall recur, these Germanic and Celtic vistas faded away and their place was taken by the history and literature of the Bible, the mythology and history and literature of Greece and Rome.

But these two great vistas in the background of English as of Western European literature generally have passed through such striking changes of perspective that it is sometimes difficult to realise that it is the same landscape we are contemplating through the windows, for example, of Chaucer's Gothic palaces and temples and those of Milton's classically builded mansions. A work like the late Churton Collins's lectures on *Greek Influence on English Poetry* produces, I think, a misleading impression of the really important relation between Greek and English literature and the right interconnection between Classical and English studies. There is little or nothing to be gained by isolating Greek from Latin, and considering only what this or that English poet may have derived from this or that Greek poet. What is of real importance is to trace the process by which Greek literature through Latin, and that not only of the Augustan but of the Silver Age, became a shaping influence in and a permanent background to the literature of Western Europe, including England and Scotland. The Renaissance was no sudden revelation of something unknown, but the gradual illumination, clearer vision bringing juster perspective, of what had always been, in some degree and shape, present to men's admiring eyes. The nations of Western Europe inherited with pride the legacy of classical learning and literature, but when it came into their hands it was already a decadent tradition. The inheritance on which they entered was not that of Roman and Greek literature in the splendour of their maturity. They were introduced to a culture in which Greek had been forgotten, in which Latin itself was in a process of decay, and the Latin authors were no longer understood aright, seen in their due perspective. The strange vicissitudes through which Virgil and classical learning passed in the early Middle Ages have been very piquantly described by the Italian scholar Comparetti. The result

was that when the vernacular literatures begin the poets
are quite confident of their knowledge of the ancient
world, as confident as of their own descent from the
Trojans, but their classical landscapes are strange and
bewildering to our eyes.   They are very decorative landscapes, and in the decorative scheme the mythology of
Greece and Rome as learned from Ovid is an important
element:

> The statue of Venus glorious for to see
> Was naked fleting in a large see,
> And fro the navel down all covered was
> With waves grene and bright as any glas.
> A citole in her right hond hadde she,
> And on her heed, ful semely for to see,
> A rose gerland, fresh and wel smellinge;
> Above her heed hir dowves flickeringe.
> Bifore hir stode hir sone Cupido,
> Upon his shuldres winges hadde he two;
> And blind he was, as it is often sene;
> A bowe he bar and arwes brighte and kene.

That is a glimpse from Chaucer's window.   And if you
had sojourned for a time with Chaucer's pilgrims on
their way to Canterbury you would have learned many
things that would seem strange.   Of ancient history,
the history of Troy and Thebes and Alexander the
Great and Rome, you would have found they claimed to
know much and in great detail.   The monk had read
it all in Homer and Virgil, and Lucan and Ovid, and
Claudian and Statius, and Dares and Dictys, and Lollius
and Guido delle Colonne—but the history would not
be what you had expected from your own reading, *e.g.*
of the story of Troy.   Achilles, you would learn, was a

brawny bully; Hector was the great hero of the story of Troy; but more famous than either, you would find, were a certain Troilus and Cressida, of whom Homer tells us nothing.

It is with the Renaissance that this strangely coloured and spaced background begins to change and to assume a more familiar perspective, but the change comes about much more slowly than our text-books would indicate. Spenser is one of the first English poets whom Churton Collins selected as an example of an English poet whose work shows that he had studied Greek literature at first hand. That may be, and certainly his poetry reveals a wider knowledge of Greek and Latin literature and philosophy than Chaucer's. Yet the classical background of the *Faerie Queene* does not differ essentially from that of Chaucer's *Knightes Tale*. It has the same Italian, Ovidian, decorative character, if the vignettes are less naïve and "primitive", more Italian renaissance in modelling and colouring. His sources are still Latin more often than Greek, of the Silver—Statius, Claudian —rather than the Golden Age. There is still the peculiar mediæval perspective that mingles in one plane classical, scriptural, and romantic figures—gods and angels and magicians and dragons. Like all the Elizabethans, Spenser treats the ancient stories and persons with the utmost freedom. He shows no suspicion of Malherbe's rule, that if you borrow from the classics you must adhere rigidly to the traditional story or characteristics; that a dead mythology admits of no developments; that to add new stories or new features only emphasises the decorative, fantastic character of your material.

And what of the classical background to Shakespeare's

plays? It is very different from what it would have been had their author been Bacon or Ben Jonson. Three vistas may be distinguished. As with Spenser and the other Elizabethans, we can look out through the windows of the earlier comedies on the sunny pleasance of Ovid—his gods and goddesses, and lovers happy and unhappy:

> Her sunny locks
> Hang on her temples like a golden fleece,
> Which makes her seat of Belmont Colchos' strand,
> And many Jasons come in quest of her.

> Now he goes
> With no less presence, but with much more love,
> Than young Alcides, when he did redeem
> The virgin tribute paid by howling Troy
> To the sea monster: I stand for sacrifice;
> The rest aloof are the Dardanian wives,
> With bleared visages, come forth to view
> The issue of the exploit. Go, Hercules!

> The moon shines bright: in such a night as this
> When the sweet wind did gently kiss the trees
> And they did make no noise, in such a night
> Troilus methinks mounted the Troyan walls,
> And sigh'd his soul towards the Grecian tents,
> Where Cressid lay that night.

Such pictures as these are in no wise different from the classic-romantic decorations of Chaucer's poems, and in *Troilus and Cressida*, though the landscape is a less sunny one, the features are even more mediæval. One who knows the tale of Troy only from Homer will be sadly disconcerted by the picture which Shakespeare presents of the Achæan heroes. It is only through some study of the mediæval story, of the *Roman de Troie* and Chaucer's *Troylus and Criseyde*, that he will be able to secure the right perspective.

The background to Shakespeare's tragedies is less mediæval but almost as unfamiliar to many classical students. Despite Churton Collins, we must admit that Shakespeare did not know the Greek tragedians. To suggestions of indebtedness based on resemblances in spirit, in situation, in phraseology, Shakespeare might reply: " Before the Greek tragedians were, I am." " Shakespeare ", says Gibbon, noting a resemblance between some lines in *A Midsummer-Night's Dream* and a poem of Gregory's, " had never read the poems of Gregory Nazianzen; he was ignorant of the Greek language; but his mother-tongue, the language of nature, is the same in Cappadocia and in Britain," in Athens and in London. But in the machinery of Shakespeare's tragedies—ghosts and witches and supernatural agencies—in their occasional motives, ruthless ambition, as in *Richard III.*, or revenge, as in *Hamlet*, and in many of the speeches the student will detect the influence of the melodramatic and declamatory tragedies of Seneca.

Lastly, Shakespeare, like all the great Renaissance authors, knows his Plutarch. The *Lives* are the stately and " embowed " windows through which he looked out on the history and the heroes of Rome. There is none of his sources whom he treats with greater respect. Yet even here Shakespeare shows no pedantic regard for Roman dignity, makes no effort to reproduce an antique atmosphere either in his stage direction or his idiom and style and verse. Caesar enters " in his nightgown ";

the Roman people welcome Coriolanus as Londoners
would the Earl of Essex:

> Stalls, bulks, windows
> Are smothered up ; leads fill'd and ridges horsed
> With variable complexions, all agreeing
> In earnestness to see him, etc.

The language the Romans speak is racy Elizabethan, or
condensed and imaginative Shakespearean.

The first poet in whom one can detect a real and
strenuous effort, attended with some measure of success,
to assimilate and adapt classical art, to reproduce a classical
atmosphere, is Ben Jonson in his comedies and tragedies
and poems.   But Jonson's art, despite the Herculean
vigour it betrays, is pedantic and clumsy; his conception
of classical poetry is governed too much by abstract and
mistaken critical dogmas;  his temperament and outlook
are still mediæval, not to say barbarian.   Chapman, the
translator of Homer, is, despite his Greek, even more of
a glorious and fantastic barbarian, apparelling Homer in
strange and outlandish garments;  at times, one is tempted
to say, tattooing his noble countenance.

It is in Milton's poetry that we look out at last on a
classical background whose perspectives and personages are
recognisable at once by a student of those authors whom we
regard to-day as the great representatives of Greek and Latin
literature—Homer and the Attic tragedians, Virgil and
Horace as well as Ovid, the "grave orators and historians".
Even in *Paradise Lost* a mediæval, or rather a patristic, link
connects the ancient gods and goddesses with devils and evil
spirits.   Nay, a careful reader of Milton's poems, from the
early Latin and Ovidian elegies to *Paradise Regained*, will
note a progressive, or regressive, change of attitude from

his early frank acceptance of the Gods and Goddesses
with all their pagan attributes and implications towards a
sterner attitude, a more disdainful rejection: as in the
invocation to Urania, the Wisdom of the Book of Proverbs,
with his slighting allusion to the Muse of the Greek poets:

> how could the Muse defend
> Her son; so fail not thou who thee implores:
> For thou art heav'nly, she an empty dream.

And, finally, in *Paradise Regained*, when Satan has
described with unsurpassable felicity all that the classical
world had come to mean for a scholar who is also a poet,

> Athens the eye of Greece,
> Mother of Arts and Eloquence,

her philosophers and poets and orators, Milton hears the
reproving voice of his Puritan conscience, the old conflict
of the Christian Fathers is renewed—"What has Christ to
do with Apollo?"—and our Lord rebukes Satan, denounces
the Greek philosophers as blind leaders of the blind, and
prefers to all the poetry of Hellas the songs of Sion.

And that brings me to the other vista in the background of *Paradise Lost*, the Biblical, the Old and New
Testament story and poetry, and all that had grown out
of these in the way of theology and mythology. The
changes which this background to our literature has
passed through are hardly less striking than those which
our classical vista underwent, in so much that there are
a great many things in our literature up to the end of the
seventeenth century which will puzzle a Protestant reader
of to-day, familiar with the Bible, but ignorant, as most of
us in Scotland are ignorant, of the great Catholic tradition
which we once shared with the whole of Western Europe.

C

The Middle Ages were more familiar with the Bible than with Homer and the greater classical poets, and understood it better, though there were few who thought that, as literature, it contained anything comparable with the majesty of Virgil and the graces of Ovid. But the Catholic Church was not a Foreign Bible and Tract Society, which put the Bible in the hand of the converted barbarian, and told him to make what he could of it. The converted nations entered a great organised institution with a highly elaborate tradition, based on the Bible but containing a large mass of superinduced articles of faith, history, and mythology, derived ultimately from many sources, Oriental and Hellenic, and it is this in whole or part which forms the chief vista in the background of our older literature. To study that background in all its elaborate detail you need only turn to Dante. There the whole system is presented with all the luminous beauty of great poetry. There you may pass through the whole definitely conceived system of the visible and the invisible world. One may descend through the earth, which is the centre of the universe, and visit the circles of Hell leading downward to the city of Dis, and the core of the earth, where is Satan holding in his triple mouth the three greatest of traitors —Judas and Cassius and Brutus. One may emerge into the sunlight on the other side of the earth, and climb the painful mountain of Purgatory, palpitating with anguish and with hope. One may meet the poet Statius, and hear how he was converted through reading the *Pollio* of Virgil, and one may feel the mountain tremble with joy at the moment of his deliverance. One may ascend from the Earthly Paradise that crowns the mountain through all the circles of Heaven, the moon and the sun, the planets and the fixed stars, till one arrive at the Empyreal Heaven that encloses all. There are the angels in their nine orders. There are the saints in the degrees of their blessedness, but all alike happy. And there, crowning all, is the presence-court of the Trinity and the Blessed Virgin, round whom are all the saved, as the petals of the Rose of Sharon. And at the last we may behold for a moment the point of intense light which is

The love that moves the Heaven and all the stars.

Human nature will probably never contemplate itself against a background at once so majestic, and so centred in man and his destiny, as was fashioned by the Mediæval Church. Modern science has enormously enlarged that background, but the vastness, and the indifference to man, of the spaces and forces revealed appal the imagination:

What be those two shapes high over the sacred fountain,
Taller than all the Muses and larger than all the mountain?
. . . The sight confuses.

These are Astronomy and Geology, terrible Muses.

But Dante's is both a learned and a shaping imagination. In simpler and more popular poets, like most of those of our own country, you will not find all this elaborate system. But you will find that its principal features—Heaven, Hell, and Purgatory, the angels and devils, the seven deadly sins, the cardinal and theological virtues, the Virgin and the saints—are taken for granted. You will find also Biblical stories and persons, but presented in a manner that is to us surprising and disconcerting. Abraham, in Cædmon's poem, will meet you in the guise of a northern warrior breathing berserker fury.

From a representative popular poem such as the *Cursor Mundi* or the cycles of Miracle Plays which follow the same selection of incidents, one gets a good idea of what the mediæval man in the street knew of the Bible. He was not as well munitioned with texts for polemical purposes as the tinkers and weavers of the seventeenth century. But he was familiar with the events of Old Testament story which led up to or symbolised the work of redemption, and with the chief incidents in the life of Christ, and the Passion and Resurrection. He knew some incidents and some characters unfamiliar to us— the story of Adam's death, what happened to Cain and his descendants, the life and death and assumption of the Virgin, the harrowing of Hell. He knew about Noah's wife, that famous shrew who sat drinking with her gossips when the flood was " fleeting in full fast "

> Hastow not herd, quod Nicolas also,
> The sorwe of Noah with his felawshipe,
> Ere that he mighte gete his wife to ship?
> Him had be lever, I dar wel undertake,
> At thilke tyme, than alle his wethers blake,
> That she had had a ship herself allone.

He thought of Herod and Pilate as notorious braggarts. He pictured the shepherds who kept watch on the night of the Nativity as English peasants blowing their nails and complaining of landlords and taxes. In addition to all this he was familiar with the lives and sufferings of the saints, from Stephen and Peter and Paul to Little Hugh of Lincoln whose throat was cut by " cursed Jewes ", as we shall never be familiar with them again. All these things formed a kind of permanent background to his life, meeting him at every turn in sermon and hymn, in story and play, in sculptured ornament and coloured glass. To picture to yourself the Biblical and religious background of our older literature almost to Shakespeare, to see what the older readers saw as they read, you must go to picture galleries, illuminated MSS., the glass and the carvings of our cathedrals or those of the Continent.

The Reformation swept away this extraneous matter, or a great deal of it; it created a new regard for the letter of the original by translating the complete Bible for the laity so that " he who runs might read ". And the English Bible began at once to constitute a fresh background; but as with the classical vista the change took place gradually. Consider Shakespeare. The Rev. Mr. Carter has written a large volume on Shakespeare's knowledge of the English Bible in the Genevan version. Many of the instances he quotes do not seem to me to prove his case. But Shakespeare did know his Bible. Consider the play from which I have already quoted to illustrate his classical outlook. Shylock was modelled on Marlowe's Barabbas; but whereas Barabbas is made to illustrate his speeches with scraps of Ovidian mythology, Shylock's sole book is the Bible. He defends usury by a reference to Jacob and the parti-coloured sheep. With quite a mediæval inconsistency Portia, when appealing to him for mercy, cites the Lord's prayer:

> Therefore, Jew,
> Though justice be thy plea, consider this—
> That in the course of justice none of us
> Should see salvation: we do pray for mercy,
> And that same prayer doth teach us all to render
> The deeds of mercy.

One of the first poets who gave to the English the new Biblical background they sought was Du Bartas as translated by Joshua Sylvester. But Milton is the first English poet the background of whose work is entirely Biblical. A few mediæval traits still linger, as in his devils and angels. But even the devils are drawn less on mediæval lines, more after the model of the characters of Greek tragedy, of the great impenitents of Dante's *Inferno*, and of the parliamentary debaters and leaders of the Commonwealth. His angels, too, as the *De Doctrina Christiana* shows, are developed from Biblical and Jewish rather than patristic suggestions.

These are the two most important vistas in the background of our literature until, at any rate, very recent days—literature and history to which a poet might refer with some confidence of being understood, and further, a certain feeling towards which of interest, respect, or reverence, was a tie that connected him with his audience, a feeling on which he could count to give values to his picture. But there was a third, not regarded with the same respect perhaps as these, but which is to many more full of enchantment than either, and which was used to invest the others with some of its own peculiar witchery. We get occasional glimpses of it in Milton, especially the earlier poems, but his later attitude towards it was a grudging one. It is a vista on which he seemed disposed to draw a curtain as affording too childish a prospect for those who have the Bible and the Classics; and critics like Bentley and Newton were to condemn him for even such measure of indulgence as he allowed himself, his ostentation of "such reading as perhaps had better never have been read". For it had been the delight of his youth,

and ever and again in *Paradise Lost* the curtain is drawn,
the window is opened, and we see a shimmering pageant
and hear a music that resounds—

> Of Uther's son
> Begirt with British and Armorick knights,
> And all who since, baptiz'd or infidel,
> Jousted in Aspramont or Montalban,
> Damasco or Morocco or Trebisond,
> Or whom Biserta sent from Afric shore,
> When Charlemain with all his peerage fell
> By Fontarabia.

This is the background of mediæval romance.  In part
it is a survival from that old Teutonic and Celtic background which the Bible and the Classics displaced in
cultivated minds, and of which so much has disappeared,
some of it to be recovered only in our own time.  It
was not altogether a loss that the classics of Greece and
Rome were only partially known and only imperfectly
understood in the Dark Ages.  It made it more possible
for the peoples of Western Europe to develop their own
tastes and to create a new literature.  And when a new
poetry began as by a kind of miracle in the south of
France, and in strange new measures the poets of Provence
and then of the north began to sing of love and of adventure, they turned for themes to the legends which still
lingered of Charlemagne and Roland and Oliver, and to
the still more bewitching Celtic legends of Arthur the
Faery King of Briton and the knights and ladies of his
court.  They gave a chivalrous, feudal setting to the
warfare and courtesy, and a Catholic, mystic tone to the
story of the Grail; and soon the names of Roland and
Oliver, of Arthur and Gawain, of Lancelot and Guine-

vere, and Tristram and Iseult, were familiar to Europe from Italy to Iceland. The romantic annexed the classical. The story of Troy became a tale of chivalry; the history of Alexander a legend of magic and marvel. The dull *Thebais* of Statius was burnished and coloured by Boccaccio and Chaucer. Allegory was interwoven with story and song, so that Arthur and Beauty, and Bielacoil and Venus, and Daunger and Daun Cupido mix and mingle in the same dance and pageant in the garden of Idleness. When Chaucer dreamed that he was awakened one May morning by the singing of birds, he found himself in a room with windows of stained glass in which were portrayed the stories

> Of Ector and King Priamus,
> Of Achilles and Lamedon,
> Of Medea and of Jason,
> Of Paris, Eleyn and Lavyne,
> And alle the walles with colours fine
> Were peynted bothe text and glose
> Of all the Romaunt of the Rose.

Such were the decorations of the chamber of mediæval romance, and they still adorn the *Faerie Queene* if the technique is more in the manner of Rubens or the Italians. The best of Shakespeare's plays " in the Faery manner " mingles the same romantic figures with the homelier creations of the people, Puck and the Fairies.

The Classicism and Puritanism of the seventeenth century banished romance and the fairies:

> But since of late Elizabeth,
>     And later, James came in,
> They never danced on any heath
>     As when the time hath bin.

> By which we knowe the fairies
> Were of the old profession,
> Their songs were Ave Maries,
> Their dances were procession.

That window was barred up or only peered through occasionally by children when their nurses told them stories of Bevis of Southampton and Guy of Warwick. But in the eighteenth century Gray and the Wartons began to reopen it as they read Spenser and the early poems of Milton and Chaucer. Gradually more and more was recovered to sight by Chatterton and Coleridge, and Scott and Tennyson, and Rossetti and Morris, and Swinburne, and that romantic background of magic and marvel, of love and chivalry, of Lancelot and Guinevere, and Tristram and Iseult, has to some extent been recovered, and has had new vistas added from Norse saga and Eastern story, and from the creative imagination of our poets themselves, Coleridge and Scott, and Keats and Rossetti.

These are the most permanent literary vistas on which the windows of English literature look out,[1] the background to the work of Chaucer, Spenser, Milton; and

[1] They are not of course the only ones. From Chaucer and Spenser, and Marlowe and Shakespeare, to Byron and Shelley, and Browning and Swinburne, English poets have loved Italy, and Italian literature and story; Italian scenery and Italian art have formed a specially beautiful and attractive vista seen through the windows of English verse and prose. After the ancient classics Italian is the language that has strongest claims upon a student of our literature.

Moreover, our own literature itself as it recedes into the past becomes a part of the background. The characters of Shakespeare's plays have become, indeed, as permanent a part of the background of the literature of Western Europe as the characters of Homer or the Greek tragedians. The late Italian poet Carducci, in a poem

if we leap forward to the reign of Queen Victoria—to
Tennyson, Browning, Arnold, Swinburne—we find the
same threefold outlook—Biblical, Classical, Romantic.
In *A Dream of Fair Women* Tennyson combines them
as Chaucer had done five hundred years earlier.   William
Morris and Rossetti stand somewhat apart from their
fellows by their effort—especially Morris's—to make the
romantic the sole or dominant vista, Morris endeavouring
to tell even classical stories in the romantic manner of
the mediæval stories of Thebes and Troy.   The result
was charming, but also not a little unreal, producing not
a little the impression of deliberate reconstruction.

---

written by the tomb of Shelley, delights himself by bringing together
in that land of the departed to which Ulysses journeyed—

" Island set around with a gleaming girdle of seas and of dreams "—

the great creations of Greek and English poetry.

" There on his spear leans Siegfried, Achilles is with him, the heroes
    Tall and golden-haired, roam in song by the sounding sea.

" And leaving her anguished lover, Ophelia brings flowers to Achilles;
    Pale from her sacrifice to Siegfried comes Iphigenia.

" The white-haired Lear recounts his woes to the wandering Oedipus,
    Who with vacant, hollow eyes gazes round him again for the Sphinx.

" Lo! with the Scottish Queen, on the shore, in the light of the moon,
    Stands Clytemnestra: they plunge white arms in the wave of the sea.

" Turbid and fervid with blood the sea rushes back, and the cry
    Of their anguish rings and rebounds from the craggy, precipitous
        shore."

Other literatures have made their contribution to the background
of our own—Don Quixote and Sancho Panza, perhaps Faust, more
certainly Mephistopheles as Goethe presents him, Perrault's and some
of Andersen's and some of Grimm's fairy stories, to mention one or
two instances.

For, charming as is the romantic background of mediæval poetry, and of modern poetry inspired by the rediscovery of the Middle Ages, it has never had quite the solidity of the classical and Biblical. Heine identified romance with Christianity, mediæval and Catholic Christianity; and, though with a different interpretation of the spirit of romance, I have heard the same thesis defended in this University. But there are more strands of tradition and sentiment in mediæval romance than the Christian strands; and mediæval Christianity was a far more comprehensive and solid structure than romance. There is Christian feeling in the *Song of Roland* and the *High History of the Holy Grail*, but no educated Christian of the time would have dreamt of thinking of either as serious documents of his faith. The literary background of that was the Bible, as interpreted by the Church, and the work of the schoolmen had been to interpret Christian belief by the methods of Greek thought. The Bible and the philosopher (*i.e.* Aristotle, the arbiter of ancient philosophy) were St. Thomas's final court of appeal. Romance might charm, but no other literature had the authority of the Bible and the Ancients. One has but to recall the vision of the books of the Old and New Testaments which passed before Dante in the Earthly Paradise. The Renaissance confirmed that view, studying both more scientifically and profoundly, and almost to our own day, to the generation of Tennyson and Browning, despite the Romantic Revival, that authority endured as a feeling on which the poet could reckon in his appeal to his audience.

In our own day that tradition has passed or is passing away. Can any writer of to-day feel confident that a

classical allusion will be understood by any wide circle of
readers, and not only understood but will awaken certain
definite emotions of respect and admiration? Can we be
sure, even in Scotland, that an allusion to the Bible will
be instantly understood, and not only understood but
regarded with the old reverence? That was what Milton
could count upon, unbounded reverence for the Bible,
unlimited admiration for the classics; and though there
had been changes and fluctuations of feeling in the long
interval Tennyson and Browning seem still to expect
the same. A poet would need to be sure of his audience
before he could do so to-day. It is not that the Bible
or the classics are less carefully studied. Modern poets
can reproduce a classical or Biblical setting with a finer
archæological accuracy and truth of spirit than Milton.
Tennyson's classical poems are more Greek, to say
nothing of Landor. There is more of the spirit and
atmosphere of the Old Testament in Browning's *Saul*
or *Epilogue* than in *Paradise Lost*; of the New Testament in *The Death in the Desert* than in *Paradise Regained*.
But this very erudition limits the audience addressed;
and the same erudition has disintegrated the old background, has shown us both the classics of Greece and
Rome and the Bible in such new relations and strange
lights, that the old simple traditional feelings have been
dispelled even in those who retain admiration and reverence for both. But above all we have lost anything like
a single definite type of education, religious or secular.
For it was a common education which created the literary
background that united the poet and his audience, a
common tradition of knowledge and feeling. The
Catholic scheme which Dante elaborates was familiar

in its main features to all.   Painter after painter could display the Virgin and the Child, and count on the beauty of his work being heightened by the halo of reverence with which the gazer would invest the group. Some of Milton's own familiarity with the text of Scripture was presupposed in every Protestant family.   And in their own place the same was true of the classics, as painting again, mediæval and renaissance, will attest.   It may be that the classical background to our literature was always a less popular one than the Biblical and romantic. But no reader could make any pretensions to culture without being familiar with it in some degree.   Shakespeare had small Latin and less Greek, but, as we have seen, the classical background to his work is not unimportant.   A liberal education up to our own day was a classical education.   Mr. Gladstone was probably the last English statesman who occasionally used a Latin quotation in the House of Commons.   The statesmen of the time of Burke, North, Fox, and Pitt did so every day.   The Bible and the classics were cited as familiar to every one; some English poets, as Shakespeare and Milton, came next.

Those days are past   Long threatened and slowly modified, our traditional education has in the last twenty years been rapidly disintegrated.   No candid man will now pretend that the majority of the Scottish people receive any definite type of religious education, Catholic or Protestant, or are familiar with the articles of their faith and the text of Scripture.   The old classical education of our grammar schools is gone.   A professor published recently a map of the Greekless areas of Scotland, and it affords a lover of the past a melancholy prospect.

At any rate no one can any longer even imagine that
every educated reader will know something of Greek or
Latin, or will understand the classical allusions in our
poets.   And the result has begun to make itself felt in
our poetry, in the poetry of the last twenty years, the
period that has elapsed since the great Victorian romantic
poets passed away or grew silent.   It is a difficult period,
and some of the older critics, perhaps Professor Saintsbury
himself, have shrunk from attempting to estimate it,
feeling themselves in a new world far removed from the
golden days of Tennyson and Browning, and Arnold
and Morris, and Swinburne—and one important difference is this want of any traditional background.

The want has made itself felt in two distinct ways.
If a poet wishes to give his work a literary background,
if he is one of those whose inspiration is caught from
books, whose imagination loves strange civilisations and
scenery remote in time or space, then he writes necessarily for a limited audience, and to some extent he
creates his own background for himself.   A poet of to-day
who deals with classical themes, like Mr. Sturge Moore,
can obtain subtleties of effect an older classical poet could
not have achieved, but he will be fully appreciated only
by those who have some intimacy with classical learning.
The same is true of a poet who like Mr. Yeats creates
a background for his own beautiful poetry out of revived
Irish legends and literature.   And so with others.   Knowing no traditional, commonly accepted background, our
poets have grown curious of strange, new vistas, Celtic
or Indian or Chinese, and their poetry has become exotic
in character.

But the more general result, the most characteristic

tendency of recent poetry, has been to eliminate any conscious reference to a literary background altogether, to give poetry a setting not of literature and tradition but of nature and actuality. Nature, of course, changing yet perennial, has always been a notable background to our poetry never at any time ignored, even at the classical or Augustan period. But along with nature modern poets have placed all the actualities, noble or mean, beautiful or ugly, of modern life. Walt Whitman heralded this movement, this rejection of everything in poetry but the actual and modern:

Dead poets, philosophs, priests,
Martyrs, artists, inventors, governments long since,
Language-shapers on other shores,
Nations once powerful, now reduced, withdrawn, or desolate,
I dare not proceed till I respectfully credit what you have left
    wafted thither,
I have perused it, own it is admirable (moving awhile among it),
That nothing can ever be greater, nothing can ever deserve more
    than it deserves,
Regarding it all intently a long while, then dismissing it,
I stand in my place with my own day here.

Browning had done something to prepare for it in this country; but the English poet who startled us out of our slumbers over romantic and classical idylls and odes was Rudyard Kipling with the strum of his banjo, the cockney accents of his soldiers, and the music-hall strains of his *Barrack-room Ballads*. Their instant popularity all over the Empire, and the endless imitations they have called forth (*Songs of a Sourdough*, *Ballads of a Cheechako*, etc.) revealed as in a flash the existence of a large class of readers even of poetry, if the poetry made no demand for a too literary and classical culture. Others followed in less raucous tones and more refined diction and metres—Henley with his Hospital poems and London Voluntaries, *The Shropshire Lad*, Thomas Hardy, John Davidson, Wilfrid Wilson Gibson, Lascelles Abercrombie, to name a few almost at random. The poet has invaded the realm of the novelist, for the novel is the form of literature which above all demands a contemporary, realistic background; hence at once the poignancy and the passingness of its appeal. And such poetry is apt to share this ephemeral character, for actuality is always changing. Only beauty endures. Is the poetry of Kipling and Henley, inspired by the actualities of English life in the 'nineties, likely to be read when these actualities are only recoverable by some careful study? That is not a question I shall attempt to answer, nor yet the larger question whether high and enduring poetry is likely to flourish in a period when there is no great common tradition, religious and æsthetic, uniting the poet to his audience. My object has been to give a bird's-eye view of our literature from a single point of view, that of the implications, scientific and literary, which at various times thus united the English poet and the English people, and leave that view to suggest for your own thought some not unimportant reflections on literature generally and on the character of our studies in their relation to other studies, historical, scientific, literary, and linguistic.

1915.

# DON QUIXOTE:

## SOME WAR-TIME REFLECTIONS ON ITS CHARACTER & INFLUENCE

### I

THE war proved for most of us a great trier of the spirits, of books as well as men. Some which we had read with amusement, even with apparent profit, failed us in our need. A few found their most complete escape in the region of pure science, detached intellectual inquiry. One friend of mine and scholar sat apparently unmoved through the weeks from Mons to the Marne and the Marne to Ypres, absorbed in the collation of manuscripts of Pelagius. Others, like Mr. Wells, felt themselves impelled to an attempt to re-read the riddle of a painful world and invent, if they could not discover, a God to clear up the mess sometime and somehow. Mysticism and the occult claimed a larger following; hence, among other causes, the popularity for a time of Dostoievsky and the Russians and the much greater popularity of *Raymond* and the literature of communication with the dead. Pious souls were sustained and comforted by what seemed to others the strangest husks, the least illuminating, consoling, or ennobling revelations of life behind the veil. For some of us, on the other hand, the most readable books were just those which were most entirely human, neither philosophical nor mystical, sentimental nor cynical, but simply human, pictures of the normal life of men and women, illuminated with playful irony but a light that is also warmed by a genial though not too obtrusive

D                    37

sympathy. Of all such books *Don Quixote* proved itself *facile princeps*. Not even Shakespeare, and certainly no other, Fielding or Jane Austen or Dickens or Charles Lamb, furnished quite the same armour of proof against outrageous fortune, provided quite the same blend of amusement with that affection and respect for humanity which alone seemed worthy of an epoch of such appalling sacrifice and suffering. To seek complete distraction at such a moment in science or art or amusement required qualities that are superhuman or inhuman; but without obscuring altogether our consciousness of the tragic background of reality, *Don Quixote* enabled us to endure by transferring us in imagination to a happier and yet a quite human world, a world where fighting and mis-adventure are not ignored or forgotten, but all is sweetened by the humanities of love and laughter and good fellowship and good cheer, which relaxes without unbracing the muscles of endurance and passionate resistance to cruelty and injustice. " Delight in several shapes " is the title which James Mabbe gave to his Elizabethan version of six of Cervantes' *Novelas Exemplares*. Delight in manifold form is the lot of the peruser of *Don Quixote* at a time like the present, a work whose satire on human nature is held in solution by a stream of unfailing humour and kindliness, whose two heroes are not more absurd than they are admirable and lovable, in all whose varied characters, from knight and priest, duke and duchess, to innkeeper and convict, none is wholly hateful.

The centenary of Cervantes fell in the middle of the world-war and evoked in this country at least two interesting appreciations, Professor Fitzmaurice-Kelly's learned address and Professor W. P. Ker's characteristically subtle analysis of the various strands which are interwoven in the great masterpiece. The present writer is not a Spanish scholar, but is tempted to record some of the impressions which a restudy of this great comedy, under war conditions, and a reconsideration of its echoes in English and European literature, have renewed and deepened. The first of these is the impression of *Don Quixote* as the parent of the modern novel. So much has been written about the slow evolution of the novel in the century and a half which followed, till all the currents united in *Clarissa* and *Tom Jones*, that it comes upon a reader as something of a surprise to realise that here, in *Don Quixote*, are all the essentials of the *genre*. Here is the proper style, theme, and material. The style, as the author himself says, "runs musically, plainly, and pleasantly, with clear, proper, and well-placed words". Malory's style is one of rare quality and beauty, but it is the style of romance, not of the novel. Cervantes is the first great master in prose of that pleasant mode of narrative in which the author seems to take you by the hand and to converse with you agreeably on the road— apostrophising, commenting, digressing, a style in which Fielding and Thackeray have been among his happiest followers; George Meredith too, were it not that Meredith's colloquial gambols are sometimes as awkward as they are fantastic. What delightful digressions those of Cervantes are themselves and have been the occasion of in others—the priest and the barber in Don Quixote's library, Parson Adams upon Homer, Fielding on the comic epic in prose! Even the more poetic flights, the descriptions of dawn, the eloquence of the knight when he dilates to Sancho or the canon, do not disturb but

enhance the harmony of the whole, and found an amusing
and variously toned echo in Fielding and Meredith, as
at the introduction of Sophia in *Tom Jones*, or the
meeting of Richard and Lucy in *Richard Feverel*.

But Cervantes' enchanting style is the natural and
beautiful vesture for his subject-matter, and that is again
just the proper subject of the novel, human nature and
the ordinary everyday life of men.   It would have been
so easy for Cervantes, in revolting from the unrealities
of romance, in seeking to bring romance into ludicrous
contact with reality, to slip either into mere burlesque or
into the tedious violence and sordid details of the *picaresque*
romance as that had already taken shape in *Lazarillo de
Tormes.*   He did neither; but, instead, he invented, as
by a divine accident, the comic epic in prose which is
just the modern novel of life and manners.   The world
of romance lies east of the sun and west of the moon,
and its epoch is that of good Haroun Alraschid or brave
King Arthur.   The world of burlesque has features of
real life at a definite era, England under the Commonwealth, or Italy in the sixteenth century; but that world
is conceived in an abstractly ludicrous and satirical fashion.
No one rises from the perusal of Butler's *Hudibras* or of
Tassoni's *La Secchia Rapita* with any such impression of
life in Puritan England or Italian city politics and wars as
*Don Quixote* conveys of Spanish life and character in the
reign of Philip the Fourth.   The sunny atmosphere of
the whole does not falsify the details.

This is the aspect of Cervantes' work which floods
the imagination with most surprise and delight when one
returns to it remembering chiefly one's early naïve
pleasure in the fantastic adventures.   Here is God's

plenty!  We linger with the same pleasure among the
people who meet us on every page as we do with the
pilgrims who rode to Canterbury, or as we make the
acquaintance of the peasants and beggars and lawyers and
ministers and gipsies who crowd the best chapters of the
Waverley Novels.  Don Quixote sets out to achieve
heroic exploits, worthy of Don Amadis, deeds that are
" to obliterate the memory of the Platirs, the Tablantes,
Olivantes and Tirantes, the Knights of the Sun and the
Belianises with the whole tribe of the famous knights-
errant of times past ".  He sees everything through the
glamour of romance, but the romance eludes him, melting
into reality, and that reality is to us who read more
delightful than any romance.  Here are innkeepers,
themselves readers of romances, but not disposed therefore
to approve of Don Quixote's omitting to pay his bill on
the ground that he is a knight-errant and the inn a castle;
frail but good-hearted chambermaids like Maritornes ;
jovial souls who toss Sancho in a blanket, " four cloth-
workers of Segovia, three needle-makers of the horse-
fountain of Cordova, and two butchers of Seville, all arch,
merry, good-hearted, and frolicsome fellows ".  We listen
to the priest and the barber as in Don Quixote's library
they talk learnedly and critically of romances and pastorals
and poems, Spanish and Italian, before they deliver them
over to the secular arm of the housekeeper.  We take the
road with Don Quixote, and traverse meadows dotted
with white-sailed windmills which he takes for armed
giants, or hear by night the roar and clanking of some
monster, and find as day breaks that the monster is a
fulling-mill turned by a water-fall, or, entering a boat,
like Lancelot and Galahad, in quest of adventure, we are

borne down a swift stream and only saved from drowning
by a flour-miller and his men. We see the village
barber scouring the plain, leaving his ass as booty for
Sancho, his basin to become Mambrino's helmet on the
head of him of the Sorrowful Countenance. We interview convicts on their way to the galleys and hear their
own account of their crimes; or companies of mounted
carriers who visit on Sancho and the knight the amorous
indiscretions of Rosinante. We dine in the open air
with shepherds and goatherds, and listen to their songs
and ballads and stories of unhappy lovers. The pastoral
element is, indeed, the only one not perfectly adjusted
to the realism of the setting, but the effect is not inharmonious. "That piping of shepherds and pretty
sylvan ballet which dances always round the principal
figures is delightfully pleasant to me," says Thackeray,
who was reading *Don Quixote* while he was writing of
Colonel Newcome. Everything else is real—the ladies
in coaches on their way to Seville to meet husbands
returning from the Spanish Indies; Benedictines on mules
protected from the dust by face-masks and glasses; a
funeral that passes by night with mounted torch-bearers
and mourners; a cart driven by a hideous devil carrying
Death and an angel with coloured wings, and a crowned
Emperor and Cupid with his bow and quiver—in short
the actors in a Corpus Christi play, for this is Spain,
and Spain is still in the Middle Ages. Or again it is a
cart conveying a present of lions to the king at Madrid;
or the puppet-show where a boy interprets as Hamlet
offered to interpret to Ophelia. Always there is abundance of good eating and drinking, with much pleasant
conversation, at Camacho's wedding, or the house of the

wealthy franklin Don Diego, or the palace of the duke, or
the inn, or in the open air, where Don Quixote and
Sancho and the Bachelor and Tom Cecial eat and talk
and sleep in the warm Spanish night by the river-side.
All the rich and varied life of Spain flows past us as we
read, giving everywhere the same impression that this
fantastic story has for setting neither the unreal world of
romance nor the harsh brutalities of *picaresque* story, but
the genial happenings of everyday, normal human life.

But this truthful, vivid picture and setting only deepens
our admiration of the art with which Cervantes has drawn
his two heroes and adjusted them to their setting, made
them real and lovable persons in a real world, allowing
for the element of exaggeration and abstraction inseparable
from comedy, not fantastic, or, as the shepherds are,
poetic intrusions from another plane. The depth of
Cervantes' picture is not less admirable than its breadth
and variety; and it is worth while considering what are
the qualities which give his two heroes their hold at once
on truth and on our affection and admiration, make
them not only realities in a world of realities but two of
the great symbolic characters of literature, like Faust and
Hamlet, types of humanity whose dreams no disillusionment can altogether destroy, humanity so material and
gross, yet so prone to faith and hero-worship.

The first great quality of Don Quixote, natural and
admirable, is his impeccable courage. No danger daunts
him, no disaster dismays, and yet there is no suggestion
of exaggeration. He remains a plain, simple Spanish
gentleman, lean, cadaverous, and of a sorrowful countenance. For his courage has its roots in two qualities of
human nature, and not least of Spanish character    His

is the traditional courage of a class and a people, the courage of those who have learnt to think of cowardice as for them impossible. "A gentleman", says Montesquieu, "may be careful of his property, never of his life." The *moral* of a battalion, it is said, depends on its traditions. To the splendid courage of the Spanish gentlemen of the sixteenth century no one has borne witness more wholeheartedly than their great enemy Sir Walter Raleigh:

> Here, I cannot forbear to commend the Spartan fortitude of the Spaniards. We seldom or never find that any nation has endured so many adventures and miseries as the Spaniards have done in their Indian discoveries; yet persisting in their enterprises with inviolable constancy, they have annexed to their kingdom so many goodly provinces as bury remembrance of all danger past. Tempests, shipwrecks, famine, overthrows, heat and cold, pestilence, and all manner of diseases, both old and new, together with extreme poverty and want of all things needful, have been the enemies wherewith every one of their most noble discoverers at one time or other hath encountered. Many years have passed over some of their heads in the search of not so many leagues; yea, more than one or two have spent their labour, their wealth, and their lives, in search of a golden kingdom, without getting further notice of it than what they had at their first setting forth. All of which notwithstanding, the third, fourth and fifth have not been disheartened. Surely they are worthily rewarded with those treasures and paradises which they enjoy, and well they deserve to hold them if they hinder not the like virtues in others; which (perhaps) will not be found.

But Don Quixote's courage has in it a finer element than that of the adventurer for El Dorado. It is also the courage of the Spanish saint and martyr, like St.

Teresa, the courage of one who follows a spiritual vision through every peril and perplexity. But a saint could not well be the hero of a comedy; and Cervantes had to make him what the saint sometimes verges on, or appears to the world to be, a madman, the victim of a fixed idea, yet no less fundamentally sane than the great saints from St. Paul (" I am not mad, most noble Festus! ") to St. Francis. Don Quixote combines all the forms of madness which Shakespeare records—the lunatic's, the lover's, and the poet's. If he does not see " more devils than vast hell can hold ", he discovers the hand of magicians in every misadventure which befalls him. The envy and evil arts of magicians are his solution of every perplexity, his refuge in every assault which threatens his illusion. He is a lover, too, in the old high way, one of those lovers

Who thought love should be
So much compounded of high courtesy
That they would sigh and quote with learned looks
Precedents out of beautiful old books;

and " he discovers Helen's beauty " in a country lass who " can pitch the bar with the lustiest swain in the parish ". He is a poet whose imagination clothes the most ordinary objects and occurrences in such vivid colours of illusion as compel belief. Nothing in the romances Cervantes was parodying is so enchantingly romantic as Don Quixote's descriptions to Sancho Panza of the achievements and adventures which await him (c. xxi.) or the *Apologia* for the credibility of his beloved romances with which he overwhelms the sceptical canon who " stood in admiration to hear the medley Don Quixote made of truth and lies, and to see how skilled he was in all matters

relating to knight-errantry " (cc. xlix., l.).   It is vain to
argue with him, for the glowing pictures which his
imagination evokes overflow the pales and forts of reason
with such a flood of enchantment that the knight is
swept away on the high tide of his own eloquence, with
Sancho Panza following in his wake like a clumsy coble
in the tow of a swift-winged yacht.   But in thus building belief upon imagination and desire Don Quixote
is typical of nine-tenths of mankind.   The fiction and
poetry we read has more effect in shaping our early
anticipations of life than the critical intellect.   If we do
not believe what we desire, we are prone to fall into the
worse delusion of believing only what we fear.   Scott
selected the same type of hero for his first romance,
Edward Waverley, misled by an early indulgence in
romance and poetry.   In each case there was something
of the author in the hero.   Lockhart's apology, in the
last chapter of his great biography, for the errors which
involved Scott's financial disasters is a sympathetic but
candid appreciation of the day-dreams which shaped the
world of Scott's activities, activities at first glance so
practical, his " romantic idealisation of Scottish aristocracy ".   Scott was himself a Don Quixote dreaming of
the past as still present or capable of being revived,
" a scheme of life, so constituted originally, and which
his fancy pictured as capable of being so revived, as to
admit of the kindliest personal conduct between (almost)
the peasant at the plough and the magnate with revenues
rivalling the monarch's.   It was the patriarchal, the clan
system that he thought of."   But Scott's portrayal of
the dreamer in Edward Waverley is restrained by didactic
considerations—he wishes to warn others against his own

errors, and the character is, like most of Scott's heroes, but half alive. Cervantes poured himself into his creation in a torrent of sympathy and humour, and made of his hero the perennial symbol of dream-ridden humanity.

But even as Scott's dreams interest us because they were the dreams of a man of sound common sense, wise judgement, and genial humour, so Don Quixote is great because he is neither a mere dreamer nor a hateful buffoon, like Hudibras, but a man of high character and fine sanity, a gentleman and a scholar. If the knight's madness moves us to laughter, it is his sanity and nobility which extort our admiration and love, and Cervantes has achieved this combination without any suggestion of unreality or sentimentality such as would inevitably have marred a character drawn on deliberately preconceived lines. On every one who encounters Don Quixote he produces the same impression of folly and sanity inextricably blended. " The canon gazed earnestly at him and stood in admiration of his strange and unaccountable madness, perceiving that in all his discourses and answers he discovered a very good understanding, and only lost his stirrups when the conversation happened to turn upon the subject of chivalry! " " Don Quixote went on with his discourse in such a manner and in such proper expressions that none of those who heard him at that time could take him for a madman." " Ah! Signor Don Quixote, have pity on yourself, and return into the bosom of discretion, and learn to make use of those great abilities Heaven has been pleased to bestow upon you by employing that happy talent you are blessed with in some other kind of reading." " Pray, sir," says Don Lorenzo to his father, " who is the gentleman you have

brought us home? For his name, his figure, and your
telling us he is a knight-errant, keep my mother and me
in great suspense." " I know not what to answer you,
son," replied Don Diego, " I can only tell you that I
have seen him act the part of the maddest man in the
world, and then talk so ingeniously that his words con-
tradict and undo all his actions."

On no theme does Don Quixote discourse more sanely
or more nobly than the motive of all his extravagances.
The romantic and fantastic aspects of his adventure are
naturally those on which the knight most often expatiates
to Sancho Panza—glory, and the gaining of kingdoms,
and the wedding of beautiful princesses, and rewarding
of squires, for Cervantes' work is a comedy, not a piece
of sentimental symbolism like *The Blue Bird*. But in
the great discourse at the inn his hero rises to a higher
conception of his task. Cervantes affords a glimpse of
the high and pure idealism which underlies the knight's
absurdities, of that aspect of his creation which Fielding
and our own eighteenth-century novelists were to
emphasise in its full significance. The hero defines his
aim in words that seem to be almost a conscious echo of
a passage in Dante's *De Monarchia*.

> In truth, gentlemen, if it be well considered, great and un-
> heard of things do they seek who profess the order of knight-
> errantry. . . . There is no doubt but that this art and pro-
> fession exceeds all that have ever been invented by men, and
> so much the more honourable is it by how much it is exposed
> to more dangers. Away with those who say that letters have
> the advantages over arms; I will tell them, be they who they
> will, that they know not what they say. For the reason they
> usually give, and which they lay the greatest stress upon, is

that the labours of the brain exceed those of the body, and that arms are exercised by the body alone; as if the use of them were the business of porters, for which nothing is necessary but downright strength; or as if in this, which we who profess it call chivalry, were not included the acts of fortitude, which require a very good understanding to execute them; or as if the mind of the warrior who has an army, or the defence of a besieged city, committed to his charge, does not labour with his understanding as well as his body. It being so then that arms employ the mind as well as letters, let us next see whose mind labours most, the scholar's or the warrior's. And this may be determined by the scope and ultimate end of each; for that intention is to be the most esteemed which has the noblest end for its object. Now the end and design of letters (I do not now speak of divinity, which has for its aim the raising and conducting souls to heaven; for to an end so endless as this no other can be compared), I speak of human learning, whose end, I say, is to regulate distributive justice, and give to every man his due, to know good laws and cause them to be strictly observed, an end most certainly generous and exalted, and worthy of high commendation, but not equal to that which is annexed to the profession of arms, whose object and end is peace, the greatest blessing men can wish for in life. Accordingly, the first good news the world received was what the angels brought on that night which was our day, when they sang in the clouds, *Glory be to God on high, and on earth peace to men of goodwill*, and the salutation which the best master of earth or heaven taught His followers and disciples was that, when they entered into any house, they should say, *Peace be to this house*: and many other times He said, *My peace I give unto you, My peace I leave with you, Peace be amongst you*. A jewel and legacy worthy of coming from such a hand; a jewel without which there can be no happiness either in heaven or earth. This peace is the true end of war; for to say arms or war is the same thing.[1] (c. xxxvii.)

This is Don Quixote at his best; but the same fine sanity, the same high Christian spirit colours much that he has to say on many and diverse themes—parents and children (c. lxviii.), marriage (c. lxxiv.), the duty of a governor (c. xciv.), to say nothing of his critical discourses on poetry and the drama.

This, then, is Don Quixote as Cervantes conceived him; but the picture remains incomplete until we see him through the eyes of his squire, for the greatest proof of Don Quixote's courage, sincerity, and goodness is the completeness of the hold which he acquires over the soul of Sancho. There is some carelessness of execution in the second part, some sacrifice of truth to burlesque; the author plays a little down to his audience. But, in general, the picture is admirably conceived and sustained. Sancho has not read chivalrous romances. He cannot read at all. His stock of wisdom is an inexhaustible store of proverbs, the peasant's philosophy of practical experience, the gnomic wisdom of a peasant poet like Hesiod. He

---

[1] In much of this Cervantes is almost translating Dante, unless there is some common scholastic source of these particular applications of texts: " Unde manifestum est, quod pax universalis est optimum eorum, quae ad nostram beatitudinem ordinantur. Hinc est, quod pastoribus de sursum sonuit, non divitiae, non voluptates, non honores, non longitudo vitae, non sanitas, non robur, non pulchritudo; sed pax. Inquit enim coelestis militia; ' Gloria in altissimis Deo, et in terra pax hominibus bonae voluntatis '. Hinc etiam ' Pax vobis ' Salus hominum salutabat. Decebat enim summum Salvatorem, summam salutationem exprimere. Quem quidem morem servare voluerunt Discipuli eius, et Paulus in Salutationibus suis, ut omnibus manifestum esse potest."—Dante, *De Monarchia* (Oxford, 1904), i. 4.

understands neither Don Quixote's chivalrous courage
nor his ideals of chivalrous love and service.  He cannot
comprehend why his master should expose himself to
unnecessary dangers, when there are no witnesses.  When
the horrors of the fulling-mill break upon their ears by
night and are interpreted by his master as indicating the
presence of some terrible monster or giant of romance,
Sancho is for beating a prompt retreat: " Sir, I do not
understand why your worship should, it is now night
and nobody sees; we may easily turn aside and get out
of harm's way . . . and as nobody sees us, much less
will there be anybody to tax us with cowardice."  When
he and his master are beaten nearly to death by the
Yangueses, and Don Quixote concludes that the mis-
adventure is due to his transgression of the laws of chivalry
in fighting with undubbed churls, and that in future
Sancho shall do all such plebeian fighting, the latter is
by no means disposed to acquiesce.  " Sir," said Sancho,
" I am a peaceable, tame, quiet man, and can dis-
semble any injury whatsoever, for I have a wife and
children to maintain and bring up; so that give me
leave, Sir, to tell you, by way of hint, that I will
upon no account draw my sword either against peasant
or against knight; and that from this time forward I
forgive all injuries any one has done, or shall do me,
or that any person is now doing me or may hereafter
do me, whether he be high or low, rich or poor,
gentle or simple, without excepting any state or condition whatsoever."

He is equally far from comprehending the nature of
Don Quixote's attachment to the fair Dulcinea, the high
theory and practice of chivalrous love.

" You perceive not, Sancho, that all this redounds the more
to her exaltation . . . for you must know that, in our style
of chivalry, it is a great honour for a lady to have many knight-
errants who serve her merely for her own sake, without ex-
pectation of any other reward of their manifold good deserts
than the honour of being admitted into the number of her
knights." " I have heard it preached ", quoth Sancho,
" that God is to be loved with this kind of love, for Himself
alone, without our being moved to it by the hope of reward
or the fear of punishment; though, for my part, I am inclined
to love and serve Him for what He is able to do for me."
" The Devil take you for a bumpkin," said Don Quixote,
" you are ever and anon saying such smart things that one
would almost think you had studied." " And yet, by my
faith," quoth Sancho, " I cannot so much as read."

Sancho is as frankly materialistic and practical as Don
Quixote is a romantic and ideal dreamer. Eating and
drinking hold a high place in his scale of values. He is
not, indeed, a symbol of the claims of the body against
a monkish asceticism, like Gargantua and Pantagruel.
He is not a bibulous and witty parasite, genial and good-
humoured, but shameless and incapable of an unselfish
impulse, like the great Sir John Falstaff, our affection
for whom is a tribute to Shakespeare's art rather than to
any intrinsic amiability of the knight's. We enjoy his
company, as we do that of Mrs. Gamp, more in imagination than we should in actuality, if we stood within
the range of his predatory activities. Sancho is neither
parasitic nor predatory, though he is not above picking
up trifles, and he does meditate the possibility of selling
the inhabitants of any island that may come his way into
slavery; but like all the above-mentioned he loves good

living, and the highest epithet in his vocabulary is reserved for that good creature wine. When he and Tom Cecial finished discussing the rabbit-pasty and that supposititious squire put the bottle into Sancho's hand, he grasped it " and setting it to his mouth stood gazing at the stars for a quarter of an hour; and having done drinking he let fall his head to one side, and fetching a deep sigh, said, ' O whoreson rogue, how *catholic* it is! ' " One seems almost to hear the voice of Mr. Belloc or Mr. Chesterton.

By what means, then, has Cervantes made credible Sancho's fidelity to his master? He has undeniably moments of doubt and hesitation. He gets his full share of the drubbings. He cannot convince himself that he has been tossed in the blanket by magicians.

" I too ", quoth Sancho, " would have revenged myself if I could, dubbed or not dubbed; but I could not; though I am of opinion that they who diverted themselves at my expense were no hobgoblins, but men of flesh and bone, as we are; and each of them, as I heard while they were tossing me, had his proper name: one was called Pedro Martinez, another Tenorio Hernandez; and the landlord's name is John Palomeque, the left-handed; so that, Sir, as to your not being able to leap over the pales, nor to alight from your horse, the fault lay in something else and not in enchantment. And what I gather from all this is that these adventures we are in quest of will at the long run bring us into so many misadventures, that we shall not know which is our right foot. So that in my poor opinion the better and surer way would be to return to our village, now that it is reaping time, and look after our business, and not run rambling from Zeca to Mecca, leaping out of the frying-pan into the fire."

He sees that the priest and the barber and the world

E

generally do not believe in his master's pretensions and promises. At times he joins them in playing upon his delusions. He parodies Don Quixote's heroic speeches. " This master of mine," he says, " by a thousand tokens that I have seen, is mad enough to be tied in his bed; and in truth I come very little behind him, nay I am madder than he is to follow and serve him, if there be any truth in the proverb that says, ' Show me thy company and I will tell thee what thou art '; or in that other, ' Not with whom thou art bred but with whom thou art fed '." But Sancho does believe in his master, and it is just this delightful blend of simplicity and shrewdness which makes him so typical a character and so unique a creation of genius.

Sancho's confidence is in the first place a reflection of Don Quixote's. Had the latter for one moment doubted of his mission, had his courage been less impeccable, Sancho's faith must have dissolved in incredulity and contempt. But Don Quixote's faith and courage are unfailing, and Sancho may well ask himself who he is, an unlearned peasant, to discredit such confidence backed by so much knowledge, so much practical good sense, such vivid descriptions. When Don Quixote launches into a rich and glowing account of adventures to come, and the glorious rewards that must ensue, Sancho's imagination kindles at his master's, and he takes up the running, though his anticipations are of a more uniformly material character. For the strongest hook in Sancho's nose is baited with an island. He may not know much about ruling, but in the last resort he can sell the inhabitants into slavery with the Moors.

" This is what I denounce, Señor Sampson," quoth Sancho, " for my master makes no more of attacking a hundred armed men than a greedy boy would do of half a dozen melons. Body of me! Signor Bachelor, there must be a time to attack and a time to retreat; and it must not be always *Saint Iago and charge Spain!* I would not have him run away when there is no need of it, nor would I have him follow on when too great superiority requires another thing. . . . But if my Lord Don Quixote, in consideration of my many good services, has a mind to bestow on me some one island of the many his worship says he shall light upon, I shall be beholden for the favour; and though he should not give me one, born I am and we must not rely upon one another but upon God, and perhaps the bread I shall eat without the Government may go down more savourily than that I could eat with it . . . yet for all that, if fairly and squarely, without much trouble or danger, Heaven should chance to throw an island or some such thing in my way, I am not such a fool as to refuse it, for it is a saying, when they give you a heifer make haste with the rope, and when good fortune comes be sure to take her aid."

It may be, Sancho argues in his confused fashion, that the whole quest is an illusion, but it may not be so, and meantime there are occasional prizes, as the hamper on the dead mule, the skimmings of the pot at Camacho's wedding, the plentiful fare at the house of Don Diego or the castle of the duke.

Sancho's faith in his master is thus, it must be confessed, a hope of good things to come. The faith of the common man is seldom entirely devoid of such material ingredients. But it would have been neither true to nature, nor likely to evoke our sympathy for Sancho, to represent this as the sole or principal motive for his loyalty. But Cervantes has taken good care not to do so. The tie which binds Sancho to his master is simply in the last resort that he loves him. Cervantes has not laboured this. He is writing pure comedy with no such blend of sentiment as colours, for example, Dickens's account of the charming relations, doubtless suggested by Cervantes' master and man, between Pickwick and Sam Weller. But the affection is there, and radiates through the light gaiety and irony of the story. When Tom Cecial, the squire to the Knight of the Looking Glass, who is the humorous Bachelor of Salamanca, declares that *his* master is crack-brained and valiant, but more knavish than valiant, Sancho replies with warmth, " Mine is not so; I can assure you he has nothing of the knave in him; on the contrary, he has the soul of a pitcher; a child may persuade him it is night at noonday; and for this simplicity I love him as my life, and cannot find in my heart to leave him, let him do never so many extravagances." When, in the second part, the Duchess challenges Sancho's sincerity his reply is the same: " By my faith, Madam," quoth Sancho, " this same scruple comes in the nick of time; please your lady-ship bid it speak out plain; for I know it says true, and had I been wise, I should have left my master long ere now, but such was my lot and such my evil errantry. I can do no more; follow him I must; we are both of the same town; I have eaten his bread; I love him; he returns my kindness; he gave me his ass colts; and above all I am faithful, and therefore it is impossible anything should part us but the sexton's spade and shovel." And if Sancho may not have the island there are innumerable proverbs to console him, and warn him of the vanity of gratified ambitions:

" They make as good bread here as in France;  and, *In the dark all cats are grey*;  and *No stomach is a span bigger than another, and may be filled*, as they say, *with straw or with hay*; and, *Of the little birds in the air God Himself takes the care*; and, *Four yards of coarse cloth of Cuença are warmer than as many of fine Segovia serge* . . . and the Pope's body takes up no more room than the sexton's, though the one be higher than the other;  for when we come to the grave we must all shrink and lie close, or be made to shrink and lie close in spite of us;  and so good night;  and therefore I say again that, if your ladyship will not give me the island because I am a fool, I will be so wise as not to care a fig for it;  and I have heard say, *The devil lurks behind the cross*;  and, *All is not gold that glitters*;  and Bamba the husbandman was taken from among his plows, his yokes and oxen, to be king of Spain;  and Roderigo was taken from his brocades, pastimes and riches to be devoured by snakes, if ancient ballads do not lie."

### 2

THE popularity of Cervantes' great work, not in Spain only but in other countries of Western Europe, was immediate, and in its influence on the literature of our own country is traceable as early as 1611.  But in none of the English imitations of the seventeenth century, including the greatest of these, Samuel Butler's *Hudibras*, is there any sign that the work was regarded as more than an amusing extravagance.  The apprehension of a higher significance in *Don Quixote*, a significance perhaps higher than the naïve genius of Cervantes himself had descried, though once or twice, as I have indicated, he seems to apprehend and suggest it, began with the great English novelists of the eighteenth century.  The debt of

Fielding's *Joseph Andrews* and *Tom Jones* to *Don Quixote* in respect to structure, incident, *e.g.* adventures on the road and at inns, dialogues upon all sorts of subjects not always relevant to the plot, inset tales, manner, style, and spirit, can hardly be overestimated. But Cervantes' work was more for Fielding than a burlesque of a romance, more even than a great comic epic in prose, a model for his own genial and humorous picture of English life; and if there never was work, as Professor Fitzmaurice-Kelly tells us, more heartily national than *Don Quixote*, more native to the heroic soil that gave it being, it is equally true that his first great literary son was the most English of all Englishmen. " Of all the works of imagination, to which the English imagination has given origin," says Sir Walter Scott, " the writings of Henry Fielding are, perhaps, most decisively and exclusively her own. They are not only altogether beyond the reach of translation, in the proper sense and spirit of the work, but we even question whether they can be fully understood, or relished to the highest extent by such natives of Scotland and Ireland as are not habitually and intimately acquainted with the characters and manners of old England." *Don Quixote* was for Fielding not merely a novel but a great and humorous satire on human life, and the Knight of the Sorrowful Countenance a type of the central figure in his own humorous and satirical picture of English life. For what, after all, one may ask, is the hero of Cervantes' romance? Is he not a type of the Christian whose Christianity is more than a speculative belief or a magical means of personal salvation, a lofty if fantastic idealist whose practical faith in his ideals no ignominy and no rebuff can destroy. " For verily," says St. Paul, " when we were with you we told you beforehand that we are to suffer afflictions; even as it came to pass and ye know." "This I can say for myself," declares Don Quixote, "that since I have been a knight-errant, I have become valiant, civil, liberal, affable, patient, a sufferer of toils, imprisonments, and enchantments; and though it be so little a while since I saw myself locked up in a cage like a madman, yet I expect, by the valour of my arm, Heaven favouring, and Fortune not opposing, in a few days to see myself king of a realm in which I may display the gratitude and liberality enclosed in this breast of mine." Is that very different in spirit from the language of the great Christian who in the service of his ideal had been " in journeyings often, in perils of mine own countrymen, in perils in the city, in perils in the wilderness, in perils in the sea, in perils among false brethren, in weariness and painfulness, in watchings often, in cold and nakedness ", and yet is a happier man than before he was the slave of Christ? And if Don Quixote's fantastic idealism needs the support of a sure and certain hope of kingdoms yet to be conquered, dreams of a golden day when he shall be received at the city gates with music and by fair damsels who will escort him to the right hand of the king whose throne and honour he has delivered from the enmity of giants and magicians and evil knights, is not St. Paul also sustained by a dream which never came true in the form he anticipated? " Then we which are alive and remain shall be caught up together with them into the clouds to meet the Lord in the air, and so shall we ever be with the Lord."

In Don Quixote Fielding found an adumbration of the type of Christian which the robuster minds of his century found more essential than either the scheme-of-

salvation theologian of the seventeenth or the Puritan
ideal as that reappeared in Richardson's novel, intent upon
the personal virtues of chastity and temperance—the man
for whom the first of Christian virtues were the social
virtues of justice and mercy; and in Don Quixote's misadventures they saw the fate of the man who endeavours to
put into practice those principles of Christian charity and
benevolence to which we all assent on Sunday.    It was
a strange delusion of Carlyle that the eighteenth century
was a waste chaos of scepticism in religion and politics, an
age of universal doubt.    In fact, there was more faith in
the little finger of some of the greatest men of that century,
Fielding and Johnson, Howard and Wilberforce, Goldsmith and Burke (with all his fears), than in the whole
body of the Victorians except Dickens, Lord Shaftesbury,
and perhaps Browning.    For intellectual scepticism is not
so fatal an enemy of faith as the spiritual pessimism of
Jeremiahs like Carlyle and Ruskin, such faint-hearts as
Tennyson, or such 'epicures of melancholy as Matthew
Arnold.    The great spirits of the eighteenth century
believed in their fellow-men.    They recognised the evils
of life without preferring an indictment against Providence.
They noted with clear and amused eye the faults and
follies of men without ceasing to love and respect their
virtues.

What, for example, is Fielding's Parson Adams but a
muscular, absent-minded Don Quixote?    He has the same
love of literature—of Homer and Aeschylus rather than of
Amadis and Palmerin (but Don Quixote also knows his
classics), and above all he has the same impeccable courage,
the same rigid adherence to the ideals he professes, the
same splendid unworldliness and immunity to disillusion-

ment.    A crucial instance is the scene in which Adams
and Joseph and Fanny discover that they have no money
wherewith to pay their bill at the inn where Joseph has
been cared for after his mishap with the highwaymen.
" They stood silent for some few minutes staring at each
other, when Adams whipped round on his toes and asked
the hostess if there was no clergyman in that parish?
She answered, ' there was '.    ' Is he wealthy? ' replied
he, to which she likewise answered in the affirmative.
Adams then, snapping his fingers, returned overjoyed to
his companions, crying out, ' Heureka! Heureka! ' which
not being understood he told them in plain English, they
need give themselves no trouble, for he had a brother in
the parish who would defray the account, and that he
would just step to his house and fetch the money and
return to them instantly."    Parson Trulliber, to whom
he proceeds, imagines at first that he has come to see the
fat pigs of which he is a breeder, and it is only after
an accident somewhat disastrous to his appearance that
Adams is enabled to explain the purpose of his visit.    " I
think, sir, it is high time to inform you of the business of
my embassy.    I am a traveller and am passing this way
in company with two young people, a lad and a damsel.
We stopped at a house of hospitality in the parish, where
they directed me to you as having the cure."    " Though
I am the curate," says Trulliber, " I believe I am as warm
as the vicar himself, or perhaps the rector of the next
parish too; I believe I could buy them both."    " Sir,"
cries Adams, " I rejoice thereat.    Now, sir, my business
is, that we are by various accidents stripped of our money,
and are not able to pay our reckoning, being seven shillings.
I therefore request you to assist me with the loan of those

seven shillings, and also seven shillings more, which peradventure, I shall return to you, but if not, I am convinced you will joyfully embrace such an opportunity of laying up a treasure in a better place than any this world affords." It is unnecessary to continue from the inimitable scene. It is sufficient to say that Don Quixote was not more mistaken when he took sheep for knights and windmills for giants than was Parson Adams when he took for granted that a Christian pastor would welcome an opportunity of laying up treasure in a better place than any this world affords. Parson Trulliber is quite prepared to take the risk of the moth and the rust.

The type of character represented by Parson Adams appears and reappears in the works of the great eighteenth-century novelists, and of those Victorian novelists whose work belongs to the same humanitarian and satiric tradition. In the same class are Roderick Random's sailor uncle, Goldsmith's Vicar of Wakefield, and, in a manner which is peculiar to Sterne, so is the tender-hearted, fantastic Uncle Toby. Cervantes, as well as Smollett and Fielding, was among the authors in the old library which Dickens found and read as a boy at Rochester; and certainly Mr. Pickwick, as he developed under the hand of his creator, became a reincarnation of the same type, a Quixote of kindness with a weakness for milk-punch and bottled beer, just as certainly as the coupling of this simple, middle-aged, good-hearted gentleman with the alert, knowing, ready-witted, good-hearted Sam Weller was suggested by the relations between Don Quixote and his squire. The same easy relations prevail between master and man, with the same occasional fits of dignified self-assertion on the part of the master. Thackeray read, and comments with

delight in a letter upon *Don Quixote*, when he was pre-
paring to write *The Newcomes*, and Colonel Newcome
is perhaps the last appearance of Don Quixote in the
varying guise in which the eighteenth- and nineteenth-
century novelists had conceived him.

In more ways than one, therefore, Cervantes in *Don
Quixote* builded better than he knew; transcended the
original intention of his work.   He invented the prototype
of the novel of everyday life and manners, the comic epic
in prose, as that was to take shape finally in the work of
the great English novelists of the eighteenth century; and,
in his hero, he depicted more than the victim of a taste
for romantic reading, he created a fantastic but yet honour-
compelling type of the idealism of the human heart rising
superior to every disillusioning experience in virtue of impeccable courage, indomitable faith, and a vivid imagination.   From the victim of a satire on romance, Don
Quixote became in the eighteenth century the hero
of a profounder satire, in which not he but the world
that ridicules him, not his ideals but the society which
professes to honour them, is arraigned, and made conscious
of the interval which divides the professions and the
practice of a so-called Christian civilisation.   In *Don
Juan* Byron sums up the thought of the past century
about Cervantes' great work, but he does so in the more
sombre tone that denotes a change of temper which was
to make the literature of the nineteenth century more
interested in another picture of the idealist in conflict with
reality and compelled in this harsh world to draw his
breath in pain:

> I should be very willing to redress
> Men's wrongs, and rather check than punish vice,

Had not Cervantes in that too true tale
Of Quixote shown how all such efforts fail.

Of all tales 'tis the saddest, and more sad
Because it makes us smile: his hero's right,
And still pursues the right: to curb the bad
His only object, and—'gainst odds to fight
His guerdon, 'tis his virtue makes him mad.
But his adventures form a sorry sight:
A sorrier still is the great moral taught
By that real epic unto all who've thought.

Redressing injury, revenging wrong,
To aid the damsel and destroy the caitiff;
Opposing singly the united strong,
From foreign yoke to free the helpless native:
Alas! must noblest views, like an old song,
Be for mere fancy's sport a theme creative.

The type of the idealist temperament in collision with
reality to which the century of Schopenhauer and Carlyle
and Ibsen and Tolstoi and the other great Russian novelists
turned by preference was that which Shakespeare had
elaborated from an old play of crime and Nemesis in the
years in which Cervantes was writing the first part of his
novel; a type which Molière drew again with sympathetic
and refined irony some sixty years later. Hamlet as
Shakespeare conceived him and Alceste in *Le Misanthrope*
(1666) are representatives of that type of idealist who at
the first touch of disillusionment, the first overthrow by
the strong and indifferent windmills of actuality, the first
acute realisation of the interval that separates what men
do from what they ought to do, loses at once and for ever
that faith in human nature in which idealism is rooted.

" Hamlet ", says a German critic, commenting on Goethe's
criticism, " is indeed a lovely vase full of costly flowers, for
he is a pure human being penetrated by enthusiasm for the
Great and Beautiful, living wholly in the ideal, and above all
things full of faith in man.    And the vase is shattered into
atoms from within; this and just this Goethe truly felt—but
what causes the ruin of the vase is not that the great deed of
avenging a father exceeds his strength, but it is the discovery
of the falseness of man, the discovery of the contradiction
between the ideal world and the actual, which suddenly
confronts him as a picture of man: it is in fact what he gradually finds in himself as the true portrait of the human nature
which he deified—in short, Hamlet perishes because the
gloomy background of life is suddenly unrolled before him,
because the sight of this robs him of his faith in life and in
good, and because he now cannot act.    Only that man can
act for others and for all who is inwardly sound, and Hamlet's
mind is out of joint after he has been robbed of his earlier
faith. . . . The great Protestant doctrine of man's need of
faith, of faith as the condition of peace, and of the fulfilment
of his mission as a moral being—this it is to which this profoundest of all the works of Shakespeare's genius owes its
origin."

Whether this be entirely Shakespeare's Hamlet or not,
it is the Hamlet which the nineteenth century took to its
heart, and which found so many counterparts in the
Russian and Scandinavian literature of disillusionment.
The Nihilist, as Prince Kropotkin has described him,
aimed at the same uncompromising sincerity as Alceste
demands; the lack of which in Polonius and Ophelia
and the courtiers deepens Hamlet's æsthetic disgust of
life.    The Nihilist probing the mystery of his own will
and of the world, violating every inhibition that he may

find if there be a Will at all other than his own, any
power behind the world of phenomena which has taken
into its keeping the cause of good against evil, if God
really *be*—what is he, as Dostoievsky describes him in
Stavrogin, the hero of *The Possessed*, but a Russian Hamlet
of the nineteenth century, finding no motive to act, no
meaning in anything?    Most interesting of all is Ibsen's
*Brand*, for it is a *Don Quixote* written by and in the spirit
of a Hamlet.    The Lutheran pastor living out his creed
of service and loyalty to his flock, even to the last sacrifice
of child and wife, is a Don Quixote without any of his
happiness, because in his heart is a great doubt, the doubt
of Stavrogin, not the faith of Don Quixote.    He wills to
pursue his ideal of "all or nothing", not because he
believes, but in despairing and passionate quest of assurance
and belief.

Nothing is more significant in *Don Quixote* than the
relation of Sancho and his master.    For what, after all, is
Sancho?    A Spanish peasant as typically Spanish as his
chivalrous master, is he not, allowing for national peculiar-
ities and for the exaggeration of comedy, just the common
man of every country, whose intrinsic worth and the
charm of whose touching simplicity this war has revealed
in camp and hospital and hut,—shrewd like Sancho and
practical, a humorist and a little material in his aims and
tastes, fond of eating and drinking when the opportunity
offers, but neither a selfish debauchee like the witty but
depraved Falstaff, nor a Rabelaisian Pantagruel, and with
an infinite capacity for faith and hero-worship?    The
common people have always believed in and followed
the idealist, Christ, Mahomet, Joan of Arc, not always
understanding the language he spoke, and prone to

interpret it literally and materially, but reverencing his high and self-forgetting spirit.    They have never understood or listened to the sceptic.    There is no character so solitary as the man who has lost his faith in his fellow-men. And *Don Quixote* is the happiest of books, the best of anodynes at a time like the present, because it renews our faith in humanity, not only by its sunny but unsentimental picture of normal everyday life and character, but because its twin heroes are of all men the most happy—the idealist whose faith no disappointment can altogether destroy, the common man who takes life as he finds it, with no philosophy beyond that of experience and proverbs, but who loves and believes in the master he follows.    Not even the necessary disillusionment of the close of Don Quixote's fantastic career, despite some careless slips of the casual creator of all this delight in many shapes, can quite take away the impression of boundless belief and hope, for Don Quixote but wakens from one dream to pass into another, the great dream of the Christian faith: "But awake he did at the end of that time, and with a loud voice said, 'Blessed be Almighty God, who has vouchsafed me so great a good; in short His mercies have no bounds, and the sins of men can neither lessen nor obstruct them.'"

1916–21.

# LORD BYRON:
## ARNOLD & SWINBURNE

### I

I T will next year be forty years [1] since Matthew Arnold, in the preface to a selection from the poetry of Byron, made the claim for Wordsworth and Byron which awakened in Swinburne a fury of eloquent anger, and served for the time to depreciate rather than to enhance the reputation of the younger but far more widely celebrated poet. "Wordsworth and Byron", he told us, "stand, it seems to me, first and pre-eminent in actual performance, a glorious pair, among the English poets of this century. Keats had probably a more consummate poetic gift than either of them; but he died having produced too little, and being as yet too immature to rival them. I, for my part, can never even think of equalling with them any other of their contemporaries, either Coleridge, poet and philosopher, wrecked in a mist of opium; or Shelley, beautiful and ineffectual angel, beating in the void his luminous wings in vain. Wordsworth and Byron stand out by themselves. When the year 1900 is turned, and our nation comes to recount her poetic glories in the century which has then just ended, the first names with her will be these."

The immediate effect of Arnold's challenge was not to enhance the reputation of Byron, but rather to dispel the glamour which still for many minds invested his almost legendary name. "Byron is dead", Carlyle and

---

[1] *Poetry of Byron chosen and arranged by Matthew Arnold,* 1881.

Jane Welsh had written to one another in 1824, in a
tone of awe; " Byron is dead ", Tennyson scratched on
a rock, " on a day when the whole world seemed darkened
for me." That feeling had departed, and not a few
readers of Arnold's selections felt as though scales had
fallen from their eyes, and they realised that for them
the poetry of Byron was valueless — wanting in art,
felicity of phrase and harmony of verse, deficient in real
depth of inspiration. " A line of Wordsworth's ", Lamb
had written, when he too heard of Byron's death, " is a
lever to lift the immortal spirit! Byron can only move
the spleen. He was at best a Satyrist,—in any other
way he was mean enough."

But this was not quite the point of view of the critics
of the eighties and nineties of last century. They did
not write as champions of Wordsworth. While paying
due respect to Wordsworth, Swinburne championed against
both poets the claims of Coleridge and Shelley; and
among those who followed Swinburne to the charge
there were not wanting depreciators of Wordsworth too.
It was no " moral Clytemnestra " that struck Byron
down again, no champion of the peculiar English blend
of honest prudery and hypocritical respectability, such
as drove him from England in 1816, nor yet of that
higher, purer spirituality which Lamb is thinking of when
he speaks of Wordsworth's verse as " a lever to lift the
immortal spirit ". It was in the name, not of morals,
but of art, that Byron was arraigned by the poets of the
" sweet new style " of Rossetti and Morris and Swinburne.
He was stricken in the house of his friends in another
sense than in 1815, treated with contumely by those
who had entered most fully into the inheritance of artistic

F

freedom, freedom in the choice of subject and the portrayal of passion, exemption from the pressure of the
spirit which would have all poetry be edifying, for which
Byron in his own way—without any theory of art for
art's sake—had fought a single-handed and splendid battle.
His was a harder fate but a robuster spirit than that of
the poet whose health of body and peace of mind were
impaired by an article on *The Fleshly School*:

> 'Tis strange the mind, that very fiery particle,
> Should let itself be snuffed out by an article,

or even of the turbulent young man the audacities of
whose *Poems and Ballads* were so purely literary and
reconstructive achievements.

For it was the author of *Poems and Ballads*, a volume
which roused the moral British public as nothing had
done since *Cain* and *Don Juan*, who led the assault; and,
forgetting the generous, discriminating, and eloquent
appreciation with which in 1866 he prefaced a happier
selection than Arnold's, proceeded now to empty upon
Byron's head the frothing vials of his shrill and exuberant
vituperation. He was followed, after a preliminary
protest in *Letters to Dead Authors*:

> Ah! were you here, I wonder would you flutter
> O'er such a foe the tempest of your wing,

by Andrew Lang; and Mr. Saintsbury, whose admiration of the Rossetti-Morris-Swinburne group is unabated,
joined in the cry and has pursued Byron's reputation ever
since with a curious rancour which has not coloured his
often equally severe criticism of Wordsworth and his
heresies. Only Henley refused to take part in the

"pogrom"; and he, alas! died before completing his work as champion, critic, and editor of Byron.

But the names of the critics who condemned as of the one who was girding himself for the defence are significant, for it is not entirely to be wondered that the school of Rossetti and Morris and Pater and Swinburne and Andrew Lang did not respond appreciatively to the challenge of Matthew Arnold and subscribe to the poetic greatness of Byron. Between his poetry and theirs was no medium except the freedom from moralist restrictions to which I have referred. In the poetry of the Pre-Raphaelites, as one may for convenience call them, one phase of the Romantic Revival—not the whole of that complex phenomenon, but an aspect which it had presented from the date of Percy's *Reliques* and Chatterton's *Rowley Poems* to *The Blessed Damozel* and *Atalanta in Calydon*—attained its most complete manifestation. Never has there been in English literature a more cunningly wrought poetry of artistic reconstruction, the reconstruction of old moods and old modes, Greek or Mediæval, especially the latter. Percy's faked ballads, Chatterton's faked Middle English, are crude things compared with the sophisticated mediævalism of *The Blessed Damozel*, the romantic historic ballad as reconstructed by Rossetti in *The King's Tragedy*, or by Swinburne in those border ballads which Mr. Gosse has published since that poet's death. And what of the same poet's *canzoni* and roundels, and *sestine* and double *sestine*, and carols and miracle play? Russell Lowell's complaint as to *Atalanta* and *Erechtheus* came just to this, that they were too like the original. But it is not a mere matter of this or that precise form revived. The whole tone and tune, spirit and art of

Morris's *Defence of Guenevere* poems, with his mediæval retelling of old stories in the manner of Chaucer, of Rossetti's ballads and *House of Life*, of Swinburne's poems, pagan or mediæval, is a reconstruction of old moods of feeling, of old fashions of utterance. Never was a poet at once so spontaneous and so purely literary as Swinburne. His poems are not, as Byron's or Burns's, the vibrating response to the agitations of experience and passion—"the dream of my sleeping passions—their somnambulism" to use Byron's own phrase, which is, I suppose, just Wordsworth's "emotion recollected in tranquillity". Swinburne's are the record of emotions begotten in the library, begotten of overmuch reading of Elizabethan plays and Greek tragedy and lyric, and Old French and Italian song, or if his inspiration is more modern he sings of liberty and babies and the sea, as Victor Hugo had done before him.

Was it any wonder that these masters of cunning technique, goldsmiths who could carve and chase with the art of a Benvenuto Cellini cups and chalices of antique fashion, or the lesser moulders of ballads in blue china, fragrant with the *pot-pourri* of the romantic Middle Ages, were startled and indignant when commanded to do reverence to the crudities of Byron's earliest verses, the flamboyant improvisations of his verse tales and even of the greater *Childe Harold*, supported by short selections from the rich and abounding life of that shocking and delightful poem *Don Juan*, that great epic of modern Europe? All attempts to rehabilitate Byron, Professor Saintsbury felt able to declare in 1896, "have certainly never yet succeeded either with the majority of competent critics or with the majority of readers of poetry" And in his vivacious record of personal adventures in the French novel he tells us roundly that while Byronism did much mischief on the Continent, " with us, though it made a great stir, it really did little harm except to some 'silly women'. . . . Counter-jumpers like Thackeray's own Pogson worshipped ' the noble poet '; boys of nobler stamp like Tennyson *thought* they worshipped him, but if they were going to become men of affairs forgot all about him; if they were to be poets took to Keats and Shelley as models, not to him. Critics hardly took him seriously, except for non-literary reasons."

But Byronism is not quite the same thing as Byron. Nor, rare and artistic poets as they are, do the names of Tennyson, Rossetti, Morris, and Swinburne represent all the qualities that make poetry great and satisfying. The *Idylls of the King* and *In Memoriam*, *The Blessed Damozel* and *The House of Life*, *Two Red Roses across the Moon* and *The Land East of the Sun and West of the Moon*, *Atalanta in Calydon*, and *Tristram of Lyonesse* —these are preciously wrought works of art such as Byron could never have composed, any more than his imagination could have lived and sported in the rarefied and enchanting atmosphere of the *Witch of Atlas* or sung the nympholeptic strains of *Epipsychidion*. But is it quite certain that they are in every respect greater poems than the last cantos of *Childe Harold* or Byron's *Prometheus* or *Cain* or *The Vision of Judgement* or *Don Juan?* Of Shelley I will speak later; but regarding the others I confess I do not feel so sure as when I was a student in the 'eighties of last century. Their beauty seems to me a beauty of things somewhat remote from life; the languid passion of Morris, the stormier music of Swinburne seem to breathe of a land indeed east of the sun and west of the moon. It is in a very timid fashion after all that Tennyson in the finished stanzas of *In Memoriam*, or even the robuster Browning of *Christmas Eve and Easter Day*, ventured into the stormy waters of doubt, death, and the tragic hints of the significance of life, timidly keeping the bathing machine of an orthodox and optimistic faith well in sight upon the beach as a shelter to run to for safety and warmth and reinvigoration:

> O yet we trust that somehow good
> Will be the final goal of ill.

And so even the exquisite art of these poems seems touched with decadence, as Shelley found the erotic poets of Greece decadent, not from any quality they possess but because of what they lack; and some of the qualities they want I seem to rediscover in the less finished, more obviously faulty, poetry of Byron—life and strength, passion and virility, wit and humour. "Close your Byron; open your Goethe," says Carlyle; but for Goethe most English readers and critics have inclined to substitute Wordsworth. "Close your Byron; open your Keats and Tennyson and Rossetti and Swinburne," says, or might say, Professor Saintsbury, "for here is art, 'the faultless and fervent melodies' of pure poetry, not the resonant improvisations and vulgar discords of Byron's rhetoric." Yet the serene wisdom and golden beauty of Goethe, the ministering medicine of Wordsworth's hills and streams and leech-gatherers, the melody and colour of Keats and Tennyson, the exotic passion and music of Rossetti and Swinburne, sometimes pall; and it is with a powerful requickening of our blood that we hear again the rolling guns and clattering squadrons of the stanzas on Waterloo, the storm and passion of the night by Lake Leman. The old thrill comes back when we read again of " the Niobe of nations ",

Childless and crownless in her voiceless woe,

her tombs and ruined Forum, the empty moonlit Coliseum; or hear the old moral, in accents of reverberating intensity, of the vanity of human life, the intoxicating sweetness of love, the sublimity and indifference of nature. Goethe and Wordsworth speak of wisdom and love, of duty and resignation:

Entbehren sollst du, sollst entbehren;

but folly and rebellion and hatred appeal to our complex nature also, and we can at times turn with relief from the *Leech-gatherer* or the second part of *Faust* to enjoy the scorn and mockery, the buoyant humour and splendid satire of *Beppo* and *The Vision of Judgement* and *Don Juan*. It is, at least, not without significance that while Arnold and Swinburne were debating and mid-Victorian criticism was passing final sentence on Byron, a young poet was just about to repeat in a measure the experience for his readers and for himself of the Byron of *Childe Harold* and the tales and some of the earlier lyrics. Mr. Kipling has been, I sometimes think, " le Byron de nos jours ", not in the sense of Browning's poem, but in virtue of the quickening and immediate effect of his poetry on an audience as wide at least as the English-speaking world, an audience not confined to the usual readers of poetry; and because Mr. Kipling, too, found the best material for romance and song, not in the reconstructed world of Greece or the Middle Ages, but in the actualities of life in his own day in India and England, the army, the workshop, and the tramp-steamer. The romantic and Hellenic revival was yet to produce some exquisite poetry, as that of Mr. Yeats; but on the whole the trend of poetry, since Mr. Arnold's prophetic date has passed, has been in the direction of a purer art, a closer touch with actuality; and it is this which has tempted me to ask myself whether, now that Byronism is certainly a thing of the past, Byron may not yet be alive, and if so what are the elements in his work which have proved most enduring.

2

THE influence of Byron on the best minds of his own generation has, I think, never been better expressed than by the late Mr. William Hale White in *The Revolution in Tanner's Lane*, and, though it is a work of fiction, one could easily make it good from the evidence of Ruskin and others. " Zachariah ", he says, speaking of his hero, " found in *The Corsair* exactly what answered to his own inmost self, down to its very depths. The lofty style, the scorn of what is mean and base, the courage—root of all virtue—that dares and evermore dares in the very last extremity, the love of the illimitable, of freedom, and the cadences like the fall of waves on a sea-shore, were attractive to him beyond measure. More than this, there was love. His own love was a failure, and yet it was impossible for him to indulge for a moment his imagination elsewhere. . . But when he came to Medora's song—

> Deep in my soul that tender secret dwells,
>   Lonely and lost to light for evermore,
> Save when to thine my heart responsive swells,
>   Then trembles into silence as before;

and more particularly the second verse—

> There, in its centre, a sepulchral lamp
>   Burns the slow flame, eternal—but unseen;
> Which not the darkness of Despair can damp,
>   Though vain its ray as it had never been,

love again asserted itself. It was not love for a person; perhaps it was hardly love so much as the capacity for love. Whatever it may be, henceforth this is what love will be in him, and it will be fully maintained, though it knows no actual object. It will manifest itself in suppressed force, seeking for exit in a thousand directions; sometimes grotesque perhaps, but always force. It will give energy to expression, vitality to his admiration of the beautiful, devotion to his worship, enthusiasm to his zeal for freedom." This is how Byron spoke to many of his own generation besides silly women and underbred Pogsons, and it goes to the heart of the matter. They heard again the authentic tones of passionate feeling; felt life and love reclaiming their rights from prudence and morality; poetry reasserting itself as something more than "the art of uniting pleasure with truth by calling imagination to the help of reason". Such an emancipation, indeed, had already begun, unmarked in Blake's poetry, disguised in the *Lyrical Ballads* by the poets' choice of theme, of other passions than that of love,— maternal affection—the affections in short rather than love as between the sexes, and a new and profound,

passionate and mystical, love of nature.   In the region
of passion, in the more limited sense of the word, Coleridge was never more than a sentimentalist, a metaphysical sentimentalist or sentimental metaphysician.
Wordsworth, it would seem, had indeed been a passionate
lover, but that phase was soon over, that impulse cut
somewhat deliberately out of his experience, and he had
become the lover who could spend his honeymoon walking
with Mary on one side and Dorothy on the other while
he contemplated nature and meditated political sonnets.
Byron was a lover, masculine and passionate, as Donne
and Burns had been before him.   He was no nympholept
like Shelley; he could never have written *Epipsychidion*.
Keats's sensuousness, the temperament to which the
"lucent syrops tinct with cinnamon" and dishes of gold
and silver " filling the chilly room with perfume light "
were as entrancing as the soul of Madeline, offended
Byron on the personal side, and he was not quite artist
enough in words to appreciate the felicity of Keats's
sensuous diction.   For Byron, strange as it may seem,
was not a sensual, he was not even a sensuous poet.   Love
was for him a passion in which soul and sense are inextricably blended.   The love he exalts is an unchangeable, a
spiritual passion:

> But this was taught me by the dove,
> To die—and know no second love.
>
> .     .     .     .     .
>
> And let the fool still prone to range
> And sneer at all who cannot change
> Partake his jest with boasting boys;
> I envy not his varied joys;

> But deem such feeble, heartless man,
> Less than yon solitary swan;
> Far, far beneath the shallow maid
> He left believing and betrayed.

In commenting on some of Burns's unpublished letters, he declares: " A true voluptuary will never abandon his mind to the grossness of reality.  It is by excluding the earthly, the material, the *physique* of our pleasures, by veiling these ideas, by forgetting them altogether or, at least, never naming them hardly to oneself, that we alone can prevent them from disgusting."

When Southey denounced the Satanic School of poetry, the school of Byron and Shelley, it was *Cain* and religious scepticism he had chiefly in view, but also *Don Juan* and this note of passion.  And it is Byron's most essential contribution to the requickening of English poetry, the note which echoed in Zachariah's heart with inspiring, liberating, ennobling effect.  For the Satanic poet, if a troubler of the waters, may give them in troubling the power to invigorate the human spirit.  He is the poet who, like Donne or Marlowe, Byron or the Swinburne of the first *Poems and Ballads*, shocks and startles and also enchants his age by the challenge which his poetry offers to the accepted moral conventions, disturbing its scale of moral values, especially the accord which every age endeavours to secure between morals and art. For art and poetry are the spontaneous expression of man's sense of values, the record of his joys, his loves and hates, his need of beauty, of pleasure, the demand of the spirit of man that he shall not only live but live well.  But the concern of morality is not so much immediate pleasure as the necessity of making us take pleasure in the right things, ἥδεσθαι οἷς δεῖ, and knowing the power of poetry the moralist would fain enlist her services, and moralise the poet's song. But if, like Plato, he is both a great moralist and a poet, he knows that it is not easy to curb the wild, free spirit of poetry, so apt to reveal to men what they really love and hate, which are not always the things society would have us hate and love; he knows that there is no room in a Republic where natural impulses are to be disciplined or eradicated for the poet who waters our natural desires. He calls the poet a liar, but what he really fears is his terrible, his revealing sincerity; it may be unconscious sincerity, for poets least of all men know what they are about.

And the moralist would be right. It would be true to say with Dryden that "supposing verses are never so beautiful and pleasing yet if they contain anything which shocks Religion or Good Manners they are at best . . . *versus inopes rerum, nugaeque canorae*"; that might be true if articulate morality in any age ever represented quite adequately the deepest and most enduring needs of our nature in conflict with, striving to curb and correct, the aberrations of feeling and the allurements of the moment. But articulate morality is in great measure the expression of the real or fancied needs of a type of society seeking to establish or protect itself, of a creed or a convention resisting troublesome inquiry and disturbance; and the human spirit faints and the sense of the joy of life is dulled; and then a Marlowe comes singing of the soaring ambitions of a Tamburlaine, of Dr. Faustus imperilling his immortal welfare that he might make blind Homer sing to him " of Alexander's love and Oenon's death ", and might see again the face

> That launched a thousand ships
> And burned the topless towers of Ilium.

He will not even, like Spenser, endeavour to disguise
his passion for beauty and power, from himself and from
others, by a veil of allegory and conventional homage to the
restrictive virtues; and so the air is cleared, the whole
gamut of passionate experience is set open to Shakespeare,
and the human spirit recovers the sense of its own infinite
capacity, the joy of energy which is life and delight.
" The road of excess leads to the palace of wisdom."

It was just so that *The Giaour* and *The Corsair* and *The
Bride of Abydos* and *Parisina* spoke to the generation of
Hale White's Zachariah, after a century of moralising,
reflective, sentimental poetry, admirable in its kind. This
is what gave to Byron's verse-tales their superior charm
to Scott's. Scott's setting and scenery are to me often
preferable to Byron's; his tone saner, more genial. But
the setting and scenery are everything, the characters and
sentiments entirely negligible, while the style, if not more
careless than Byron's, has more of cheap and facile phrasing and filling. With Byron the Greek and Mediterranean setting is in itself of small importance. The
appeal that the south, the Mediterranean, made to Byron,
as to Marlowe and to Goethe, was that of lands where
passions are more intense and more unrestrained. And
if the Byronism of Byron's tales has lost its appeal, rather
repels now than attracts us, one must not go to the other
extreme and lose sight of the sincerity and intensity of
feeling which quickened and still quickens these faulty
poems, gave them in their first freshness such power and
beauty. Byron has delineated, as Wordsworth and his
contemporaries shrank from doing, passion and energy.

His central theme is the infinite worth of love and courage and endurance. If the immediate result in English poetry was a hasty crop of crude and absurd Oriental tales, yet the true inheritors of the spirit of Byron were, firstly, those poets who after the reaction to edification and sentiment of the first Victorian generation reasserted the rights in poetry of passion and the free imagination, Rossetti, Swinburne, Morris, greater artists but less potent personalities; and, secondly, Kipling and his generation, who brought poetry back from a too exotic cult of technique and strange moods to the passions and humours, loves and hates of the world around us. Byron did in these poems, as Tennyson said, " give the world another heart and new pulses, and so we are kept going ".

## 3

But the passionate quality of Byron's tales and lyrics has suffered for us from the comparative poverty both of the thought in which the feeling becomes articulate and of the language in which the thought is clothed. Donne's songs and sonnets have reasserted their worth, after a long interval, because passion made Donne a subtle and at times even a profound thinker, and because his style, if harsh and careless, is never banal, and often splendidly felicitous. Byron has occasional splendid felicities too:

> She walks in beauty like the night
> Of cloudless climes and starry skies.

> There be none of Beauty's daughters
>   With a magic like thee,
> And like music on the waters
>   Is thy sweet voice to me.

In fact the few of Byron's lyrics which are really excellent stand out by themselves in an anthology of contemporary lyrics somewhat as Jonson's do in an Elizabethan collection; not better than their fellows, indeed in many respects less exquisitely lyrical than the songs of Shakespeare and Dekker, of Shelley and Scott, but with a rhetoric, a combined felicity and force, momentum, which is all their own.  But in the tales Byron's style, compared with the best work of Wordsworth or Coleridge or Keats, is vehement declamation verging at times on the banal.  We feel as though some fierce blind mood were blundering round the bars of language unable to win its way to the light; as if the poet were unable to find and to give the relief which would come from more perfect expression, from lines like Shakespeare's:

> I am dying, Egypt, dying; only,
> I here importune death awhile, until
> Of many thousand kisses the poor last
> I lay upon thy lips.

Shakespeare finds the perfect words; Byron just misses.[1]  Like the tiger of his own comparison he springs, but is baffled and goes growling back to his lair.  Yet that is not quite the whole truth, for verse is itself expression, and the pulse and movement even of this early verse betrays the passion which the words do not quite adequately convey.  "No verse narrative", says Professor Elton, "has the same pace and energy and flame."  For flame

---

[1] Shakespeare and Byron were alike in finding revision and polishing difficult, because as a critic (E. E. Kellet, *Suggestions*) has indicated, speaking of Shakespeare: "No sooner had he begun to revise than the fury of creation seized him and he rewrote."  Byron could hardly correct a proof without making fresh insertions.

one would be tempted to substitute fire, the dark fire of which Donne speaks, which heats but does not illuminate; but not alone no narrative but no English verse, narrative or lyrical, had given such an impression of momentum (except it be some parts of Dryden's and Pope's satire) and none such an impression of speed as Byron's octosyllabics or the anapæsts of *The Destruction of Sennacherib*; and no poet reproduced the same impression until Swinburne. Swinburne's achievement as a metrist might be described as a union of the music of Shelley with the momentum and speed of Byron, the music more elaborately orchestral, the speed more winged, yet with loss as well as gain, the music of brass and wood for the wail of Shelley's violin, the speed but not all the momentum of Byron's fierce and tormented temperament.

An orator, and a great, passionate improviser, that is what Byron appears when one thinks of his octosyllabics and " Christabel " measure, his Spenserians and later, better decasyllabics compared with the more delicate and perfect harmonies of Coleridge and Shelley, the rich and felicitous sensuousness of Keats and his Victorian followers; but it is to these oratorical qualities, this strain of passionate improvisation that his poetry owed its immediate effectiveness, its success with circles in which the inspired " silly sooth " of Wordsworth, the rarefied harmony of Shelley, "singing hymns unbidden in the light of thought ", the sensuous and imaginative felicities of the *Ode to a Nightingale* and the *Grecian Urn* made small appeal. Byron spoke to such readers—and he still, I find, speaks to many if they read poetry at all—and spoke with some of the oratorical force of Dryden and the more passionate strain of Donne and Marlowe, because he spoke as a

poet who was also a man and a man of the world.    Just
as Burns was a great poet who was also a peasant, a
peasant who really lived the life and shared the joys of
peasants, not like Clare a poet born by accident in a
peasant's hut and " gifted for poetry by those very qualities
which made him ineffective as a peasant ", and as Mr.
Kipling is—if one may say so admiringly and without
offence—a poet who is also a brilliant journalist, so
Byron was a poet who was also a man among men and
a man of the world, seeing the world with which he was
at war through the world's eyes.    Poetry such as this
will necessarily lack some of the finest shades and
harmonies.    It will generally lack the note of pure song—
unless, like the peasant song of Burns, tradition has kept
song pure and simple in feeling—and it will want the
note of mystic, inward reverie.    Not for quite common
ears, either of peasant or man of the world, are such
strains as:

> Golden lads and girls all must,
> As chimney-sweepers, come to dust,

or:

> Liquid Peneus was flowing,
> And all dark Tempe lay
> In Pelion's shadow outgrowing
> The light of the dying day,

nor the inward tones of Shakespeare's lines on

> The cloud-capped towers, the gorgeous palaces,

or Wordsworth's on the yew trees:

> Beneath whose sable roof
> Of boughs, as if for festal purpose decked
> With unrejoicing berries—ghostly Shapes

G

May meet at noontide: Fear and trembling Hope,
Silence and Foresight; Death the Skeleton
And Time the Shadow;—there to celebrate,
As in a natural temple scatter'd o'er
With altars undisturbed of mossy stones,
United worship; or in mute repose
To lie, and listen to the mountain-flood
Murmuring from Glaramara's inmost caves.

The accents of poetry which appeals to audiences on which the " melodies unheard " of such pure poetry of the spirit are wasted are those of the orator and those of the talker. Byron began in the one; he ended in the other. His greatest success was achieved when he found a measure—not the Spenserian, though it was with the intention of using it thus to express his varying moods, " to be either droll or pathetic, descriptive or sentimental, tender or satirical ", that he began *Childe Harold*—but the *ottava rima*, in which he could write poetry as he talked or as he wrote racy letters to his friends. But to say that Byron's serious poems are oratorical in tone is not, it seems to me, to condemn them as *rhetorical* in the depreciatory sense of the word, for the style may be appropriate to the subject, and the sincere expression of the poet's emotion. Pope's *Eloisa to Abelard* is a brilliant exercise in passionate eloquence, yet it is not just *so*, we feel, that love speaks with most convincing power. On the other hand, when Swinburne writes of liberty as though she were his mistress:

Ask nothing more of me, sweet;
  All I can give you I give.
    Heart of my heart, were it more,
More would be laid at your feet:

> Love that should help you to live
> Song that should spur you to soar,

one is, I think, justified in asking whether such a strain
is as appropriate and effective as Byron's:

> Yet, Freedom! yet thy banner, torn, but flying,
> Streams like the thunderstorm *against* the wind;
> Thy trumpet-voice, though broken now and dying,
> The loudest still the Tempest leaves behind;
> Thy tree hath lost its blossoms, and the rind,
> Chopp'd by the axe, looks rough and little worth,
> But the sap lasts,—and still the seed we find
> Sown deep, even in the bosom of the North;
> So shall a better spring less bitter fruit bring forth.

There are emotions whose source and sphere is the
individual soul alone with itself and God, or in individual
contact with other individual souls, and the poetry which
expresses these is like the still, small voice, not heard but
overheard; but there are also feelings which belong to
us as " political animals ", whose source and sphere is
national and civic life, the love of liberty, of justice, the
passion of power, the hatred of oppression; and such
passions find their fittest utterance in the trumpet tones
of the orator.

### 4

LOVE is hardly one of these.  Its natural tones are not
the strident tones of the orator except at moments when,
driven back on itself by conflict or check, it quickens
the intellect and makes eloquent the lips with the language
of argument and expostulation.  But these are the
moments which the poet who is also an orator, Corneille

or Dryden or Pope in his one brilliant achievement, has always preferred, and most of Byron's entirely serious love poetry is of this kind, vehement and eloquent, not tender and musical. But the eloquence of the lovers in Dryden's heroic plays interests us now only as the school in which he acquired the splendid and shattering vigour of argument and satire and declamation apparent in the later satires and didactic poems,—the character of Zimri, the panegyric on the Catholic Church in *The Hind and the Panther*. Here was the proper sphere for sonorous eloquence and sustained, incisive ratiocination. And Byron in like manner was revealed for the first time in something of his true proportions when he emerged on the rostrum of the last two cantos of *Childe Harold* as the orator of the world's woes and his own. *Childe Harold*, that is these cantos, and *Don Juan*—these are the two chief pillars on which Byron's fame rests, the two *foci* of his poetry round one or other of which the best of his shorter poems, *Prometheus*, *Manfred*, *Cain*, or *Beppo* and *The Vision of Judgement*, move like satellites which the accidents of an ever-eruptive force have thrown out from the central mass. These are the great representative poems, the one of the orator, turbid, vehement, eloquent, and withal a poet, the other of the most splendid talker and raconteur in English verse. The very scenes which are selected in *Childe Harold* for elaboration show an orator's recognition of telling " topics "—Waterloo, the Rhine, the Alps, Venice, Rome; Napoleon, Rousseau, Gibbon, Cromwell, Washington, Hannibal—one must recall what these meant to England and to Europe in 1816–17, to the Europe of the Revolution, Napoleon and the Restoration, to an England restored, after twenty

years of exile, to the Continent, which had acquired from
Gibbon and from experience a new sense of the pomp
and pageantry, the dramatic significance and the futility
of human history.   As a descriptive poem alone, in the
tradition of *The Seasons*, *The Task*, and the yet unpublished *Prelude* and *The Excursion*, *Childe Harold* is the
greatest of its kind, the noblest panoramic poem in our
literature.   But this is only one aspect of the poem, the
other is Byron himself.   Scenes and events and persons
are all topics in a great declamation the central theme of
which is Byron himself, his wrongs and sorrows and
sombre reflections upon life.   And the strange thing,
if one considers it, is that Byron made his readers feel
that he was large enough to stand thus face to face with
these sublime topics—the Alps, Venice, Rome, the Sea—
and comment in passionate tones, and in a single breath,
on them and on himself.   In a lesser man, as Rogers,
it would have been absurd, and he makes in *Italy* no such
attempt.   Cowper in *The Task* is an egotist, but the
scenes through which he wanders pensively, the windings
of the Ouse and level plains of Bedfordshire, have no such
place in the history and imagination of Europe.   Wordsworth is an indefatigable egotist, but if one can learn to
read and enjoy *The Prelude* as a whole it is because the
long stretches of uninspired garrulity are always leading
by unexpected ways to sublime and mystical vistas in
which Wordsworth's private personality is merged in
something greater and more awe-inspiring, the mind of
the poet and the seer.   But Byron remains himself, his
private wrongs and sorrows are ever kept before us,
and yet the effect is never absurd, at least never so affects
the imagination of the reader, whatever cooler judge-

ment one may pass with Meredith or Arnold on this pageant of the bleeding heart. The closest parallel is Milton, who is always with us throughout his poem, amid the horrors of Hell and Chaos, the glories of Heaven, the sublime pastoral scenes of Eden, who pauses between Heaven and Hell to sing of his own blindness; and is with us, not even as Dante, under the guidance of a master to whom he listens and submits, but as a protagonist in the poem; for Milton is, as a French critic has recently claimed, the true hero of *Paradise Lost*, the only worthy rival of Satan, from the beginning of the poem to the end. The central motive of *Paradise Lost* and the poems which followed is this conflict; and it is a conflict in Milton's own soul, between faith and questioning, acquiescence and rebellion. And a like conflict, as I have tried to show in a later essay, is the theme of Byron's serious poems written after the exile—*Childe Harold, Manfred, Prometheus, Sardanapalus, Cain*. It is the conflict of Byron's sense of sin, as interpreted by the Calvinistic, pietistic creed of his day, with his pride and his sense of justice. Neither Milton nor Byron achieved a victory in that conflict, ever in their poetry reached that highest level in which the conflict is suspended in a complete self-surrender:

> In la sua voluntade è nostra pace,

and so the mind knows

> That blessed mood
> In which the burthen of the mystery,
> In which the heavy and the heavyweight
> Of all this unintelligible world
> Is lightened. . . .

> We are laid asleep
> In body, and become a living soul
> While with an eye made quiet by the power
> Of harmony, and the deep power of joy
> We see into the life of things.

Poor Byron never, in verse at any rate, got beyond the defiance of *Prometheus* or the mockery of *Don Juan*:

> A firm will, and a deep sense
> Which even in torture can descry
> Its own concenter'd recompense,
> Triumphant where it dares defy,
> And making Death a victory.

Milton in *Samson Agonistes* does succeed in, at least apparently, subduing this spirit of fierce defiance, the spirit of Capaneus in the *Inferno*, c. xiv.:

> O Capaneo, in ciò che non s' ammorza
> La tua superbia, sei tu più punito:
> Nullo martirio, fuor che la tua rabbia
> Sarebbe al tuo furor dolor compito.

Milton is able, through the chorus of *Samson Agonistes*, to strike the note of faith and acquiescence:

> All is best though we oft doubt
> What the unsearchable dispose
> Of highest wisdom brings about
> And ever best found in the close.

But that close was a terrible act of vengeance; and the thought continues to haunt us that Milton's victory was one of the will rather than of insight and humility, that he never forgave, or ever thought it possible he himself had been in error. " Is it therefore infallibly agreeable

to the Word of God, all that *you* say?   I beseech you in
the bowels of Christ, think it possible you may be mistaken." Cromwell, whom too Milton finally found
wanting, might have addressed these words to the poet
who had been his secretary as well as to the General
Assembly of the Kirk of Scotland.

Be that as it may, Milton is a greater poet than Byron,
because whatever his moods he can express them more
adequately.   Yet Byron's best serious poetry, the two
last cantos of *Childe Harold*, has great qualities.   It is
idle to censure Byron because his Spenserians have not
the melody and sweetness of Spenser's—the greatest
master of pure melody in our language.   Byron's use of
the stanza is oratorical—it would be a poor measure that
admitted of only one mode of fingering—and if his worst
stanzas, those in which he endeavours to argue, are
twisted and tormented, in the finest he achieves a richer
language, a fuller compass of eloquence than the intolerable monotony of the rhetorical couplet permitted.   I
am a great admirer of the poetic oratory of Dryden and
Pope, but I know no passage of such splendid eloquence,
so serious and sublime, in which the changes of mood
are so finely managed as the verses on Waterloo, the finest
poem of battle ever written.   *Childe Harold* must be read,
and *The Prelude*, so different in tone and temper, must
also be read, as a rhapsody with all the inequalities of a
rhapsody.   The third canto has the turbid flow of a
stream of lava, choked at times with the *débris* and scoriæ
of imperfect phrasing and tortured rhythms, again flowing
clear and strong but dark, and yet again growing in-
candescent in felicitous and magnificent lines and stanzas.
The fourth has more of the movement of the Rhine as

he describes it, an "exulting and abounding river",
reflecting in its stream the blue of the heavens, the snows
and storms of the Alps, the cities and the ruins and the
passions of human history, till it loses itself in the "image
of eternity", the sea. Nor is the passion unillumined
by thought, though Byron's argumentative stanzas are
his worst. His characters of Napoleon—the sceptred
cynic—of Voltaire, Rousseau, Gibbon, are not the work
of one deprived of insight or the gift of expression, or,
despite his too careless improvisations, the power of
felicitous phrasing,—Gibbon

> Sapping a solemn creed with solemn sneer,

or, in a later poem, George III.

> An old man
> With an old soul, and both extremely blind.

But it is difficult, even as oratorical poetry, to say much
for Byron's dramas and blank verse. *Manfred* and *Cain*,
the glamour and the horror which once invested these
has dispersed. Their interest is biographical. Even
Milton's strong wing is apt to flag when he grows metaphysical; Byron falls plumb; poetry is "quenched in a
boggy Syrtis". Nor can he, like Shelley, when he feels
himself growing bogged, escape upon the wings of song,
pinnacled dim in the intense inane, but pouring forth a
flood of ineffable harmony.


# 5

FOR if Byron had no philosophy, there may be a philosophy
in that very want. The advantage is not entirely with
Shelley in the scene which Byron described to Kennedy,

when, in his room, Shelley and a friend argued with
such eloquence on high themes of " fate, freewill, foreknowledge absolute ", that each converted the other.
Theoretic philosophies which admitted of such revolu-
tions of opinion made little appeal to his clear and sceptical
vision; and if he found no escape by way of the imagination and the heart such as Blake and Wordsworth and
Shelley discovered or dreamed they had discovered, he
was less prone to identify poetic with real values. If
the world of imagination was closed to him he had a
firmer hold on the world in space and time, of men and
women as they live in the world that is subject to and at
war with Urizen, the spirit of natural reason and moral
individuality. As a man, he found escape from the confused conflicts of that world, not in any such imaginative
vision of the infinite as Blake's, or interpretation of
Nature as Wordsworth's, or in Shelley's dream of a golden
age when man shall be

> Sceptreless, free, uncircumscribed, but man
> Equal, unclassed, tribeless and nationless.

He found it in the call to heroic action and self-control
in the cause of concrete liberty and humanity: and as a
poet he found himself, not in " metaphysical " or historical
poems and dramas, but in the only poem of the romantics
to which the title of epic may justly be applied. In
*Childe Harold* he had given a vivid and impassioned, if
unequal and too hastily improvised, panorama of Western
Europe, scenic and historical. In *Don Juan* and its
attendant satellites, *Beppo* and *The Vision of Judgement*,
he wrote the comic epic of modern Europe, rendering
the very spirit of the world of kings and politicians, where

men " sit down to eat and to drink and rise up to play ". And he did so because he had found the proper medium for that blend of gravity and gaiety which he contemplated when he began to write *Childe Harold*, a measure in which he could write as he talked, orally and in correspondence, could express all his keen sense of human life, with consummate ease and naturalness, in buoyant and moving verse.   For when we turn to *Beppo*, *The Vision of Judgement*, and *Don Juan* much of the criticism of Byron's technique becomes irrelevant.   In these poems he proves himself master of a style entirely his own, the author of poems as unique in their kind—it may not be the highest kind—as the *Ode to a Nightingale* or the *Ode to the West Wind*.   The orator of *Childe Harold* gives place to the talker whose conversation was, as Colonel Stanhope described it, a " stream sometimes smooth, sometimes rapid, and sometimes rushing down in cataracts— a mixture of philosophy and slang—of everything ".

*Beppo* is by far the best of his verse-tales, though Byron's art as a story-teller was always improving, and *The Island* is excellent in description—as of the waterfall, on which Ruskin comments—and in the management of the decasyllabic couplet.   But to write really well Byron must draw straight from his own experience, and *Beppo* is the record, vivid, dramatic, humorous, of his Venetian experiences.   It is the only verse-tale since Chaucer wrote which might stand unabashed among the *Canterbury Tales*.   Compare the dialogue of the closing stanzas with that of Chaucer's Shipman's Tale.   *The Vision of Judgement* is a greater satire than anything of Pope's, and if not greater than Dryden's *Mac Flecknoe* yet the range of feeling it comprises is wider,—something of the finer fun of Chaucer in the Summoner's Tale and others like it; of the fiercer fun and savage denunciation of Swift:

> " Passion! " cried the phantom dim,
> " I loved my country and I hated him ";

and a touch of Miltonic sublimity, blended with a magnanimity and pathos that are Byron's own, in the interview between Lucifer and Michael. But *Don Juan* is the fullest expression of the later Byron, able in his poetry to be all himself; and the first great quality to note is its variety, the compass, the register of Byron's voice.

Take as a single instance the closing stanzas of the third canto, when the modern Greek has sung, not the

> Long low island song
> Of ancient days, ere tyranny grew strong,

but the ringing stanzas on the Isles of Greece. What a medley ensues! Poetic fame; Milton and Mrs. Milton; Shakespeare and deer-stealing; Lord Bacon and bribery; Southey and Coleridge and Pantisocracy and the two milliners of Bath; Wordsworth and his " drowsy, frowsy poem, the Excursion ":

> " Pedlars ", and " Boats ", and " Wagons "! Oh! ye shades
> Of Pope and Dryden, are we come to this?
> .     .     .     .     .     .
> The " little boatman " and his *Peter Bell*
> Can sneer at him who drew " Achitophel "!

and then in a trice we are back to the lovers and the hour of evening:

Ave Maria! blessed be the hour!
　The time, the clime, the spot, where I so oft
Have felt that moment in its fullest power
　Sink o'er the earth—so beautiful and soft—
While swung the deep bell in the distant tower,
　Or the faint dying day-hymn stole aloft,
And not a breath crept through the rosy air,
And yet the forest leaves seem'd stirred with prayer.

．　　．　　．　　．　　．　　．　　．

Sweet Hour of Twilight! in the solitude
　Of the pine forest, and the silent shore
Which bounds Ravenna's immemorial wood,
　Rooted where once the Adrian waves flowed o'er,
To where the last Caesarean fortress stood,
　Evergreen forest! which Boccaccio's lore
And Dryden's lay made haunted ground to me,
How have I loved the twilight hour and thee!

．　　．　　．　　．　　．　　．　　．

Soft Hour! which wakes the wish and melts the heart
　Of those who sail the seas, on the first day
When they from their sweet friends are torn apart;
　Or fills with love the pilgrim on his way
As the far bell of Vesper makes him start,
　Seeming to weep the dying day's decay;
Is this a fancy which our reason scorns?
Ah! surely Nothing dies but Something mourns!

To me there is more of the appeal of the human voice
in these verses than in the more rapt but shriller or remoter
strains of the *Lines written among the Euganean Hills*,
so rich in cloud effects, clouds metaphysical as well as
physical.

For Shelley moves among the clouds; Byron never
quits the earth. This is his second and greatest achieve-

ment, to have written a poem which is a poem yet is
concerned from first to last with realities and nothing but
realities, mundane realities, real persons and scenes and
happenings.    This is what Shelley himself felt when he
wrote of *Don Juan* fulfilling " in a certain degree what
I have long preached of producing—something wholly
new and relative to the age and yet surpassingly beautiful ".
The effect is so completely realised and with such sustained ease that it is not difficult to underrate it, to think
that it requires no imagination but simply the power to
record, to contend that Byron has simply turned into
verse the material of diaries and correspondence, like those
of Horace Walpole and Lady Mary, as some of it *did*
come from Byron's grand-uncle's book and a Frenchman's
Russian history.    As a fact, few even of the novelists
have achieved the same effect so fully—Cervantes, Fielding, in a measure Thackeray, and, a little under the line,
Anthony Trollope.    My comparison does not include
depth of modelling.    The novelists have elaborated more
complete characters than Byron's, which are no more
than sketches, though vivid and perfectly natural sketches.
I refer only to the general and sustained impression of
mundane reality, of the form and pressure of life;  and
I feel that the effect is one of more authentic imagination
than *Prometheus Unbound*, for Shelley's scenes and characters have neither the reality of *Don Juan* nor yet the equal
or greater reality of the scenes and characters of the
*Paradiso*, neither earthly nor unearthly reality.    And this
veracity, this not painful but buoyant and vivid realism,
animated by many moods, pathos and melancholy as well as
humour and irony, includes nature as well as human life.
Nowhere is Byron's treatment of nature so felicitous, so

natural as in *Don Juan*.  The melodramatic, rhetorical note
audible in the stanzas on the Alps and on the sea is silent.
With Wordsworth's great visionary scenes, the sunrise on
the way home from the dance, the frosty evening when

> every icy crag
> Tinkled like iron;  while far distant hills
> Into the tumult sent an alien sound
> Of melancholy not unnoticed,

or the spectral apparition in the mist among the hills of
*The Excursion*, nothing in *Childe Harold* will compare,
but in the scene of Haidee's nuptials Nature seems to
take the pen and write, in simpler and more passionate,
if less pontifical, strains than when she dictated to Wordsworth:

> It was a wild and breaker-beaten coast,
>     With cliffs above, and a broad sandy shore,
> Guarded by shoals and rocks as by an host,
>     With here and there a creek, whose aspect wore
> A better welcome to the tempest-tost;
>     And rarely ceased the haughty billow's roar,
> Save on the dead long summer days, which make
> The outstretched Ocean glitter like a lake.

> .    .    .    .    .    .    .

> The coast—I think it was the coast that I
>     Was just describing, yes, it was the coast—
> Lay at this period quiet as the sky,
>     The sands untumbled, the blue waves untossed,
> And all was stillness save the sea-bird's cry,
>     And dolphin's leap, and little billow crossed
> By some low rock or shelve, that made it fret
> Against the boundary it scarcely wet.

It was the cooling hour, just when the rounded
    Red sun sinks down behind the azure hill,
Which then seems as if the whole earth it bounded,
    Circling all Nature, hushed, and dim, and still,
With the far mountain-crescent half-surrounded
    On one side, and the deep sea calm and chill
Upon the other, and the rosy sky
With one star sparkling through it like an eye.

And thus they wandered forth, and hand in hand,
    Over the shining pebbles and the shells,
Glided along the smooth and hardened sand,
    And in the worn and wild receptacles
Worked by the storms, yet worked as it were planned,
    In hollow halls, with sparry roofs and cells,
They turned to rest; and, each clasped by an arm,
Yielded to the deep Twilight's purple charm.

They looked up to the sky, whose floating glow
    Spread like a rosy Ocean, vast and bright;
They gazed upon the glittering sea below
    Whence the broad Moon rose circling into sight;
They heard the waves splash and the winds so low,
    They saw each other's dark eyes darting light
Into each other—and beholding this
Their lips drew near and clung into a kiss.

   .    .    .    .    .    .    .

They were alone, but not alone as they
    Who shut in chambers think it loneliness;
The silent Ocean, and the starlight bay,
    The twilight glow, which momently grew less,
The voiceless sands, and dropping caves, that lay
    Around them, made them to each other press,
As if there were no life beneath the sky
Save theirs, and that their life could never die.

Is there any love-poetry of the romantics which vibrates with so full a life of sense and soul as these verses?   Compared with it, " I arise from dreams of thee " or " A slumber did my spirit seal " are the love strains of a disembodied spirit or a rapt mystic.   There is nothing like it in English poetry except some of the songs of Burns and the complex, vibrant passion, sensual and spiritual, of Donne's songs and elegies.   And considering the descriptive element alone—to use the English language so simply and naturally to produce an effect so vivid, vivid to every sense, and not the eye alone, for one hears the plash of the waves, one feels the cool, strong air of the salt sea-wind, the wet, hard sand beneath one's feet, the glow of the sky in the inner chambers of the soul— to do this seems to me as unique an achievement as to write the *Ode to a Nightingale* or the *Ode to the West Wind*.   And Byron does the same kind of thing throughout the poem, in descriptions of interiors as well as of Nature, of battle by land and shipwreck by sea, of characters like Julia and Haidee and Johnson and Lady Adeline, the Duchess of Fitz-Fulke and Aurora, sketches, but extraordinarily natural and vivid.   No poem gives such a sense of mundane life as *Don Juan*, and yet it is a poetic effect, for the metre and movement are an integral part of the whole impression.   When we call a poem prosaic we mean—we should mean, I think—not only that it lacks some of the highest imaginative qualities of great poetry, but that it would be better written in prose, as is the case with many of Crabbe's tales; that nothing would be lost, there might rather be actual gain, if the vesture of verse were slipt and the story went its way in the naked naturalness and ease of prose.   Byron's

H

would lose enormously, for the measure which he manages with such careless power retains all the momentum if not the speed of the earlier octosyllabics, the passion if not the rhetoric of the Spenserians. There are stanzas which vibrate with feeling like the atmosphere on a hot day

> I know not why, but in that hour to-night,
>   Even as they gazed, a sudden tremor came,
> And swept, as 'twere, across their hearts' delight,
>   Like the wind o'er a harp-string, or a flame,
> When one is shook in sound, and one in sight:

and the movement of the whole with its shifting and passionate and humorous moods is neither that of the lava stream to which one might compare the more fiery and turbid stanzas of *Childe Harold* and *Prometheus* nor the broad, heaven-reflecting river of the finer stanzas, but is, as Swinburne described it in his earlier, less prejudiced criticism, the movement of the sea itself: " Across the stanzas of *Don Juan* we swim forward as over ' the broad backs of the sea ' They break and glitter, hiss and laugh, murmur and move, like waves that sound or that subside. There is in them a delicious resistance, an elastic motion which salt water has and fresh has not. There is about them a wide, wholesome air full of vivid light and constant wind which is only felt at sea."

But if Byron's poem, despite its mundane theme and realistic rendering, moves with the passionate pulse of poetry it is because the spirit of the work is *not* mundane. Byron is in the world and yet not of it. He and Shelley were the twin protagonists of Southey's Satanic School. We have cleared Shelley—though Professor Babbit demurs —and have assigned him a throne and harp among the

angels.  Byron himself rather suspected the cloven hoof
in Shelley.  "Goethe's Mephistopheles", he writes,
"calls the serpent who tempted Eve 'my aunt, the
renowned snake', and I always insist that Shelley is
nothing but one of her nephews walking about on the
tip of his tail".  To Byron, at the same time, Shelley
seemed "the one perfectly unworldly man he ever
knew", a man who "possessed one of the first Christian
virtues, charity and benevolence.  His benevolence was
universal and his charity far beyond his means."  But
Byron had no sympathy with Shelley's shrill atheism,
or his taste for abstract dialectics.  Yet in their relation
to the world they are at once poles apart and radically
at one.  Byron was in the world.  He never really rises
above the mundane sphere to a vision of the pure ideas
beyond.  He never came out and stood upon the back
of heaven and beheld the world beyond, of which no
earthly poet has sung or ever will sing in a worthy manner.
Shelley's eyes were dazzled with that vision, or what he
took for authentic revelation.  But between him and the
world to which he desired to speak of what he saw
was a dome of viewless glass against which he beat his
ineffectual wings in vain.  He did not understand the
heart of men.  He craved for a perfect sympathy which
he could neither give nor obtain; and so if he strove,
as Professor Moorman says, to rebuild as well as to
destroy, it is as one builds castles in the air, or clouds
pile themselves up at sunset with burning battlements
"pinnacled dim in the intense inane".  But Byron in the
world was as fiercely at war with it as Shelley, and on
the same count of "man's inhumanity to man".  When
he left England in 1816 Byron was not yet an active

politician, though a Foxite Whig by tradition, a humanitarian by sympathy.   Since that time he had learned to view England from the point of view of a continental liberal, had realised the extent to which England had betrayed the cause of liberty in Italy and Spain, had betrayed the cause of justice and reform at home.   Hence the scorn with which in the old manner of Dryden and Churchill he reviews in *The Age of Bronze* the politicians and kings of Europe and the Holy Alliance:

> those who play their " tricks before high heaven ".
>    .      .      .      .      .      .      .
> Ah, how much happier were good Aesop's frogs
> Than we! for ours are animated logs,
> With ponderous malice swaying to and fro,
> And crushing nations with a stupid blow;
> All duly anxious to leave little work
> Unto the revolutionary stork.

Hence his picture of the landlords of England anguished at the fall of war-time rents:

> Safe in their barns, these Sabine tillers sent
> Their brethren out to battle—why? for rent, etc.

But *Don Juan* is not only a greater poem than *The Age of Bronze* but a greater satire, not because of the splendid vehemence of the vituperative stanzas on Castlereagh or the mocking lines on Wellington and others, but because there is less of individual and occasional satire, and what we have instead is a picture of the governing classes of Europe and England by one of themselves. "It is impossible", he told Kennedy, "you can believe the higher classes of society worse than they are in England, France, and Italy, for no language can sufficiently paint

them." To paint them as he found them was the main
purpose of *Don Juan*, though into that brilliant medley
he wove many strands of romance and poetry and philosophy. "Here they are!" he seems to say, and the
poem closed just as he had begun to deal with the society
he knew best; "here they are, the brilliant coteries under
whom as a great Colossus common men must

> peep about
> To find themselves dishonourable graves,

in all their external glitter, the same at St. Petersburg as
at London, with the cynical disregard for human happiness of their eternal game of diplomacy and war, and
under this brilliant surface the one great preoccupation,
'the orgiastic whirlpool'." The principal object of
Byron's satire in *Don Juan*, as of Swift's in *Gulliver's
Travels*, is human nature as revealed in the bungled,
cruel business of government and war:

> "Let there be Light," said God, "and there was Light!"
>     "Let there be Blood," says man, and there's a sea!
> The fiat of this spoiled child of the Night
>     (For Day ne'er saw his merits) could decree
> More evil in an hour, than thirty bright
>     Summers could renovate, though they should be
> Lovely as those which ripened Eden's fruit;
> For war cuts up not only branch but root.
>
> .     .     .     .     .     .     .
>
> Suwarrow now was conqueror—a match
>     For Timour or for Zinghis in his trade.
> While mosques and streets, beneath his eyes, like thatch
>     Blazed, and the cannon's roar was scarce allayed,
> With bloody hands he wrote his first dispatch;
>     And here exactly follows what he said:

" Glory to *God* and to the Empress! " (*Powers
Eternal! such names mingled*) " Ismail's ours ".

Methinks these are the most tremendous words
　　Since " Mene, Mene, Tekel " and " Upharsin ",
Which hands or pens have ever traced of swords.
　　Heaven help me! I'm but little of a parson:
What Daniel read was short-hand of the Lord's,
　　Severe, sublime; the prophet wrote no farce on
The fate of nations; but this Russ so witty
Could rhyme, like Nero, o'er a burning city.

He wrote this Polar melody, and set it,
　　Duly accompanied by shrieks and groans,
Which few will sing, I trust, but none forget it—
　　For I will teach, if possible, the stones
To rise against Earth's tyrants. Never let it
　　Be said that we still truckle unto thrones;—
But ye—our children's children! think how we
Showed *what things were* before the World was free!

That hour is not for us, but 'tis for you;
　　And as, in the great joy of your Millennium,
You hardly will believe such things were true
　　As now occur, I thought that I would pen you 'em;
But may their very memory perish too!—
　　Yet if perchance remembered, still disdain you 'em
More than you scorn the savages of yore,
Who *painted* their *bare* limbs but *not* with gore.

　　The poet who wrote these stanzas was as much at
war with the world in which he lived and moved as
the author of *Prometheus Unbound*, that voice crying in
ineffable music

O cease! must hate and death return?
Cease! must men kill and die?

and he was a more effective fighter.   For the Byron of
*Don Juan* as of *Childe Harold* was as great as his theme.
In the one as in the other one feels that a less potent
personality would have been overweighted, been compelled to be either a voice like Shelley singing unheeded
outside the haunts of men; or to play with his subject
like Moore, a literary mosquito buzzing about the face
of the omnipotent politicians and soldiers.   But Byron
had to be heard and was heard.   He was as big as those
he assailed.   On the stage which Napoleon had quitted
Byron's was the most interesting figure.   His political
activity began with his departure from Venice for Ravenna;
and he was prepared to go to all lengths had not the
Italians recoiled.   The expedition to Greece was not
the outcome of a sudden impulse to escape from idleness
and ennui.   It was a second chapter in the history of
his endeavour to serve the cause of emancipation with
his sword as well as his pen.   Milton and Swift are the
only other Englishmen of Letters whose writings have
been not only literary works but deeds.   The former
exercised but little influence on the actual course of
events, but a careful study of his last poems in relation
to the political pamphlets and *De Doctrina* will show that
they were more to their author than works of art alone.
They were great political acts; declarations by the poet
intended to be trumpet-calls to action, a vindication of
freedom conceived as obedience to reason and reason
only, addressed to the English people and the Christian
world, and if they failed to find such hearing as he desired,

yet before *Paradise Lost* had been published Milton's name had a European reputation, " and the only inducement of several foreigners that came over into England was chiefly to see Oliver Protector and Mr. John Milton ". Swift was a pamphleteer, but his pamphlets ended a European war and shook the government of Ireland, and it was not the satire alone which did so but the personality, the fearless pride and strength of the man who launched them. And Byron's voice rang through Europe. His every poem, his every action, was an historical event. When he went to Greece it was not only a man and an English peer who went but a power in Europe. Nor is Byron's satire and eloquence disposed of by declaring that his conception of liberty was purely negative, for he was not a metaphysician but a poet and a politician. A free government, says Burke, is, for practical purposes, what the people think so. The Europe for which Byron spoke knew well that it was not free, and understood and appreciated Byron's attacks on Holy Alliances and Congresses better than Shelley's metaphysics or Wordsworth's enlightenment.

6

THE issue between Arnold and Swinburne was the ever-recurring one of the relative values in poetry of technique and inspiration, art and life. It was as a great poetic virtuoso, perhaps the greatest virtuoso in English poetry, that Swinburne poured contempt on Byron's crudities of style, the shortcomings of his Spenserian stanzas, his halting and harsh " Christabel " measure, his inharmonious blank-verse; and exalted the wonderful achievement

ARNOLD & SWINBURNE 109

of Coleridge's *Christabel* and *Kubla Kkan*, the lyrical triumphs of the poet of the *West Wind* and the *Hymn to Pan*. For in the great development of poetic technique, the enrichment of diction and verse, in which Coleridge and Keats and Shelley led the way, to be followed by Tennyson and Browning and the Pre-Raphaelites themselves, Byron had no share. His failure to recognise what Keats and Shelley were in different ways doing; his short-sighted commendations of Campbell and Rogers and Moore, reveal how little he appreciated the revolution in poetic technique that was in progress. "Keats was not, nor ever will be a popular poet," said Shelley. Keats has been, without any exception, the greatest influence in English poetry for a whole century. To his example and inspiration are due all the wonderful sensuous felicity, the splendour of exotic phrasing and harmony of Tennyson's 1842 volumes; the bold and varied experiments of Browning's *Bells and Pomegranates*; the curious subtleties of *The Blessed Damozel* and *The House of Life*; *The Defence of Guenevere* and *The Earthly Paradise*; *Poems and Ballads*, and *Atalanta in Calydon*. If poetry be first and last a sensuous pleasure, then Keats and his successors are the greatest of our poets since Spenser, and the Marlowe of *Hero and Leander*, the Shakespeare of *Venus and Adonis* and the "sugared sonnets"; as virtuosi of phrase and harmonies perhaps greater even than these. Compared with wines of such rare bouquet Wordsworth's simplicity and purity of language and verse tastes no better, if no worse, than a draught from a mountain stream, and Byron's turbulent rhetoric and fierce invective has the effect of such water dashed with whisky or his favourite gin.

But water has been turned to wine, and the wine
that the poet pours is a sacramental wine, a spiritual
even more than a sensuous pleasure; and such is Wordsworth's poetry at its best.   And the poetry and criticism
of Arnold were a protest against the over-exaltation in
poetry of craftsmanship, of exotic and sensuous beauty,
of indifference to subject or even a preference for subjects remote from actual experience, lending themselves
to subtle and precious craftsmanship.   Hence the stress
he laid for a time upon the great subject; hence his
tendency to look past the romantic poets with their
passionate illusions and intoxicating harmonies and phrasing to Greek poetry in which beauty of craftsmanship
was combined with sanity of thought and depth of feeling.
Hence the emphasis he laid on Wordsworth as a poet of
the soul, and on Byron as a poet, despite all his shortcomings, of actual experience, a poet of the Europe of
Castlereagh and the Holy Alliance.

In the main, one may admit that Swinburne was in
the right.   With all the stress that he laid upon the real
as opposed to the personal estimate Arnold's judgements
were often even obviously personal.   He had not out-
grown either the Wordsworthian tradition of his circle—
" I am a Wordsworthian myself "— or the Byronic
tradition of his youth.   He could sympathise with the
romantic enthusiasm for Byron of Lord Beaconsfield,
perhaps the last great representative in literature and
politics of the Napoleonic and Byronic tradition.   The
appeal to the Continent on which Arnold characteristically relied has gone against him.   Byronism is a fashion
of the past.   Byron no longer interests the French,
says Estève; and Professor Farinelli tells the same tale

of Italy: " Il narcotico di quei versi che agiva ancora sul Michelet (' Je l'ai dévoré. Impossible de faire autre chose ') ha perso ogni efficacia. E pensiamo con malinconia stringente al consumarsi rapido di ogni gloria nostra più fulgida, e al disperdersi ai venti dei tesori di poesia raccolti, che credemmo incorruttibili e eterni." We have so much to learn, Arnold was ever insisting, from continental criticism, but continental criticism has of late learned a good deal from us and come to a juster appreciation of Wordsworth and Byron, Shelley and Keats.

And yet Arnold was not altogether wrong when he insisted on the subject as well as the form in poetry, on subject and form as distinguishable but not separable; his insistence on thought as an element in poetry as well as sensuous imagery and harmonies; and therefore the appeal of Wordsworth's spirit of wisdom and contemplation, of Byron's vivid and sensitive reflection of his troubled age. And the proof may be felt by a little consideration of the work of those who arraigned Byron, the poetry of Swinburne, and Rossetti and their school. If the poetic spirit in Wordsworth and Byron is too often obscured by a limited and unequal art, I am not sure that Rossetti and Swinburne are not too perfect artists, too great virtuosi. After the first tremendous impression of the daring as well as the craftsmanship of *Poems and Ballads*, and *Atalanta in Calydon*, the experience of a reader of Swinburne was of growing disillusionment till even *Songs before Sunrise* read as " a tale of little meaning though the words be strong ". A sense of echoing emptiness haunts the student who turns back on much of the exquisite, exotic, sensuous craftsmanship of these last of the romantics. What after all does the " fundamental brain-work " in *The House of Life*, that aumbry full of chased and burnished vessels of gold, heavy with the fragrance of frankincense, amount to; is there any such clear, passionate thinking about love and its many moods and contradictions as in the *Songs and Sonnets* of an older poet?   Compared with *Atalanta* and *The Blessed Damozel* and *The Land East of the Sun and West of the Moon*, Byron's *Childe Harold* and *Beppo* and the best parts of *Don Juan* have at least this advantage, that they read like the record of an actual, vivid experience.

When all is said and done Byron remains a great poet because his poetry possesses certain great qualities in a fuller measure than his in many other ways more richly dowered contemporaries.   They are not the purest, the highest gifts of the poet, but they are qualities which his poetry shares with that of some of our greatest older poets more fully than does the poetry of Wordsworth or Shelley or Coleridge or Keats.   It is no intention of mine to endeavour to restore Byron's whilom reputation as the greatest of English poets after Shakespeare and Milton. Not all the king's horses and all the king's men can do that.   In the finest qualities of poetry—the imagination which at once creates and transfigures; the magical perfection of phrasing, whether pure or severe as in Wordsworth, or delicate and sensitive as with Coleridge, or winged and ethereal as with Shelley, or so rich in sensuous beauty that we may use Keats' own words and say that " summer has o'erbrimmed their clammy cells "; the deep inner music which is the very soul of poetry—in all these Byron has been surpassed by all these poets, *at their best*, and the Continent, at least that part of it which studies our poetry seriously, is learning to recognise the

fact.   But poetry has many qualities and moves on more
than one level.   There may be good poetry which does
not aim at entering the seventh heaven of ecstasy and
vision, or dissolving into music, but is able to absorb and
assimilate the real world of men and women, good sense,
and earthly passions and humour and wit and oratory
and talk.   And this is where Byron's poetry joins hands
with that of Chaucer and Shakespeare and Milton and
Dryden and Pope if it fails to ascend the highest heavens.
It has force, passion, humour and wit, narrative and
descriptive power, oratorical fire and conversational ease
and flow.   I can imagine Chaucer writing *Beppo*, I can
think of Shakespeare or Milton or Dryden composing
the tremendous onslaught upon Castlereagh—I cannot
think of any of the romantics writing either, to say
nothing of the interplay of wit and gaiety and pathos
and poetic description and superabundant vitality of
*Don Juan* and *The Vision of Judgement*, or the vehement
eloquence and colour of the best things in *Childe Harold*.
*Childe Harold* and *Don Juan* have more of the epic quality,
the solidity of *Paradise Lost*, than any of the Romantic
or Victorian longer poems — *The Revolt of Islam*,
*Endymion*, *Idylls of the King*, *Aurora Leigh*, *The Ring and
the Book*.   The love story of Don Juan and Haidee has
a virility which the sublimated love-tales of the Victorians,
*Maud*, and *The Angel in the House* and *The Ring and the
Book*, with all their beauty, somewhat lack.   Virility,
vehemence, colour, humour, wit, eloquence and a perfect
naturalness of conversational writing—these will not
doubtless compensate for the lack of the supreme qualities.
But compared with Byron's a great deal of both Victorian
and Georgian poetry seems a little anæmic.   " In the

physical force of words Byron excels all other English poets," said George Macdonald, who did not love him; no one can. "Quand on voit le style naturel, on est tout étonné et ravi, car on s'attendait de voir un auteur et on trouve un homme." Byron has been over-estimated and under-estimated—the fact remains that English poetry would be greatly the poorer without the passionate, humorous, essentially human voice that declaims in *Childe Harold* and flows like a torrent in *Don Juan*.

1920–25.

# THE METAPHYSICAL
# POETS

METAPHYSICAL POETRY, in the full sense of the term, is a poetry which, like that of the *Divina Commedia*, the *De Natura Rerum*, perhaps Goethe's *Faust*, has been inspired by a philosophical conception of the universe and of the rôle assigned to the human spirit in the great drama of existence. These poems were written because a definite interpretation of the riddle—the atoms of Epicurus rushing through infinite empty space, the theology of the schoolmen as elaborated in the catechetical disquisitions of St. Thomas, Spinoza's vision of life *sub specie aeternitatis*, beyond good and evil—laid hold on the mind and the imagination of a great poet, unified and illumined his comprehension of life, intensified and heightened his personal consciousness of joy and sorrow, of hope and fear, by broadening their significance, revealed to him in the history of his own soul a brief abstract of the drama of human destiny. "Poetry is the first and last of all knowledge—it is as immortal as the heart of man." Its themes may be the simplest experiences of the surface of life, sorrow and joy, love and battle, the peace of the country, the bustle and stir of towns, but equally they may be the boldest conceptions, the profoundest intuitions, the subtlest and most complex classifications and "discourse of reason", if into these too the poet can "carry sensation", make of them passionate experiences communicable in vivid and moving imagery, in rich and varied harmonies.

It is no such great metaphysical poetry as that of Lucretius and Dante that the present essay deals with. Of the poets whom Johnson classed as " metaphysical ", Donne is familiar with the definitions and distinctions of Mediæval Scholasticism; Cowley's bright and alert, if not profound, mind is attracted by the achievements of science and the systematic materialism of Hobbes.    Donne, moreover, is metaphysical not only in virtue of his scholasticism, but of his deep reflective interest in the experiences of which his poetry is the expression, the new psychological curiosity with which he writes of love and religion.    The divine poets who follow Donne have each the inherited metaphysic, if one may so call it, of the Church to which he is attached, Catholic or Anglican.    But none of the poets has for his main theme a metaphysic like that of Epicurus or St. Thomas passionately apprehended and imaginatively expounded.    Donne, the most thoughtful and imaginative of them all, is more aware of disintegration than of comprehensive harmony, of the clash between the older physics and metaphysics on the one hand, and on the other the new science of Copernicus and Galileo and Vesalius and Bacon:

> The new philosophy calls all in doubt,
> The element of fire is quite put out;
> The sun is lost and the earth, and no man's wit
> Can well direct him where to look for it.
> And freely men confess that this world's spent,
> When in the planets and the firmament
> They seek so many new; they see that this
> Is crumbled out again to his atomies.
>
> Have not all souls thought
> For many ages that our body is wrought

> Of air and fire and other elements?
> And now they think of new ingredients;
> And one soul thinks one, and another way
> Another thinks, and 'tis an even lay.

The greatest English poet, indeed, of the century was, or believed himself to be, a philosophical or theological poet of the same order as Dante. *Paradise Lost* was written to be a justification of " the ways of God to men ", resting on a theological system as definite and almost as carefully articulated in the *De Doctrina Christiana* as that which Dante had accepted from the *Summa* of Aquinas. And the poet embodied his argument in a dramatic poem as vividly and intensely conceived, as magnificently and harmoniously set forth, as the *Divina Commedia*. But in truth Milton was no philosopher. The subtleties of theological definition and inference eluded his rationalistic, practical, though idealistic, mind. He proved nothing. The speech in the third book, which expounds Milton's justification of God's ways to men, simply lays down in the hardest, most dogmatic fashion a view of the relation between foreknowledge and freewill, the difficulties inherent in which he might have learned from Chaucer and Chaucer's master Boethius; and the metaphysical doctrine of the divine " retreat " in which M. Saurat would have us find Milton's ultimate explanation of individual liberty is as incomprehensible as any doctrine of the " procession of the Holy Ghost ". What Milton did was to give by his poetic handling a new concreteness, vividness and dramatic power to the myth of the fall of Lucifer and of Adam, which, as he presented it, was for more than a century to dominate the mind and imagination of pious Protestants, few of whom suspected the

I

heresies which lurked beneath the imposing and dazzling poem in which was retold the Bible story of the Fall. Unfortunately, if he failed in his metaphysical justification of God's ways to men, he failed more disastrously to justify them to the heart and the imagination, to suggest, if he divined it, an underlying mystery of divine love.

Metaphysical in this large way, Donne and his followers to Cowley are not, yet the word describes better what is the peculiar quality of their poetry than any other, *e.g.* fantastic, for poetry may be fantastic in so many different ways, witness Skelton, and the Elizabethans, and Hood, and Browning. It lays stress on the right things—the survival, one might say the reaccentuation, of the metaphysical strain, the *concetti metafisici ed ideali* (as Testi calls them in contrast to the simpler imagery of classical poetry), of mediæval Italian poetry; the more intellectual, less verbal, character of their wit compared with the conceits of the Elizabethans; the finer psychology of which their conceits are often the expression; their learned imagery; the argumentative, subtle evolution of their lyrics; above all, the peculiar blend of passion and thought, feeling and ratiocination which is their greatest achievement. In these poets' often trivial songs survives something of the mental habit of the schoolmen who had carried subtle deductive reasoning to a higher pitch than it had, or ever since has, attained, for Bacon signalised the breach of modern with mediæval thought when he transferred the emphasis from deduction to induction. The distinctive note of " metaphysical " poetry is the blend of passionate feeling and paradoxical ratiocination. The evolution of a lyric by Donne is not quite that which Wordsworth indicates when he speaks of " the manner

in which we associate ideas in a state of excitement ".    It
is rather the subtle elaboration of a passionately conceived
hyperbole or paradox.

The Italian influence which Wyatt and Surrey brought
into English poetry at the Renaissance gave it a more
serious, a more thoughtful colour.    They caught, especially Wyatt in some of the finest of his sonnets and
songs, that spirit of " high seriousness " which Chaucer
with all his admiration of Italian poetry had failed to
apprehend.    English mediæval poetry is often gravely
pious, haunted by the fear of death and the judgement,
melancholy over the " Falls of Princes ";    it is never
serious and thoughtful in the introspective, reflective,
dignified manner of Wyatt and Sackville, and our " sage
and serious " Spenser, and the first group of Elizabethan
courtly poets, Sidney and Raleigh and Dyer.    One has
but to recall " My lute, awake! perform the last ",
" Forget not yet the tried intent ", " My mind to me a
kingdom is ", and to contrast them in mind with the
songs which Henry VIII. and Cornish were still composing and singing when Wyatt began to write, in order
to realise what Italy and the Renaissance did to deepen
the strain of English lyric poetry as that had flowed under
French influence from the thirteenth to the sixteenth
centuries.    But French influence, the influence of
Ronsard and his fellows, renewed itself in the seventies,
and the great body of Elizabethan song is as gay and
careless and impersonal as the earlier lyric had been,
though richer in colour and more varied in rhythm.    Then
came Donne and Jonson (the schoolman and the humanist
one might say, emphasising for the moment single aspects
of their work), and new qualities of spirit and form

were given to lyrical poetry, and not to lyrical poetry alone.

In dealing with poets who lived and wrote before the eighteenth century we are always confronted with the difficulty of recovering the personal, the biographical element, which, if sometimes irrelevant and even disturbing and disconcerting, may yet be essential to a complete understanding of their work. Men were not different from what they are now, and if there be hardly a lyric of Goethe's or Shelley's that does not owe something to the accidents of their lives, one may feel sure it was in varying degrees the same with poets three hundred years ago. Poems are not written by influences or movements or sources, but come from the living hearts of men. Fortunately, in the case of Donne, one of the most individual of poets, it is possible to some extent to reproduce the circumstances, the inner experiences from which his intensely personal poetry flowed.

He was in the first place a Catholic. Our history text-books make so little of the English Catholics that one is apt to forget they existed and were, for themselves at any rate, not a political problem, but real and suffering individuals. " I had my first breeding and conversation ", says Donne, " with men of a suppressed and afflicted religion, accustomed to the despite of death and hungry of an imagined martyrdom." In these circumstances, we gather, he was carefully and religiously educated, and after some years at Oxford and Cambridge was taken or sent abroad, perhaps with a view to entering foreign service, more probably with a view to the priesthood, and visited Italy and Spain. And then, one conjectures, a reaction took place, the rebellion of a full-blooded and highly

intellectual temperament against a superimposed bent.
He entered the Inns of Court in 1592, at the age of
nineteen, flung himself into the life of a young man about
town, Jack Donne, " not dissolute but very neat," says
Sir Richard Baker, " a great visiter of ladies, a great
frequenter of plays, a great writer of conceited verses ";
and another adds, " Neither was it possible that a vulgar
soul should dwell in such promising features ".   But
Donne was a student as well as a gallant.   " In the most
unsettled days of his youth his bed was not able to detain
him beyond the hour of four in the morning, and it was
no common business that drew him out of his chamber
till past ten;  all which time was employed in study;
although he took great liberty after it."   He joined the
band of reckless and raffish young men who sailed with
Essex to Cadiz and the Islands.   He was taken into the
service of Sir Thomas Egerton.   Ambition began to vie
with the love of pleasure, when a hasty marriage closed a
promising career, and left him bound in shallows and in
miseries, to spend years in the suitorship of the great, and
to find at last, not altogether willingly, a haven in the
Anglican priesthood, and reveal himself as the first great
orator that Church could boast of.

The record of these early years is contained in Donne's
Satires—harsh, witty, lucid, full of a young man's scorn
of fools and low callings, and a young thinker's consciousness of the problems of religion in an age of divided faiths,
and of justice in a corrupt world—and in his Love Songs
and Elegies.   The satires were more generally known;
the love poems the more influential in courtly and literary
circles.

Donne's genius, temperament, and learning gave to his

love poems certain qualities which immediately arrested attention and have given them ever since a power at once fascinating and disconcerting despite the faults of phrasing and harmony which, for a century after Dryden, obscured, and to some still outweigh, their poetic worth. The first of these is a depth and range of feeling unknown to the majority of Elizabethan sonneteers and song-writers. Over all the Elizabethan sonnets, in greater or less measure, hangs the suggestion of translation or imitation. Watson, Sidney, Daniel, Spenser, Drayton, Lodge, all of them, with rarer or more frequent touches of individuality, are pipers of Petrarch's woes, sighing in the strain of Ronsard or more often of Desportes. The best of them, Sidney, Spenser, Drayton, Shakespeare— the first and the last of these pre-eminently—give an individual note to the traditional themes; but Donne's love-poetry is startlingly unconventional if at times he may dally, half ironically, with the hyperboles of Petrarchian adoration. His songs are the expression in unconventional, witty language of all the moods of a lover that experience and imagination have taught him to understand—sensuality aerated by a brilliant wit; fascination and scornful anger inextricably blended:

> When by thy scorn, O murdress, I am dead
> And that thou think'st thee free
> From all solicitations from me,
> Then shall my ghost come to thy bed;

the passionate joy of mutual and contented love:

> All other things to their destruction draw,
>   Only our love hath no decay;
> This no to-morrow hath nor yesterday,

Running it never runs from us away,
    But truly keeps his first, last, everlasting day;

the sorrow of parting which is the shadow of such joy:

So, so, break off this last lamenting kiss
Which sucks two souls and vapours both away;

the gentler pathos of temporary separation in married life:

Let not thy divining heart
    Forethink me any ill,
Destiny may take thy part,
    And may thy fears fulfil;
        But think that we
    Are but turn'd aside to sleep;
    They who one another keep
        Alive ne'er parted be;

the mystical heights and the mystical depths of love:

Study me then you who shall lovers be
At the next world, that is, at the next Spring:
For I am every dead thing
In whom love wrought new Alchemy.

If Donne had expressed this wide range of intense feeling
as perfectly as he has done at times poignantly and startlingly; if he had given to his poems the same impression
of entire artistic sincerity that Shakespeare conveys in
the greater of his sonnets; in short, if his wit and fancy
had been a little more under the control of a sense of
fitness and beauty, his regard for form a little more
dominant, he would have been, as in range and poignancy
he surely is, the greatest of love poets, the greatest poet
of love as a real, untransmuted, overwhelming experience.
But there is a second quality of his poetry which made it

the fashion of an age, but has been inimical to its general acceptance ever since, and that is its metaphysical wit. "He affects the metaphysics", says Dryden, "not only in his satires but in his amorous verses where nature only should reign; and perplexes the minds of the fair sex with nice speculations of philosophy when he should engage their hearts and entertain them with the softnesses of love." "Amorous verses", "the fair sex", and "the softnesses of love" are the vulgarities of a less poetic and passionate age than Donne's, but metaphysics he does affect. Now a metaphysical strand, *concetti metafisici ed ideali*, had run through the mediæval love-poetry of which the Elizabethan sonnets are a descendant. It had attained its fullest development in the poems of Dante and his school, had been subordinated to rhetoric and subtleties of expression rather than thought in Petrarch, and had lost itself in the pseudo-metaphysical extravagances of Tebaldeo, Cariteo, and Serafino. Donne was no conscious reviver of the metaphysics of Dante, but to the game of elaborating fantastic conceits and hyperboles which was the fashion throughout Europe, he brought not only a full-blooded temperament and acute mind, but a vast and growing store of the same scholastic learning, the same Catholic theology, as controlled Dante's thought, but jostling already with the new learning of Copernicus and Paracelsus. The result is startling and disconcerting,—the comparison of parted lovers to the legs of a pair of compasses, the deification of his mistress by the discovery that she is only to be defined by negatives or that she can read the thoughts of his heart, a thing "beyond an angel's art"; and a thousand other subtleties of quintessences and nothingness, the mixture of souls and the significance of numbers, to say nothing of the aerial bodies of angels, the phœnix and the mandrake's root, Alchemy and Astrology, legal contracts and *non obstantes*, " late schoolboys and sour prentices ", " the king's real and his stamped face ".   But the effect aimed at and secured is not entirely fantastic and erudite.   The motive inspiring Donne's images is in part the same as that which led Shakespeare from the picturesque, natural or mythological, images of *A Midsummer-Night's Dream* and *The Merchant of Venice* to the homely but startling phrases and metaphors of *Hamlet* and *Macbeth*, the " blanket of the dark ", the

> fat weed
> That rots itself in ease on Lethe wharf,

" the rank sweat of an enseamed bed ".   It is the same desire for vivid and dramatic expression.   The great master at a later period of dramatic as well as erudite pulpit oratory coins in his poems many a startling, jarring, arresting phrase:

> For God's sake hold your tongue and let me love:

> Who ever comes to shroud me do not harm
>   Nor question much
> That subtle wreath of hair, which crowns my arm:

> I taught my silks their rustling to forbear,
> Even my opprest shoes dumb and silent were.

> I long to talk with some old lover's ghost
> Who died before the God of love was born;

> Twice or thrice had I loved thee
> Before I knew thy face or name,
> So in a voice, so in a shapeless flame,
> Angels affect us oft and worshipped be;

> And whilst our souls negotiate there
> We like sepulchral statues lay;
> All day the same our postures were
> And we said nothing all the day.

> My face and breast of haircloth, and my head
> With care's harsh, sudden hoariness o'erspread.

These vivid, simple, realistic touches are too quickly merged in learned and fantastic elaborations, and the final effect of almost every poem of Donne's is a bizarre and blended one; but if the greatest poetry rises clear of the bizarre, the fantastic, yet very great poetry may be bizarre if it be the expression of a strangely blended temperament, an intense emotion, a vivid imagination.

What is true of Donne's imagery is true of the other disconcerting element in his poetry, its harsh and rugged verse. It is an outcome of the same double motive, the desire to startle and the desire to approximate poetic to direct, unconventional, colloquial speech. Poetry is always a balance, sometimes a compromise, between what has to be said and the prescribed pattern to which the saying of it is adjusted. In poetry such as Spenser's, more sensuous than passionate, the musical flow, the melody and harmony of line and stanza, is dominant, and the meaning is adjusted to it at the not infrequent cost of diffuseness— if a delightful diffuseness—and even some weakness of phrasing logically and rhetorically considered. In Shakespeare's tragedies the thought and feeling tend to break through the prescribed pattern till blank verse becomes almost rhythmical prose, the rapid overflow of the lines admitting hardly the semblance of pause. This is the kind of effect Donne is always aiming at, alike in his satires and lyrics, bending and cracking the metrical pattern to the rhetoric of direct and vehement utterance.  The result is often, and to eighteenth-century ears attuned to the clear and defined if limited, harmony of Waller and Dryden and Pope was, rugged and harsh.  But here again, to those who have ears that care to hear, the effect is not finally inharmonious.  Donne's verse has a powerful and haunting harmony of its own.  For Donne is not simply, no poet could be, willing to force his accent, to strain and crack a prescribed pattern; he is striving to find a rhythm that will express the passionate fullness of his mind, the fluxes and refluxes of his moods; and the felicities of his verse are as frequent and startling as those of his phrasing.  He is one of the first masters, perhaps *the* first, of the elaborate stanza or paragraph in which the discords of individual lines or phrases are resolved in the complex and rhetorically effective harmony of the whole group of lines:

> If yet I have not all thy love,
> Dear, I shall never have it all,
> I cannot breathe one other sigh, to move;
> Nor can entreat one other tear to fall.
> And all my treasure, which should purchase thee,
> Sighs, teares, and oaths, and letters I have spent,
> Yet no more can be due to me,
> Then at the bargain made was meant,
> If then thy gift of love were partial,
> That some to me, some should to others fall,
>     Dear, I shall never have Thee All.
>
> But I am None; nor will my sun renew.
> You lovers, for whose sake the lesser Sun
>     At this time to the Goat is run
> To fetch new lust and give it you,

Enjoy your summer all;
Since she enjoys her long night's festival,
Let me prepare towards her, and let me call
This hour her Vigil and her Eve, since this

Both the year's | and the day's | deep mid | night is.

The wrenching of accent which Jonson complained of is not entirely due to carelessness or indifference. It has often both a rhetorical and a harmonious justification. Donne plays with rhythmical effects as with conceits and words and often in much the same way. Mr. Fletcher Melton's interesting analysis of Donne's verse has not, I think, established his main thesis, which like so many " research " scholars he over-emphasises, that the whole mystery of Donne's art lies in his use of the same sound now in *arsis*, now in *thesis*; but his examples show that this is one of many devices by which Donne secures two effects: firstly, the troubling of the regular fall of the verse stresses by the intrusion of rhetorical stress on syllables which the metrical pattern leaves unstressed; and, secondly, an echoing and re-echoing of similar sounds parallel to his fondness for resemblances in thoughts and things apparently the most remote from one another. There is, that is to say, in his verse the same blend as in his diction of the colloquial and the bizarre. He writes as one who *will* say what he has to say without regard to conventions of poetic diction or smooth verse; but what he has to say is subtle and surprising, and so are the metrical effects with which it is presented. There is nothing of unconsciousness or merely careless harshness in such an effect as this:

Poor soul, in this thy flesh what dost thou know?
Thou know'st thyself so little that thou knowst not
How thou didst die, nor how thou wast begot.
Thou neither know'st how thou at first camest in,
Nor how thou took'st the poison of man's sin;
Nor dost thou though thou know'st that thou art so
By what way thou art made immortal know.

Here the sounds " oh " and " ow ", approximate yet distinct, ring through the lines like two tolling bells. Such a result is not purely accidental.   Mr. Melton has collected, and any careful reader may discover for himself, many similar subtleties of poetical rhetoric; for Donne is perhaps our first great master of poetic rhetoric, of poetry used, as Dryden and Pope were to use it, for effects of oratory rather than of song, and  the advance which Dryden achieved was secured by subordinating to oratory the more passionate and  imaginative qualities which troubled the balance and movement of Donne's packed but imaginative rhetoric.

It was not indeed in lyrical verse that Dryden followed and developed Donne, but in his eulogistic, elegiac, satirical, and epistolary poems.   The progress of Dryden's eulogistic style is traceable from his earliest metaphysical extravagances, through lines such as those addressed to the Duchess of York, where Waller is his model, to the beautiful verses on the death of Oldham in which a more natural and classical strain has entirely superseded his earlier extravagances and elegancies.   In truth Donne's metaphysical eulogies and elegies and epistles are a hard nut to crack for his most sympathetic admirers.   And yet they have undeniable qualities.   The metaphysics are developed in a more serious, a less paradoxical, strain than

in some of the songs and elegies.    In his letters he is an
excellent, if far from a perfect, talker in verse; and the
personality which they reveal is a singularly charming
one, grave, loyal, melancholy, witty.    If some of the
elegiac pieces are packed with tasteless and extravagant
hyperboles, the *Anniversaries* (especially the second) remains, despite all its faults, one of the greatest poems on
death in the language, the fullest record in our literature
of the disintegrating collision in a sensitive mind of the
old tradition and the new learning.    Some of the in-
vocational passages in *Of the Progresse of the Soule* are
among the finest examples of his subtle and passionate thinking as well as of his most elaborate verse
rhetoric.

But the most intense and personal of Donne's poems,
after the love-songs and elegies, are his later religious
sonnets and songs; and their influence on subsequent
poetry was even more obvious and potent.    They are as
personal and as tormented as his earlier " love-song weeds ",
for his spiritual Aeneid was a troubled one.    To date
Donne's conversion to Anglicanism is not easy.    In his
satires there is a veiled Roman tone.    By 1602 he dis-
claims to Egerton " all love of a corrupt religion ", but
in the autumn of the previous year he had been meditating
a satire on Queen Elizabeth as one of the world's great
heretics.    His was not a conversion but a reconciliation,
an acquiescence in the faith of his country, the established
religion of his legal sovereign, and the act cost him some
pangs.    " A convert from Popery to Protestantism ", said
Dr. Johnson, " gives up so much of what he has held as
sacred as anything that he retains, there is so much
laceration of mind in such a conversion, that it can hardly

be sincere and lasting." Something of that laceration of mind is discernible in Donne's religious verse:

Show me dear Christ that spouse so bright and clear.

But the conflict between the old and the reformed faiths was not the only, nor perhaps the principal trouble for Donne's enlightened mind ready to recognise in all the Churches "virtual beams of one sun", "connatural pieces of one circle". A harder fight was that between the secular, the "man of the world" temper of his mind, and the claims of a pious and ascetic calling. It was not the errors of his youth, as the good Walton supposed, which constituted the great stumbling-block, though he, unlike some of his later clerical critics, never ignores these:

O might those sighs and tears return again
Into my breast and eyes, which I have spent,
That I might in this holy discontent
Mourn with some fruit, as I have mourned in vain.

It was rather the temperament of one who, at a time when a public career was more open to unassisted talent, might have proved an active and useful, if ambitious, civil servant, or professional man, at war with the claims of a religious life which his upbringing had taught him was incompatible with worldly ambition. George Herbert, a much more contented Anglican than Donne ever became, knew something of the same struggle before he bent his neck to the collar.

The two notes then of Donne's religious poems are the Catholic and the personal. He is the first of our Anglo-Catholic poets, and he is our first intensely personal religious poet, expressing always not the mind simply of the Christian as such, but the conflicts and longings of one troubled soul, one subtle and fantastic mind. Donne's technique is the same in the religious as in the love poems. There are the same arresting phrases and startling, mediæval, and metaphysical conceits; there is the same packed verse with its bold, irregular fingering and echoing vowel sounds. The echoing and re-echoing " i " sounds in the following lines cannot be altogether accidental:

> O might those *sighs* and tears return again
> Into my breast and *eyes*, which *I* have spent,
> That *I* might in this holy discontent
> Mourn with some fruit, as *I* have mourned in vain;
> In mine *Idolat'ry* what showers of rain
> *Mine eyes* did waste? What griefs *my* heart did rent?
> That sufferance was *my* sin; now *I* repent
> Cause *I* did suffer *I* must suffer pain.

In the remaining six lines the same sound never recurs.

A metaphysical, a philosophical poet, to the degree to which his contemporaries Sir John Davies or Fulke Greville might be called such, Donne was not. He expounds no coherent system. The thought in his poetry is not his primary concern but the feeling. No scheme of thought, no interpretation of life became for him a complete and illuminating experience. The central theme of his poetry is ever his own intense personal moods, as a lover, a friend, an analyst of his own experiences worldly and religious. His philosophy cannot unify these experiences. It is used to record the reaction of his restless and acute mind on the intense experience of the moment, to supply a reading of it in the light now of one, now of another philosophical or theological dogma or thesis caught from his multifarious reading, developed with audacious paradox or more serious intention, an expression, an illumination of that mood to himself and to his reader Whether one choose to call him a metaphysical or a fantastic poet, the stress must be laid on the word " poet " Whether verse or prose be his medium, Donne is always a poet, a creature of feeling and imagination, seeking expression in vivid phrase and complex harmonies, a poet whose acute and subtle intellect was the servant, if sometimes the unruly servant, of passion and imagination.

2

DONNE'S influence was felt in his own day by two strangely different classes of men, both attached by close ties to the Court.    For the Court, the corrupt, ambitious, intriguing, dissolute but picturesque and dazzling court of the old pagan Elizabeth, of the pedantic and drunken James, of the dignified and melancholy and politically blinded Charles, was the centre round which all Donne's secular interests revolved.    He can speak of it as bitterly and sardonically as Shakespeare in *Hamlet*:

> Here's no more news, then virtue, I may as well
> Tell you Cales or St. Michael's tale for news, as tell
> That vice doth here habitually dwell.
>
> .    .    .    .    .    .    .
>
> But now 'tis incongruity to smile,
> Therefore I end; and bid farewell a while,
> *At Court*, though *From Court* were the better style.

He knows its corruptions as well as Milton and commends Lady Bedford in just such terms as Milton might have commended Alice Egerton.    All the same, to be shut

K

out from the Court, in the city or the country, is to inhabit
a desert, or sepulchre, for *there*:

> The Princes favour is defus'd o'er all,
> From which all Fortunes, Names, and Natures fall.

.    .    .    .    .    .    .    .

> And all is warmth and light and good desire.

It was among the younger generation of Courtiers
that Donne found the warmest admirers of his paradoxical
and sensual audacities as a love-poet, as it was those
divines who looked to Laud and the Court for Anglican
doctrine and discipline that revered his memory, enshrined
by the pious Izaak Walton, as of a divine poet and preacher.
The " metaphysicals " were all on the King's side.    Even
Andrew Marvell was neither Puritan nor Republican.
" Men ought to have trusted God " was his final judgement on the Rebellion, " they ought to have trusted the
King with the whole matter."    They were on the side
of the King, for they were on the side of the humanities;
and the Puritan rebellion, whatever the indirect constitutional results, was in itself and at the moment a
fanatical upheaval, successful because it also threw up
the John Zizka of his age; its triumph was the triumph
of Cromwell's sword:

> And for the last effect
> Still keep the sword erect.

> Besides the force it has to fright
> The spirits of the shady night,
> > The same arts that did gain
> > A power must it maintain.

To call these poets the " school of Donne " or " metaphysical " poets may easily mislead if one takes either

phrase in too full a sense.   It is not only that they show little of Donne's subtlety of mind or " hydroptic, immoderate thirst of human learning ", but they want the complexity of mood, the range of personal feeling which lends such fullness of life to Donne's strange and troubled poetry, justifies his subtle and fantastic misapplication of learning.   His followers, amorous and courtly, or pious and ecclesiastical, move in a more rarefied atmosphere; their poetry is much more truly " abstract " than Donne's, the witty and fantastic elaboration of one or two common moods, of compliment, passion, devotion, penitence.   It is very rarely that one can detect a deep personal note in the delightful love-songs with which the whole period from Carew to Dryden abounds.   The collected work of none of them would give such an impression of a real history behind it, a history of many experiences and moods, as Donne's Songs, Elegies, and, as one must still believe, the sonnets of Shakespeare record.   Like the Elizabethan sonneteers they all dress and redress the same theme in much the same manner, though the manner is not quite the Elizabethan, nor the theme.   Song has superseded the sonnet, and the passion of which they sing has lost most of the Petrarchian, chivalrous strain, and become in a very definite meaning of the words, " simple and sensuous ", at time humorous or scornful.   And if the religious poets are rather more individual and personal, the personal note is less intense, troubled, and complex than in Donne's Divine Poems;   the individual is more merged in the Christian, whether Catholic or Anglican.

Donne and Jonson are probably in the main responsible for the unconventional purity and naturalness of their diction, for these had both "shaken hands with " Spenserian archaism and strangeness, and with the "rhetoric" of the sonneteers and of poems like *Venus and Adonis*; and their style is untouched by any foreshadowing of Miltonic diction or the jargon of a later poetic vocabulary. The metaphysicals are the masters of the " neutral style ", of a diction equally appropriate, according as it may be used, to prose and verse.    If purity and naturalness of style is a grace, they deserved well of the English language, for few poets have used it with a more complete acceptance of the established tradition of diction and idiom.    There are no poets till we come perhaps to Cowper, and he has now quite escaped from jargon, or Shelley, and his imagination operates in a more ethereal atmosphere, whose style is so entirely that of an English gentleman of the best type, natural, simple, occasionally careless, but never diverging into vulgar colloquialism, as after the Restoration, or into conventional, tawdry splendour, as in the century of Akenside and Erasmus Darwin.    If one sets even a good verse from Gray beside a poem by Herbert, if one reads first:

> Still is the toiling hand of Care;
>     The panting herds repose:
> Yet hark how through the peopled air
>     The busy murmur glows!
> The insect-youth are on the wing,
> Eager to taste the honied spring,
> And float amid the liquid noon:
> Some lightly o'er the current skim,
> Some show their gaily-gilded trim
>     Quick-glancing to the sun.

and then:

Sweet day so cool, so calm, so bright,
The bridal of the earth and sky,
The dew shall weep thy fall to-night,
For thou must die; &c.,

one cannot fail to realise what a charm resides in simplicity and perfect purity of diction.

"The language of the age is never the language of poetry ", Gray declares, and certainly some of our great poets have created for themselves a diction which was never current, but it is equally true that some of the best English poetry has been written in a style which differs from the best spoken language only as the language of feeling will naturally diverge from the language of our less exalted moods. It was in the seventeenth-century poets that Wordsworth found the best corrective to the jargon of the later eighteenth-century poetry, descriptive and reflective, which he had admired in his youth and imitated in his early poems; for as Coleridge pointed out, the style of the " metaphysicals " is the reverse of " that which distinguishes too many of our most recent versifiers; the one conveying the most fantastic thoughts in the most correct language, the other in the most fantastic language conveying the most trivial thoughts ".

But even the fantastic thoughts, the conceits of these courtly love-poets and devout singers, are not to be dismissed so lightly as a later, and still audible, criticism imagined. They played with thoughts, Sir Walter Scott complained, as the Elizabethans had played with words. But to play with thoughts it is necessary to think. " To write on their plan," says Dr. Johnson, " it was at least necessary to read and think. No man could be born a metaphysical poet, nor assume the dignity of a writer, by descriptions copied from descriptions, by imitations borrowed from imitations, by traditional imagery and hereditary similes, by readiness of rhyme and volubility of syllables." Consider a poem by such a minor poet as Thomas Stanley, who with Sir Edward Sherburne really merits the title of Marinist once misapplied to Donne. *The Repulse* is no frigid conceit, but develops, in a delightfully simple yet elaborated measure, a real and thrilling experience, the discovery that you might have fared worse in love than not to be loved, you might have been loved and then abandoned. Carew's *Ask me no more* is an enchanting coruscation of hyperboles, but

> Now you have freely given me leave to love,
>     What will you do?

is a fresh and effective appeal to the heart of a woman. And this is what the metaphysicals often succeed in doing. In their unwearied play with conceits, humorous, naughty, extravagant, fantastic, frigid—they light or stumble upon some thought which reveals a fresh intuition into the heart, or states an old plea with new and prevailing force. And the divine poets express with the same blend of argument and imagination the deep and complex currents of religious feeling which were flowing in England throughout the century, institutional, theological, mystical, while in the metaphysical subtleties of conceit they found something that is more than conceit; they found symbols in which to express or adumbrate their apprehensions of the infinite.

The debt of the courtly poets to Ben Jonson is, it has been argued, small, but it is not entirely negligible. He taught Carew and Herrick at least a better ordered evolution, to achieve a more concentrated sweetness; and not only Herrick, but more " metaphysical " poets, like Carew himself and Stanley, owe much both of their turn of conceit and their care for form to Jonson's own models, the Latin lyrists, Anacreon, the Greek Anthology, neo-Latin or Humanist poetry so rich in neat and pretty turns. Some of them, as Crashaw and Stanley, and not only these, were familiar with Italian and Spanish poetry, Marino and Garcilasso and their elegantly elaborated confections.  But their great master is Donne.  If he taught them many heresies, he instilled into them at any rate the pure doctrine of the need of passion for a lover and a poet.  What the young courtiers and university wits admired and reproduced in different degrees and fashions were his sensual audacity and the peculiar type of evolution which his poems accentuated, the strain of passionate paradoxical reasoning which knits the first line to the last and is perhaps a more intimate characteristic than even the far-fetched, fantastic comparisons.  This intellectual, argumentative evolution had been of course a feature of the sonnet which might fancifully be called, with its double quatrain and sestet, the poetical analogy of the syllogism.  But the movement of the sonnet is slow and meditative, a single thought expanded and articulated through the triple division, and the longer, decasyllabic line is the appropriate medium:

> Then hate me when thou wilt; if ever, now;
> Now while the world is bent my deeds to cross,
> Join with the spite of Fortune, make me bow,
> And do not drop in for an after-loss;

> Ah, do not when my heart hath scaped this sorrow,
> Come in the rearward of a conquer'd woe,
> Give not a windy night a rainy morrow,
> To linger out a purpos'd overthrow.
> If thou wilt leave me, do not leave me last
> When other petty griefs have done their spite,
> But in the onset come; so shall I taste
> At first the very worst of Fortune's might;
> And other strains of woe which now seem woe,
> Compared with loss of thee will not seem so.

What Donne had done was to quicken this movement, to intensify the strain of passionate ratiocination, passionate, paradoxical argument, and to carry it over from the sonnet to the song with its shorter lines, its winged and soaring movement, although the deeper strain of feeling which Donne shares with Shakespeare made him partial to the longer line, at least as an element in his stanzas, and to longer and more intricate stanzas.    Lightening both the feeling and the thought, the courtly poets simplified the verse, attaining some of their most wonderful effects in the common ballad measure [4, 3] or the longer [4, 4] measure in couplets or alternate rhymes.    But the form and content are intimately associated.    It is the elaboration of the paradoxical argument, the weight which the rhetoric lays on those syllables which fall under the metrical stress, that give to these verses, or seem to give, their peculiar *élan*:

> My love is of a birth as rare
>   As 'tis for object strange and high;
> It was begotten by Despair
>   Upon Impossibility.

The audacious hyperboles and paradoxical turns of thought give breath to and take wings from the soaring rhythm.

It is needless here to dwell on the individual poets at length  Their range is not wide—love, compliment, elegy, occasionally devotion.  Herrick had to leave the Court to learn the decorative possibilities of the country-side and of the old rites and superstitions and fairy-tales which still lingered there.  Lord Herbert of Cherbury, philosopher and coxcomb, was just the person to dilate on the Platonic theme of soul and body in the realm of love on which Donne occasionally descanted in half-ironical fashion, Habington with tedious, thin-blooded seriousness, Cleveland and others with naughty irreverence. But Lord Herbert's *Ode upon a Question moved, whether Love should continue for ever*, which had been, till recently, very badly edited, seems to me the finest thing inspired by Donne's *Ecstasy* and more characteristic of the romantic taste of the Court of Charles.  But the poetic ornament of that Court is Thomas Carew.  This young careless liver was a careful artist with a deeper vein of thought and feeling in his temperament than a first reading of his poems suggests.  His masque reveals the influence of Bruno.  In Carew's poems and Vandyke's pictures the artistic taste of Charles's Court is vividly reflected, a dignified voluptuousness, an exquisite elegance, if in some of the higher qualities of man and artist Carew is as inferior to Wyatt or Spenser as Vandyke is to Holbein. His *Ecstasy* is the most daring and poetically the happiest of the imitations of Donne's clever if most outrageous elegies; Cartwright's *Song of Dalliance* its nearest rival. His letter to Aurelian Townshend on the death of the King of Sweden breathes the very enchanted air of

Charles's Court while the storm was brewing as yet unsuspected. The text of Richard Lovelace's *Lucasta* (1649) is frequently corrupt, and the majority of the poems are careless and extravagant, but the few good things are the finest expression of honour and chivalry in all the Cavalier poetry of the century, the only poems which suggest what " Cavalier " came to mean when glorified by defeat. His *Grasshopper* has suffered a hard fate by textual corruption and from dismemberment in recent anthologies. Only the fantastic touch about " green ice " ranks it as " metaphysical ", for it is in fact an experiment in the manner of the Horatian ode, not the heroic ode, but the lighter Epicurean, meditative strain of " Solvitur acris hiems " and " Vides ut alta stet nive candidum ", description yielding abruptly to reflection. A slightly better text or a little more care on the poet's part would have made it perfect. The gayest of the group is Sir John Suckling, the writer of what might be called *vers de société*, a more careless but more fanciful Prior. His beautiful *Ballad on a Wedding* is a little outside the scope of metaphysical poetry. Thomas Stanley, classical scholar, philosopher, translator, seems to me one of the happiest of recent recoveries, elegant, graceful, felicitous, and if at times a little flat and colourless, not always flat like the Catholic puritan William Habington.

But the strongest personality of all is Andrew Marvell. Apart from Milton he is the most interesting personality between Donne and Dryden, and at his very best, for he is unequal, a finer poet than either. Most of his descriptive poems lie a little outside my beat, though I have claimed *The Garden* as metaphysical,

> Annihilating all that's made
> To a green thought in a green shade,

and I might have claimed *The Nymph and the Faun*.    But
his few love-poems and his few devotional pieces are
perfect exponents of all the " metaphysical " qualities—
passionate, paradoxical argument, touches of humour,
learned imagery, and withal genuine poetic feeling:

> As lines, so loves oblique, may well
>     Themselves in every angle greet:
> But ours so truly parallel,
>     Though infinite, can never meet;

but above all the sudden soar of passion in bold and felicitous
image, in clangorous lines:

> But at my back I always hear
> Time's wingèd chariot hurrying near,
> And yonder all before us lie
> Deserts of vast eternity.
> Thy beauty shall no more be found;
> Nor in thy marble vault shall sound
> My echoing song: then worms shall try
> That long preserv'd virginity;
> And your quaint honour turn to dust;
> And into ashes all my lust.
> The grave's a fine and private place,
> But none I think do there embrace.

These lines seem to me the very roof and crown of the
metaphysical love-lyric, at once fantastic and passionate.
Donne is weightier, more complex, more suggestive of
subtle and profound reaches of feeling, but he has not one
single passage of the same length that combines all the
distinctive qualities of the kind, in thought, in phrasing,

in feeling, in music; and Rochester's most passionate lines are essentially simpler, less metaphysical.

> When wearied with a world of woe,

might have been written by Burns with some differences. The best things of Donne and Marvell could only have been composed—except, as an imitative *tour de force*, like Watson's

> Bid me no more to other eyes—

in the seventeenth century.  But in that century there were so many poets who could sing, at least occasionally, in the same strain.  Of all those whom Professor Saintsbury's ardent and catholic but discriminating taste has collected there is none who has not written too much indifferent verse, but none who has not written one or two songs showing the same fine blend of passion and paradox and music.  The "metaphysicals" of the seventeenth century combined two things, both soon to pass away, the fantastic dialectics of mediæval love poetry and the "simple, sensuous" strain which they caught from the classics—soul and body lightly yoked and glad to run and soar together.  Modern love poetry has too often sacrificed both to sentiment.

### 3

ENGLISH religious poetry after the Reformation was a long time in revealing any distinctive note of its own. Here as elsewhere, Protestant poetry took the shape mainly of Biblical paraphrases or dull moralisings less impressive and sombre than the *poema morale* of an earlier century.  Sylvester's translation of Du Bartas's

*Weeks and Days* eclipsed all previous efforts and appealed
to Elizabethan taste by its conceits and aureate diction.
Catholic poets, on the other hand, like Robert Southwell,
learned from the Italians to write on religious themes in
the antithetic, " conceited ", " passionating " style of the
love-poets of the day.   His *Tears of St. Peter*, if a poem
of greater lyrical inspiration than the poem by which it
was suggested, Tansillo's *Le Lagrime di San Pietro*, is
composed in the same feverish strain and with a super-
abundance of the conceits and antitheses of that and other
Italian religious poems of the sixteenth century:

> Launch forth, my soul, into a main of tears,
>     Full-fraught with grief, the traffic of thy mind;
> Torn sails will serve, thoughts rent with guilty fears;
>     Give Care the stern, use sighs in lieu of wind:
> Remorse thy pilot; thy misdeeds thy card;
> Torment thy haven, shipwreck thy best reward.

His best poem, *The Burning Babe*, to have written which
Jonson "would have been content to destroy many of
his", has warmth and colour, but is marred by the
grotesque elaboration of a physical conceit.   It is in
Donne's poems, *The Crosse*, *The Annuntiation and Passion*,
*The Litanie*, that the Catholic tradition which survived in
the Anglican Church becomes articulate in poetry; it is
in his sonnets and hymns that English religious poetry
becomes for the first time intensely personal, the record
of the experiences and aspirations, not of the Christian
as such merely, but of one troubled and tormented soul.
But the Catholic tradition in Donne was Roman rather
than Anglican, or Anglican with something of a conscious
effort; and Donne's passionate outpourings of penitence

and longing lack one note of religious poetry which is audible in the songs of many less complex souls and less great poets, the note of attainment, of joy and peace. The waters have gone over him, the waters of fear and anguish, and it is only in his last hymns that he seems to descry across the agitation of the waves by which he is overwhelmed a light of hope and confidence:

> Swear by thyself that at my death thy Son
>   Shall shine as he shines now and heretofore;
> And having done that thou hast done,
>   I fear no more.

The poet in whom the English Church of Hooker and Laud, the Church of the *via media* in doctrine and ritual, found a voice of its own, was George Herbert, the son of Donne's friend Magdalen Herbert, and the younger brother of Lord Herbert of Cherbury. His volume *The Temple, Sacred Poems and Private Ejaculations, By Mr. George Herbert*, was printed at Cambridge in the year, 1633, that a disorderly collection of the amorous, satirical, courtly, and pious poems of the famous Dean of St. Paul's, who died in 1631, was shot from the press in London as *Poems, by J. D., with Elegies on the Author's Death*. As J. D. the author continued to figure on the title-page of each successive edition till that of 1669; nor were the additions made from time to time of a kind to diminish the complex, ambiguous impression which the volume must have produced on the minds of the admirers of the ascetic and eloquent Dean. There is no such record of a complex character and troubled progress in the poetry of Herbert. It was not, indeed, altogether without a struggle that Herbert bowed his neck to the collar, abandoned the ambitions and vanities of youth to become the pious rector of Bemerton.    He knew, like Donne, in what light the ministry was regarded by the young courtiers whose days were spent

> In dressing, mistressing, and compliment.

His ambitions had been courtly.    He loved fine clothes. As Orator at Cambridge he showed himself an adept in learned, elegant, and outrageous flattery, and he hoped " that, as his predecessors, he might in time attain the place of a Secretary of State ".    When he resolved, after the death of " his most obliging and powerful friends ", to take Orders, he " did acquaint a court-friend " with his resolution, " who persuaded him to alter it, as too mean an employment, and too much below his birth, and the excellent abilities and endowments of his mind ". All this is clearly enough reflected in Herbert's poems, and I have endeavoured in my selection to emphasise the note of conflict, of personal experience, which troubles and gives life to poetry that might otherwise be too entirely doctrinal and didactic.    But there is no evidence in Herbert's most agitated verses of the deeper scars, the profounder remorse which gives such a passionate, anguished *timbre* to the harsh but resonant harmonies of his older friend's *Divine Poems*:

> Despair behind, and death before doth cast
> Such terror, and my feeble flesh doth waste
> By sin in it, which it t'wards hell doth weigh.

Herbert knows the feeling of alienation from God; but he knows also that of reconcilement, the joy and peace of religion:

You must sit down, says Love, and taste my meat:
    So I did sit and eat.

Herbert is too in full harmony with the Church of his country, could say, with Sir Thomas Browne, "There is no Church whose every part so squares unto my Conscience; whose Articles, Constitutions, and Customs seem so consonant unto reason, and as it were framed to my particular Devotion, as this whereof I hold my Belief, the Church of England ":

Beauty in thee takes up her place,
And dates her letters from thy face,
    When she doth write.

A fine aspect in fit array,
Neither too mean, nor yet too gay,
    Shows who is best.

.    .    .    .    .    .

But, dearest Mother (what those miss),
The mean, thy praise and glory is,
    And long may be.

Blessed be God, whose love it was
To double moat thee with his grace,
    And none but thee.

It was from Donne that Herbert learned the "metaphysical" manner. He has none of Donne's daring applications of scholastic doctrines. Herbert's interest in theology is not metaphysical but practical and devotional, the doctrines of his Church—the Incarnation, Passion, Resurrection, Trinity, Baptism—as these are reflected in the festivals, fabric, and order of the Church and are capable of appeal to the heart. But Herbert's central

theme is the psychology of his religious experiences.    He
transferred to religious poetry the subtler analysis and
record of moods which had been Donne's great contribution to love poetry.    The metaphysical taste in
conceit, also, ingenious, erudite, and indiscriminate, not
confining itself to the conventionally picturesque and
poetic, appealed to his thoughtful and acute mind, and to
the Christian temper which rejected nothing as common
and unclean.    He would speak of sacred things in the
simplest language and with the aid of the homeliest
comparisons:

> Both heav'n and earth
> Paid me my wages in a world of mirth.

Prayer is:

> Heaven in ordinary, man well drest,
> The milky way, the bird of Paradise.

Divine grace in the Sacramental Elements:

> Knoweth the ready way,
> And hath the privy key
> Op'ning the soul's most subtle rooms;
> While those, to spirits refin'd, at door attend
> Dispatches from their friend.

Night is God's " ebony box " in which

> Thou dost inclose us till the day
> Put our amendment in our way,
> And give new wheels to our disorder'd clocks.

> Christ left his grave-clothes that we might, when grief
> Draws tears or blood, not want an handkerchief.

These are the " mean " similes which in Dr. Johnson's
view were fatal to poetic effect even in Shakespeare.    We

L

have learned not to be so fastidious, yet when they are
not purified by the passionate heat of the poet's dramatic
imagination the effect is a little stuffy, for the analogies
and symbols are more fanciful or traditional than natural
and imaginative. Herbert's nature is generally " metaphysical ",—" the busy orange-tree ", the rose that
purges, the " sweet spring " which is " a box where sweets
compacted lie ". It is at rare moments that feeling and
natural image are imaginatively and completely merged
in one another:

> And now in age I bud again,
> After so many deaths I live and write;
> I once more smell the dew and rain,
> And relish versing: O my only light,
> It cannot be
> That I am he
> On whom thy tempests fell all night.

But if not a greatly imaginative, Herbert is a sincere and
sensitive poet, and an accomplished artist elaborating his
argumentative strain or little allegories and conceits with
felicitous completeness, and managing his variously
patterned stanzas—even the symbolic wings and altars
and priestly bells, the three- or seven-lined stanzas of his
poems on the Trinity and Sunday—with a finished and
delicate harmony. If *The Temple* breathes the spirit of
the Anglican Church at its best, primitive and modest,
it is yet no *Christian Year*, but the record of a troubled
and sensitive soul seeking and finding peace and expressing
its experiences in poems whose quaintness is often transcended by their depth of feeling and felicity of word,
image, and cadence.

Herbert's influence is discernible in the religious verse of all the minor Anglican poets of the century, but his two greatest followers were poets of a temper different from his own. Henry Vaughan had written verses of the fashionable kind, mildly amorous, reflective, eulogistic, elegiac, before the influence of Herbert converted his pen to the service of Heaven; but all his *poetry* is religious. In *Silex Scintillans* he often imitates his predecessor in name and in choice of theme, but his best work is of another kind. The difference between Herbert and Vaughan, at his best, is the difference on which Coleridge and Wordsworth dilated between fancy and imagination, between the sensitive and happy discovery of analogies and the imaginative apprehension of emotional identity in diverse experiences, which is the poet's counterpart to the scientific discovery of a common law controlling the apparently most divergent phenomena. Herbert's " sweet day, so cool, so calm, so bright " is a delightful play of tender fancy. Vaughan's greatest verses reveal a profounder intuition, as when Night is:

> God's silent, searching flight;
> When my Lord's head is fill'd with dew, and all
> His locks are wet with the clear drops of night;
> His still, soft call;
> His knocking-time; the soul's dumb watch
> When spirits their fair kindred catch.

Vaughan is a less effective preacher, a far less neat and finished artist than Herbert. His temper is more that of the mystic. The sense of guilt which troubles Donne, of sin which is the great alienator of man's soul from God in Herbert's poems, is less acute with Vaughan, or is merged in a wider consciousness of separation, a veil

between the human soul and that Heaven which is its
true home.   His soul is ever questing, back to the days
of his own youth, or to the youth of the world, or to the
years of Christ's sojourn on earth, when God and man
were in more intimate contact:

> In Abraham's tent the winged guests
> —O how familiar then was heaven!—
> Eat, drink, discourse, sit down and rest,
> Until the cool and shady even;

or else he yearns for the final reconciliation beyond the
grave:

> Where no rude shade or night
> Shall dare approach us; we shall there no more
> Watch stars or pore
> Through melancholy clouds, and say,
> " Would it were Day! "
> One everlasting Sabbath there shall run
> Without succession, and without a sun.

To this mystical mood Nature reveals herself, not as a
museum of spiritual analogies, a religious *materia medica*,
but as a creature simpler than man, yet, in virtue of that
simplicity and innocence, in closer harmony with God.
" Etenim res creatae exserto capite observantes exspectant
revelationem filiorum Dei."   At brief moments Vaughan
writes of Nature and childhood as Wordsworth and
Blake were to write, but generally with the addition
of some little pietistic tag which betrays his century.   It
is indeed only in short passages that Vaughan achieves
adequate imaginative vision and utterance, but the spirit
of these passages is diffused through his religious verse,
more quietistic, less didactic, in spirit than Herbert's.

Vaughan's quietist and mystical, Herbert's restrained and ordered, temper and poetry are equally remote from the radiant spirit of Richard Crashaw. Herbert's conceits are quaint or homely analogies, Vaughan's are the blots of a fashion on a style naturally pure and simple. Crashaw's long odes give the impression at first reading of soaring rockets scattering balls of coloured fire, the " happy fireworks " to which he compares St. Teresa's writings. His conceits are more after the confectionery manner of the Italians than the scholastic or homely manner of the followers of Donne. Neither spiritual conflict controlled and directed by Christian inhibitions and aspirations, nor mystical yearning for a closer communion with the divine, is the burden of his religious song, but love, tenderness, and joy. In Crashaw's poetry, as in the later poetry of the great Dutch poet Vondel, a note is heard which is struck for the first time in the seventeenth century, the accent of the convert to Romanism, the joy of the troubled soul who has found rest and a full expansion of heart in the rediscovery of a faith and ritual and order which give entire satisfaction to the imagination and affections. And that is not quite all. The Catholic poet is set free from the painful diagnosis of his own emotions and spiritual condition which so preoccupies the Anglican Herbert:

How should I praise thee, Lord! how should my rhymes
Gladly engrave thy name in steel,
If what my soul doth feel sometimes
    My soul might ever feel!

Although there were some forty heav'ns or more.
Sometimes I peer above them all;
Sometimes I hardly reach a score,
    Sometimes to hell I fall.

The Catholic poet loses this anxious sense of his own moods in the consciousness of the *opus operatum* calling on him only for faith and thankfulness and adoration.    It is this *opus operatum* in one or other of its aspects or symbols, the Cross, the name of Christ, the Incarnation, the Eucharist, the life of the saint or death of the martyr, which is the theme of all Crashaw's ardent and coloured, sensuous and conceited odes, composed in irregular rhythms which do not progress but rise and fall like a sparkling fountain. All other moods are merged in faith and love:

> Faith can believe
> As fast as Love new laws can give.
> Faith is my force.    Faith strength affords
> To keep pace with those powerful words.
> And words more sure, more sweet than they
> Love could not think, Truth could not say.

Crashaw's poetry has a limited compass of moods, but it has two of the supreme qualities of great lyric poetry, of poetry such as that of Shelley and Swinburne, ardour and music.

Of the other divine poets not much need be said. Quarles hardly belongs to the " metaphysical " tradition. In his paraphrases of Scripture he continues the Elizabethan fashion of Drayton and the later Giles Fletcher, but in the *Emblemes* [1635, 1639, 1643] he is a religious lyrist of real if unequal power, with the taste for quaint and homely analogy of Herbert.    The poems, "Why dost thou shade thy lovely face? " — Rochester's impudent parody of which has found its way into the *Oxford Book of Verse*—and " Ev'n like two little bank-dividing brooks ", are as sincere and ardent as they are throughout felicitous and musical.    To include Milton's *Hymn* in an anthology of metaphysical poems will seem less warrantable, for Milton is not enamoured of the quaint, the homely, or the too ratiocinative evolution, though he was also an erudite poet.    Yet it would be to fail in literary perspective not to recognise that in this poem Milton wrote in a manner he was not to use again, that his models here are Italian rather than classical (the poem may owe something to Tasso's *Canzone sopra la Cappella del Presepio*), that the verses are a sequence of poetical and delightful conceits, some of which, as that of the blushing earth and the snow, or the

> Glimmering Orbs did glow,
> Until their Lord himself bespake, and bid them go,

are not very remote from the blushing dagger on which Boileau commented.    Milton's style was to become more uniformly classical, but with the conceits departed alas! also the tenderness of spirit that gives to this early poem an ineffable charm.

Milton's young friend Andrew Marvell imbibed no more of Milton's classical inspiration than his graceless nephews and pupils, the Phillipses.    In his religious as in his amorous and descriptive verses he is a " metaphysical " dallying with poetic conceits in pure and natural English.    But the temper of these few poems is of the finest that the Puritan movement begot, as devoted to the " restrictive virtues " as Milton's, with less of polemical narrowness and arrogance; the temper of one in the world yet not of the world, recognising and loyal to a scale of values that is not the world's:

> Earth cannot show so brave a sight
> As when a single soul does fence
> The batteries of alluring sense,
> And Heaven views it with delight.

In no poetry more than the religious did the English genius in the seventeenth century declare its strong individuality, its power of reacting on the traditions and fashions which, in the Elizabethan age, had flowed in upon it from the Latin countries of Europe. There are individual poets who have risen to greater heights of devotional and mystical feeling as well as being more consummate artists—some of the mediæval hymn-writers, Dante, perhaps John of the Cross. The sufferings of Germany in this same century begot hymns of a more passionate and poignant simplicity:

> O Haupt voll Blut und Wunden,
> Voll Schmerz und voller Hohn!
> O Haupt, zu Spott gebunden
> Mit einer Dornenkron!

Our " metaphysicals " could not write hymns. But no country or century has produced a more personal and varied devout poetry, rooted in the basal religious experience of a consciousness of alienation from God and the longing for reconciliation but complicated by ecclesiastical and individual varieties of temperament and interpretation, than the country and century of Giles Fletcher, of John Donne, of Herbert and Vaughan, of Traherne and Crashaw and Andrew Marvell, of John Milton, to say nothing of those whose medium was prose, Andrews, Donne in his sermons and devotions, Bunyan and Baxter and Barclay and Sir Thomas Browne.

4

W<small>HEN</small> Dryden and his generation passed judgement, not merely on the conceits, but on the form of the earlier poetry, what they had in view was especially their use of the decasyllabic couplet in eulogistic, elegiac, satiric, and narrative verses. " All of them were thus far of Eugenius his opinion that the sweetness of English verse was never understood or practised by our fathers . . . and every one was willing to acknowledge how much our poesy is improved by the happiness of some writers yet living, who first taught us to mould our thoughts into easy and significant words, to retrench the superfluities of expression, and to make our rhyme so properly a part of the verse, that it should never mislead the sense, but itself be led and governed by it." " Donne alone ", Dryden tells the Earl of Dorset, " of all our countrymen had your talent: but was not happy enough to arrive at your versification; and were he translated into numbers and English, he would yet be wanting in the dignity of expression." Sweetness and strength of versification, dignity of expression—these were the qualities which Dryden and his generation believed they had conferred upon English poetry. " There was before the time of Dryden no poetical diction, no system of words at once refined from the grossness of domestic use, and free from the harshness of terms appropriated to particular arts. . . . Those happy combinations of words which distinguish poetry from prose had been rarely attempted; we had few elegances or flowers of speech, the roses had not yet been plucked from the brambles, or different colours had not been joined to enliven one another." Johnson is amplifying and emphasising Dryden's "dignity of expression", and it is well to remember that Scott at the beginning of the next century is still of the same opinion. It is also worth remembering, in order to see a critical period of our poetical history in a true perspective, that Milton fully shared Dryden's opinion of the poetry of his time, though he had a different conception of how poetic diction and verse should be reformed. He, too, one may gather from his practice and from occasional references, disapproved the want of selection in the "metaphysicals'" diction, and created for himself a poetic idiom far removed from current speech. His fine and highly trained ear disliked the frequent harshness of their versification, their indifference to the well-ordered melody of vowel and consonant, the grating, "scrannel pipe" concatenations which he notes so scornfully in the verse of Bishop Hall:

> " Teach each hollow grove to sound his love
> Wearying echo with one changeless word.

And so he well might, and all his auditory besides, with his ' teach each ' " (*An Apology for Smectymnuus*). But the flowers which Milton cultivated are not those of Dryden, nor was his ear satisfied with the ring of the couplet. He must have disliked as much as Dryden the breathless, headlong overflow of Chamberlayne's *Pharonnida* (if he ever read it), the harsh and abrupt crossing of the rhythmical by the rhetorical pattern of Donne's *Satires*, but he knew that the secret of harmonious verse lay in this subtle crossing and blending of the patterns, "apt numbers, fit quantity of syllables, and the sense variously drawn out from one verse into another". Spenser was Milton's poetic father, and his poetic diction and elaborately varied harmony are a development of Spenser's art by one who has absorbed more completely the spirit, understood more perfectly the art, of Virgil and the Greeks, who has taken Virgil and Homer for his teachers rather than Ariosto and Tasso.    Dryden's reform was due to no such adherence to an older and more purely poetic tradition though he knew and admired the ancients. His development was on the line of Donne and the metaphysicals, their assimilation of poetic idiom and rhythm to that of the spoken language, but the talk of which Dryden's poetry is an idealisation is more choice and select, less natural and fanciful, and rises more frequently to the level of oratory.    Like other reforms, Dryden's was in great measure a change of fashion.    Men's minds and ears were disposed to welcome a new tone and tune, a new accent, neither that of high song,

> passionate thoughts
> To their own music chanted,

nor of easy, careless, but often delightful talk and song blended, which is the tone of the metaphysical lyric, but the accent of the orator, the political orator of a constitutional country.

It was in the Satires of Hall, Marston, and Donne, especially the last, that what Professor Saintsbury calls the "unscrewing" of the decasyllabic couplet began, partly as a deliberate effort to reproduce the colloquial ease of Horace and the abrupt harshness of Persius and Juvenal. Drayton's couplets in the *Heroical Epistles* had been as smooth and balanced almost as those of Pope himself. But the new, looser, rougher rhythm, with overflow and medial pauses, generally quite inartistically managed, became the fashion in the eulogistic and elegiac poems which everybody had on occasions to produce. It would be hard to get together from any other source a body of poetry quite so bad in its own way—there are other ways of being bad—than could be collected from the eulogistic verses prefixed to every collection of plays or poems which issued from the press, or from the elegies composed on the death of poor Prince Henry. Nor are there many of the innumerable satirical poems which the political events called forth—Cleveland's, Marvell's, Oldham's—which have artistic as well as historic interest.

After Spenser Elizabethan narrative poetry suffered almost without exception from the " uncontented care to write better than one could ", the sacrifice of story and character to the elaboration of sentimental and descriptive rhetoric. Shakespeare's *Venus and Adonis* and *Rape of Lucrece* are no exception to this failure to secure that perfect balance of narrative, dramatic, and poetic interest, which makes Chaucer's tales unsurpassed models in their kind. The "metaphysical" fashion changed merely the character of the rhetoric, shifting the weight from diction and verse to wit, to διάνοια. The result may be studied in Davenant's *Gondibert* and Cowley's *Davideis*, where in place of vivid, dramatic narrative we get an ever-flowing stream of witty comment and embroidery. The most readable—if with somewhat of a wrestle—is Chamberlayne's *Pharonnida*. The story is compounded of the tedious elements of Greek romance—shepherds and courts and loves and rapes and wars—but no one can take the smallest interest in the characters. The verse is breathless and the style obscure, as that of Mr. Doughty is, because the writer uses the English language as if he had found it lying about and was free of it without regard to any tradition of idiom or structure.   Still Chamberlayne does realise the scenes which he describes, as Cowley does not, and he decorates them with all the arabesques of a fantastic and bewildering yet poetic wit:

> The Spring did, when
> The princess first did with her pleasure grace
> This house of pleasure, with soft arms embrace
> The Earth—his lovely mistress—clad in all
> The painted robes the morning's dew let fall
> Upon her virgin bosom;  the soft breath
> Of Zephyrus sung calm anthems at the death
> Of palsy-shaken Winter, whose large grave,
> The earth, whilst they in fruitful tears did lave,
> Their pious grief turned into smiles, [did] throw
> Over the hearse a veil of flowers;  the low
> And pregnant valleys swelled with fruit, whilst Heaven
> Smiled on each blessing its fair hand had given.

But the peculiar territory of the metaphysical poets, outside love-song and devout verse, was eulogy and elegy. They were pedants but also courtiers abounding in compliments to royal and noble patrons and friends and fellow-poets.   Here again Donne is the great exemplar of erudite and transcendental, subtle and seraphic compliments to noble and benevolent countesses.   One may doubt whether the thing ought to be done at all, but there can be no doubt that Donne does it well, and no one was better aware of the fact than Dryden, whose eulogies, whether in verse or in prose, as the dedication of the *State of Innocence* to Mary of Modena, which Johnson denounces as blasphemous, "an attempt to mingle earth and heaven by praising human excellence in the language of religion", are in the same seraphic vein and indeed contain lines that are boldly " lifted " from Donne.    They are not made vivid by the accumulation of concrete details, though there are some not easily to be surpassed, as Ben Jonson's favourite lines:

> No need of lanterns, and in one place lay
> Feathers and dust, to-day and yesterday.

But the most vivid impressions are secured not by objective detail, but by the suggestion of their effect upon the mind. The nervous effect of storm and calm is conveyed by Donne's conceits and hyperboles in a way that is not only vivid but intense.

One cannot say much for the metaphysical eulogies of Donne's imitators.    Even Professor Saintsbury has omitted many of them from his collection of the other poems by their authors, as Godolphin's lines on Donne and on Sandys's version of the Psalms, which are by no means the worst of their kind.    He has, on the other hand, included one, Cleveland's on Edward King, some lines of which might be quoted to illustrate the extravagances of the fashion:

> I like not tears in tune, nor do I prize
> His artificial grief who scans his eyes.
> Mine weep down pious beads, but why should I
> Confine them to the Muses' rosary?
> I am no poet here; my pen's the spout
> Where the rain-water of mine eyes run out
> In pity of that name, whose fate we see
> Thus copied out in grief's hydrography.
> The Muses are not mermaids, though upon
> His death the ocean might turn Helicon.

.    .    .    .    .    .    .

> When we have filled the roundlets of our eyes
> We'll issue 't forth and vent such elegies
> As that our tears shall seem the Irish Seas,
> We floating islands, living Hebrides.

The last word recalls the great poem which appeared along with it:

> Where'er thy bones are hurl'd,
> Whether beyond the stormy Hebrides,
> Where thou perhaps under the whelming tide
> Visit'st the bottom of the monstrous world.

Cleveland is not much worse than Joseph Beaumont on the same subject, and neither is quite so offensive as Francis Beaumont in his lines on the death of Mrs. Markham:

> As unthrifts grieve in straw for their pawned beds,
> As women weep for their lost maidenheads
> (When both are without hope of remedy),
> Such an untimely grief have I for thee.

It would be difficult to imagine anything in worse taste, yet, from the frequency with which the poem recurs in manuscript collections, it was apparently admired as a flight of " wit ".   There are better elegies than these, as Herrick's and Earle's and Stanley's on Beaumont and Fletcher, Cleveland's (if it be his) on Jonson, Carew's noble lines on Donne, but in proportion as they become readable they cease to be metaphysical.   Donne's *a priori* transcendentalism few or none were able to recapture. Their attempts to rise meet the fate of Icarus.   The lesser metaphysical poets are most happy and most poetical when their theme is not this or that individual but death in general.   Love and death are the foci round which their thoughts moved in eccentric cycles and epicycles. The mood their poems express is not the sombre mediæval horror of " Earth upon earth ", nor the blended horror and fascination of Donne's elegies, or of his greater sermons. They dwell less in the Charnel House. The strain is one of pensive reflection on the fleetingness of life, relieved by Christian resignation and hope:

> Like as the damask rose you see,
> Or like the blossom on the tree,
> Or like the dainty flower in May,
> Or like the morning of the day,
> Or like the sun, or like the shade,
> Or like the gourd which Jonas had—
> Even such is man: whose thread is spun,
> Drawn out and cut and so is done.

> If none can scape Death's dreadful dart,
> If rich and poor his beck obey,
> If strong, if wise, if all do smart,
> Then I to scape shall have no way.
>   O grant me grace, O God, that I
>   My life may mend since I must die.

In Abraham Cowley " metaphysical " poetry produced its last considerable representative, and a careful study of his poetry reveals clearly what was the fate which overtook it. His wit is far less bizarre and extravagant than much in Donne, to say nothing of Cleveland and Benlowes. But the central heat has died down. Less extravagant, his wit is also less passionate and imaginative. The long wrestle between reason and the imagination has ended in the victory of reason, of good sense. The subtleties of

the schoolmen have for Cowley none of the significance
and interest they possessed for Donne:

> So did this noble Empire waste,
> Sunk by degrees from glories past,
> And in the School-men's hands it perished quite at last.
> Then nought but words it grew,
> And those all barbarous too.
> It perish't and it vanisht there,
> The life and soul breath'd out, became but empty air.

The influence of the new philosophy simplified with such
dogmatic simplicity by Hobbes has touched him,—atoms
and determinism, witness the ode *To Mr. Hobbes* and the
half-playful, charming *Destinie*; and though that philosophy
might appeal to the imagination, the intellectual imagination, by its apparent simplicity and coherency, it could
make no such appeal to the spiritual nature as the older,
which had its roots in the heart and conscience, which had
endeavoured to construct a view of things that should
include, that indeed made central, the requirements and
values of the human soul.    Cowley is not wanting in
feeling any more than in fancy, witness his poem *On the
Death of Mr. William Hervey*, and he was a Christian,
but neither his affections nor his devotion expressed themselves imaginatively as these feelings did in Donne's most
sombre or bizarre verses and those of his spiritual followers;
his wit is not the reflection of a sombre or bizarre, a
passionately coloured or mystically tinted conception of
life and love and death.    The fashion of " metaphysical "
wit remains in Cowley's poems when the spirit that gave
it colour and music is gone.    Yet Cowley's poetry is not
merely frigid and fantastic.    The mind and temper which

M

his delightful essays, and the poems which accompany them, express has its own real charm—a mind of shy sensitiveness and clear good sense.   It was by a natural affinity that Cowley's poetry appealed to Cowper.   But wit which is not passionate and imaginative must appeal in some other way, and in Dryden it began to do so by growing eloquent.   The interest shifted from thought to form, the expression not the novelty of the thought, wit polished and refined as an instrument of satire and compliment and declamation on themes of common interest. Dryden and Pope brought our witty poetry to a brilliant close.   They are the last great poets of an age of intense intellectual activity and controversy, theological, metaphysical, political.   "The present age is a little too warlike", Atterbury thought, for blank verse and a great poem.   With the peace of the Augustans and the Georgians the mood changed, and poetry, ceasing to be witty, became sentimental; but great poetry is always metaphysical, born of men's passionate thinking about life and love and death;  the poetry of what we call the romantic revival was again to be, in the work of its greater spirits, "tout traversé de frissons métaphysiques ".

1921

# BYRON

# & ENGLISH SOCIETY

It is generally admitted that Byron's fame as a poet, so far as it survives, rests upon the poems composed in the years of exile following the violent rupture of his marriage. The first cantos of the *Childe Harold* and the verse tales served to disturb the waters of English poetry with a quickening influx of passionate feeling, but the melodramatic tones of these earlier poems, their deficiency in the finer qualities of poetry, beauty of phrase and rhythm, have consigned them to general oblivion, if readers may still find something stirring and arresting in the passionate speed of Byron's octosyllabics, the colour and animation of these records of travel and strange climes and turbulent moods.

But in the later cantos of *Childe Harold*, in *Manfred*, in *Prometheus* and *Darkness*, in the lyrical epistles to his sister, Byron's poetry acquired a new and deeper accent, his voice a *timbre* that shook the heart of Europe; and when with *Beppo* he found a new medium, and this man of many moods and sparkling wit began to pour himself forth in the most brilliant and buoyant conversation in verse that perhaps any literature can lay claim to, it was then that he became the spokesman of a disillusioned Europe and the arraigner and satirist of aristocratic society and English Evangelical morals and piety.

For to read Byron's later poetry aright one must consider its relation to the English society which cast him out, against which it is one passionate or scornful

167

protest, the more passionate and scornful because that
society had for Byron an attraction and authority it never
possessed for Shelley, and conversely that society, even
in holding up its hands in horror and indignation, was
fascinated by Byron's poetry while Shelley's musical cry
passed over their heads unheeded. What I wish to
attempt is an analysis of this mutual attraction and repul-
sion. Byron was an Englishman—with Scottish blood
in his veins—and he never forgot it. His eyes were
ever on England; and for Englishmen in Italy Byron
was one of the sights. Whatever part he played, in
anticipation or actually, on the stage of Italian or Greek
politics, the first thought in his mind was of the impression the new *rôle* would make upon his countrymen.
And if Byron's poetry is little read to-day, the interest
in Byron is never quite extinguished. His spirit is too
dæmonic—as is that of Shelley, though there is a world
of difference between their angels—ever to be exorcised
by a purely technical criticism of his faults of style and
defects of harmony.

Byron left the shores of England in a tumult of con-
tending emotions. A flood of light has been shed in the
last few months upon his life during the fatal years between
his return to England in 1811 and his final departure in
1816. By some strange irony the full truth about Byron
and about Wordsworth has been made known at the
same time. It is not an unfortunate circumstance that
the revelation was so long delayed, for both men are now
so far removed from us that moral judgements are super-
fluous, and what we may contemplate with interest is
the fresh and poignant light thrown upon the poetry of
two great poets. We know now that Byron was not

" le fanfaron de vices qu'il n'avait pas "; but that his passionate, uncontrolled, not altogether sane temperament —there was a strain of madness in all his ancestral lines, Byrons, Gordons, Duffs—drove him into vices which were not the deliberate choice of his soul but left him a prey to remorse and self-contempt. He had sinned against those he loved the best; and his marriage was a final catastrophe because it entailed a bondage that drove him frantic, and because it left upon one unforgetting mind an impression of the worst in Byron's character as the essential fundamental element. To Lady Byron her husband was the incarnation of evil. If her vengeance was delayed it has been wreaked to the full, and by the irony of circumstances, which can always go one better than our imagining, from Byron's own blood was fashioned the instrument of his final exposure.

But it was because Byron was not all of a piece in villainy, that he was not essentially what it was so easy to make him out from his own words and from those many acts in which his evil genius turned him against his own better instincts, made him the " agent of his proper woe ", that Byron's poetry in these years is the expression, furious or scornful, of a deadly inner conflict, a conflict in which his sympathies were strangely divided, as he understood and even shared the prejudices of those with whom he was at war in a manner altogether incomprehensible to the more single and impervious mind of Shelley. It was this conflict which gave Byron's mature poetry a new *timbre*, a deeper melancholy, a fiercer scorn; but the conflict itself has a more than personal interest. Strange champion for such a cause, Byron was yet enlisted in the cause of justice and enlightenment,

political and spiritual.   The spirit of the poet and prophet
is often contained in a very imperfect earthly vessel.   It
is not quite true that a good orator, and *a fortiori* a good
poet, must be a good man as we judge of good men.   It
was a noble thought of Milton that " he who would
not be frustrate of his hope to write well hereafter in
laudable things ought himself to be a true poem: that is,
a composition and pattern of the best and honourablest
things:  not presuming to sing high praises of heroic men,
or famous cities, unless he have in himself the experience
and the practice of all that which is praiseworthy ".
There is in this an element of truth.   Byron could never
have written *Paradise Lost* or the *Divina Commedia*;
nor would Dante or Milton have deigned to write *Don
Juan.*   But human nature is a strange, mingled yarn,
and the relation between a man's character, as we can
measure it, and his work is not so simple as Milton's
words imply.   God's gifts are not so unequally dis-
tributed.   Great art is sincere.   The man himself may
be insincere and vain and inconstant, yet when he speaks
" in the spirit ", as Blake would say, he speaks, like
Balaam, truth despite himself.   Shylock and Satan take
on heroic proportions despite their creator's intention,
becoming symbols of truths which social usage or rigid
creeds have ignored, but which the kindled imagination
of a poet divines.   The would-be blasphemer may do
more honour to the Idea of Good than the pious hymn-
writer;  the cynical but passionate and sincere satirist
may bear more effective witness to the Ideal than dreamers
of Utopias or all the lyrical raptures of a *Prometheus
Unbound.*

Byron left England at war with the society which had

flattered and caressed and then cast him out with contumely; at war with the predominant political sentiment
of his country, for the great deliverance of Waterloo
seemed to him to mark the triumph of the spirit of reaction
against which he had already enlisted under the banner
of Fox and Sheridan; but above all at war with his own
soul, conscious of irremediable wrong done to those he
loved and respected, conscious of the waste of great powers
and finer susceptibilities and nobler impulses:

The expense of spirit in a waste of shame.

But it was not only his pride which sustained the conflict
with remorse and shame, but also his sense of justice,
his critical judgement; and so—as I hope to elucidate—
he was at war with the creed by help of which he envisaged
his own wrongdoing and its significance, the creed of
his early upbringing which he never rejected in the
thorough-going fashion of Shelley. This was the inner
conflict which drove Byron like a man possessed through
Switzerland, uttering the cries which are the last cantos
of *Childe Harold*, *Prometheus*, *Manfred*; and flung him
into the debauchery of his life at Venice, " crying out and
cutting himself with knives ". To understand aright
all Byron's later poetry of any great significance it is
necessary to realise the two main forces which had shaped
and coloured his life, and with which he now found himself involved in an inextricable and passionate conflict.
He was not at war, as was Shelley, with an evil that
stood outside his own mind, inexplicable and baffling,
but with forces around but also within himself, whose
power to attract as well as to repel he fully realised,
against which indeed he had nothing positive to set but

only a fierce protest, a passionate sense of injustice and cruelty:

> a firm will, and a deep sense,
> Which even in torture can descry
> Its own concentred recompense.

The two forces with which Byron was at war are the two great forces which dominated English life in the later eighteenth and early nineteenth centuries—aristocratic society—its ideals, privileges, policy; and that pietistic, Evangelical Christianity which, quickened by the Wesleys, had become the great shaping and inspiring religious influence in the life of serious English people within and without the Established Church. To both these influences Byron stood exposed in a peculiar way which made him at once deeply sensitive and passionately rebellious. The latter set its impress upon his early training; he passed under the influence of the former as he entered Harrow, or indeed from the moment that he burst into tears when the name of " Byron Dominus " was called in the roll of the Aberdeen Grammar School. And his attitude to the two was strangely similar. He was never religious, but the religion whose power he felt and combated was the evangelical creed in which he was educated at Aberdeen and under his turbulent mother. He was palpably and even painfully proud of his position as a peer of England; and he was the scornful and indignant satirist of aristocratic government and aristocratic morality.

What the English aristocracy had been in the eighteenth century and still was at the close of the Napoleonic wars, its power and privilege, its morals and manners, is hard for us to realise to-day, but an accurate impression may be recovered by any student of history, memoirs,

letters, and fiction. For my purpose it will be sufficient
to quote from the illuminating description given by Sir
George Trevelyan in his *Early History of Charles Fox*.
And first, as to the attractions and advantages which such
a society had to offer a young man who entered its privileged circle. " Moral considerations apart, no more
desirable lot can well be imagined for a human being
than that he should be included in the ranks of a highly
civilised aristocracy at the culminating moment of its
vigour. A society so broad and strongly based that,
within its own borders, it can safely permit absolute
liberty of thought and speech;—whose members are so
numerous that they are able to believe with some show
of reason that the interests of the state are identical with
their own, and at the same time so privileged that they
are sure to get the best of everything which is to be had;—
is a society uniting, as far as those members are concerned,
most of the advantages and all the attractions both of a
popular and an oligarchical form of government. It is
in such societies that existence has been enjoyed most
keenly, and that books have been written which communicate a sense of that enjoyment most vividly to
posterity. . . . A student who loves to dwell upon times
when men lived so joyously that their past seems to us
as their present, will never tire of recurring to the Athens
of Alcibiades, the Rome of Mark Anthony and Cicero,
the London of Charles Townshend and Horace Walpole."
That is one side of the picture, the good things, the solid
advantages which membership of a proud and privileged
society has to offer. But there is another. The morals
of English aristocratic society in the eighteenth and early
nineteenth century—indeed until the accession of Queen

Victoria—were in essentials those of the Restoration, and hardly less flagrantly paraded. "The frivolity of the last century was not confined to the youthful, the foolish, or even the idle. There never will be a generation which cannot supply a parallel to the lords who, in order that they might better hear the nonsense which they were talking across a tavern table, had Pall Mall laid down with straw at the cost of fifty shillings a head for the party; or to the younger brother who gave half a guinea every morning to the flower-woman who brought him a nosegay of roses for his button-hole. These follies are of all times; but what was peculiar to the period when Charles Fox took his seat in Parliament and his place in society, consisted in the phenomenon (for to our ideas it is nothing else) that men of age and standing, of strong mental powers and refined cultivation, lived openly, shamelessly, and habitually, in the face of all England, as no one who had any care for his reputation would now live during a single fortnight of the year at Monaco." These were the years of Lord Weymouth, the Earl of Sandwich, the Duke of Grafton, Sir Francis Dashwood, and Lord George Sackville. "Gambling in all its forms was then rather a profession than a pastime to the leaders of the London world." "No one can study the public or personal history of the eighteenth century without being impressed by the truly immense space which drinking occupied in the mental history of the young, and the consequences of drinking in that of the old."

The society which Byron entered was not in every respect the same as that of which Fox was the ornament and scandal, nor did Byron, despite his rank, enter its portals under quite such favourable circumstances as the son of Lord Holland. With Pitt's ministry the era of absolutely subservient and personally scandalous ministries had closed, and purifying forces were at work in society. Yet in all essential respects the aristocratic society of the Regency was still both the privileged and the corrupt society which Sir George Trevelyan describes. It was not unnatural that Byron should be proud and sensitive of his rank—to be an English nobleman was no small thing in the world's eye—nor is it surprising that the ideals of this society shaped and coloured his feelings and conduct and at the same time evoked his scorn and hatred. We must take human nature as we find it. Those who criticise Byron's snobbishness forget that all English people are snobs. That he was proud of his rank was apparent to every one who met Byron. Scott's description indicates with his usual discrimination the inconsistent strain in Byron's temperament. " On politics he used sometimes to express a high strain of what is now called Liberalism; but it appeared to me that the pleasure it afforded him as a vehicle of displaying his wit and satire against individuals in office was at the bottom of this habit of thinking, rather than any real conviction of the political principles on which he talked. He was certainly proud of his rank and ancient family, and in that respect as much an aristocrat as was consistent with good breeding. Some disgusts, how adopted I know not, seemed to me to have given this peculiar and, as it appeared, contradictory cast of mind; but at heart I would have termed Byron a patrician on principle." The disgusts bred in the mind of one whose education had not fitted him to take the position to which he succeeded with ease and without embarrassment, while his fortunes were

unequal to the demands of that position, was certainly
an element in Byron's inconsistency; but it was not
the whole. His clear intuitions made it impossible for
Byron to be the quite complacently privileged aristocrat.
But he never could transcend the inconsistency. " He
has many generous and exalted qualities," said Shelley,
" but the canker of aristocracy wants to be cut out, and
something, God knows, wants to be cut out of us all."
" Certain it is that Lord Byron has made me feel bitterly
the inferiority which the world has presumed to place
between us and which subsists nowhere in reality but in
our talents, which are not ours but Nature's—or in our
rank, which is not our own but Fortune's." Byron's
uneasiness made him the more prone to assert his position
and to adopt the manners and the pose of his class. If
he gambled and drank, it was in part because this was
the correct thing. The difference between the tone and
life of Byron's set at Cambridge, as reflected in his letters,
and that of Tennyson and Hallam's set some thirty years
later, is the difference between Georgian and Victorian
England. If Byron, so far from concealing, boasted of
his amours and dissipation, that had been for a century
the habit of his class. They were privileged not only
to indulge their vices but to make a parade of the indulgence. It was as a man of rank that he spoke with
at least affected scorn of literature and men of letters.
The English aristocracy never shared their French
compeers' respect for talent. Of Hume's reception in
Paris Sir George Trevelyan writes: " English people of
fashion, who were accustomed to see authors kept in
their proper place, could not understand why such a fuss
should be made about a man with nothing but his talents

to recommend him." Byron was always uneasy about his literary friends, of whom Rogers and Moore alone he ranked with himself. "The pity of these men", he wrote, after a contemptuous note on most of the authors of the day, "is that they never lived in high life or in solitude: there is no medium for the knowledge of the busy or the still world. If admitted into high life for a season, it is merely as spectators—they form no part of the mechanism thereof. Now Moore and I, the one by circumstances, the other by birth, happened to be free of the corporation, and to have entered into its pulses and passions—*quarum partes fuimus.*" (September 12, 1821.) "The truth is, my dear Moore, you live near the *stove* of society, where you are unavoidably influenced by its heats and vapours. I did so once—and too much—and enough to give a colour to my whole future existence." (March 4, 1822.) Byron was not altogether wrong. His sketches of society, especially in the later cantos of *Don Juan*, have a quality, hard to define but unmistakable, which is only felt again in the work of the great Russian aristocrat, Count Tolstoi: Thackeray and Meredith obviously formed "no part of the mechanism" themselves. But if English men of letters have lost something by their very partial admission to the best society, English society has lost in interest by its contempt for talent. It is chiefly in Meredith's novels that their conversation has intellectual brilliance. In reality its wit at the best is good-natured "chaff", its eloquence declamation on a narrow range of topics supplied by prejudice. In the upper as in other classes good talkers are few, but the former draw from a wider and more piquant range of experience and have the greater charm of manner.

Cynicism was the aristocratic trait in Byron's mind which most jarred upon the sensitiveness of Shelley. Byron's cynicism was of course partly a protection for his intense sensitiveness, as intense as Shelley's own, and more proud, more apt to beget rage. It was also an excuse for the indulgence of the wit and pure gaiety of which there was in Byron, as in Swift, a deep vein. But cynicism was also an aristocratic canker, part of the pose which his class-consciousness demanded, for cynicism is an almost necessary product of such a privileged, self-centred society as Trevelyan describes. Chesterfield, Walpole, La Rochefoucauld — all in different fashion express the cynical contempt for humanity which is begotten of the egoism of a life in which everything must yield to personal ambition; begotten also, one imagines, of the consciousness of enjoying privileges altogether independent of, or out of proportion to, any sense of personal merit. If one enjoys endless advantages for which one can claim no personal merit, it is a comfort to reflect that there is no such thing as real merit. An aristocrat — I speak, of course, of a real aristocracy, privileged and governing—can hardly become an idealist, an enthusiast for humanity, without practically or theoretically forgoing his privileges and claim of superiority, like Prince Gautama, or Lord Shaftesbury or Count Tolstoi, or, in his measure, Shelley.

This, then, was one great section of English society whose traditions shaped and coloured Byron's life and character, and of which he was to become the fierce and scornful satirist. But it was not the only one. Byron was touched, and that more deeply than his letters indicate, by the other great force in the moral and spiritual life

of England in his day.   To understand Byron one must
read, not only the letters of Walpole and Chesterfield and
George Selwyn, but the journals of John Wesley, the
letters and poems of Cowper, the whole history of the
Methodist movement without and the Evangelical movement within the Anglican Church, the lives of John
Newton, Hannah More, Joseph and Isaac Milner, John
Bowdler, Thomas Gisborne, the Clapham sect.   The
greatest moral and religious power in the eighteenth and
nineteenth centuries was Evangelical Christianity, of
which Victorian England was the social product, for even
the High Church movement came out of Evangelicalism.

   It was not an intellectual but a moral and spiritual
movement.   That was at once the strength and weakness of Evangelicalism.   It had its root in two things:
the need of the individual soul for more than a secular
and sceptical view of human life; and secondly, a profound
sympathy with the poor and suffering in an age when,
in the words of an historian, " the masses were ignorant
and brutalised, and their numbers and demoralisation
increased rapidly. . . . A governing class intent only
on pleasure or politics, a Church occupied chiefly with
patronage and controversy, felt the force of a great religious wave which was to beat on every wall of privilege."
Evangelicalism recognised no need of an intellectual
reinterpretation or vindication of the Christian faith.
"Wesley", says Leslie Stephen, "takes his creed for
granted, and it was the creed, so far as they had one,
of the mass of the nation.   He is shocked by perjury,
drunkenness, corruption, and so forth, but has not seriously
to meet scepticism of the speculative variety.   If Wesley
did not, like the leader of another Oxford movement,

feel bound to clear up the logical basis of his religious beliefs he had, of course, to confront deism, but could set it down as a mere product of moral indifference." That was the line taken in Evangelical apologetics, *e.g.* by Kennedy in his conversations with Byron. Scepticism is the result of moral indifference and failure to study the Scriptures in a reverent spirit. Their acceptance of the verbal inspiration of the Bible confined the spirit of religious England in a closer cage than perhaps even the creed of the Catholic Church from which the Bible had been its weapon of deliverance in the sixteenth century. All stood for them on the same level. No one dreamed of the glaciation which had welded together the different strata which composed the Old and the New Testaments. God's goodness was equally revealed in the craft of Jacob, the penalty of Cain, the exploits of Jael, the murder of Agag, the pogroms in the Book of Esther,—and in the spiritual aspirations of the Psalms, the divine love and wisdom of the Gospels.

To say that Byron was touched by the sweep of the Evangelical wave may seem strange, but it is true. His early years had been spent, not in aristocratic, but in middle-class and pious circles; and aristocratic circles themselves felt the influence, witness Lady Byron. At Aberdeen he acquired the elements of that intimate knowledge of the Bible which he manifested throughout his life, and imbibed the Calvinist doctrine of predestination. For him to be religious meant to be Evangelical or Methodist. When Scott told him " That if he lived a few years he would alter his sentiments, he answered rather sharply, ' I suppose you are one of those who prophesy I will turn Methodist'. I replied: 'No—I don't expect your conversion to be of such an ordinary kind. I would rather look to see you retreat upon the Catholic faith, and distinguish yourself by the austerity of your penances. The species of religion to which you must, or may one day, attach yourself must exercise a strong power upon the imagination.' He smiled gravely, and seemed to allow I might be right." Scott's was a shrewd remark, and in distinguishing his position from Shelley's, Byron told Moore: " I am no enemy to religion, but the contrary. . . . I am educating my daughter a strict Catholic . . . for I think people can never have enough of religion if they are to have any. I incline myself very much to the Catholic doctrines." But Byron knew nothing of Catholicism in his early, impressionable days. For him, as he entered life, there were two views of life, and two only, to choose between for one who had none of Shelley's power to find in his own spirit the principles and way by which he was to live, and these were the irreligious, licentious ideals of his own order and the pieties of middle-class Evangelicals. His passions and his pride alike drove him into the one, but not without a constant protest on the part of his better nature. " Don't suppose that I took any pleasure in all these excesses, or that parsons A., K., and W. were associates to my taste." The second he tended always to treat with amused contempt: " I remember a Methodist preacher who, on perceiving a profane grin on the faces of part of his congregation, exclaimed, ' No hopes for them as laughs ' ". Byron was very much one of " them as laughs ". Yet he never could quite disown or shake off its influence. And when he was driven into exile, cast off by his country and the aristocracy to which he belonged,

N

his first conflict was not with these—that came later—
but in his own heart with the sense of wrongdoing,
and with the creed by which he had been taught to
envisage and arraign his own wrongdoing.  The central
experience of *Childe Harold*, *Prometheus*, *Manfred*, *Cain*,
*Sardanapalus*, is the sense of sin and the injustice of the
decree which arraigns sin as guilt, a consciousness and
conflict inexplicable to the " invincible ignorance " or the
purer and more enlightened eyes of Shelley.

*Childe Harold* is, of course, much beside a confession
of Byron's sense of sin and conflict with the creed of his
childhood.  It is an almost classical—wanting indeed
classical clarity of thought and perfection of form—an
almost classical expression of the mind of Europe when
the long period of high hopes and fierce conflicts which
the French Revolution inaugurated had ended with
Waterloo in shattering and complete disillusionment.
Great men—Napoleon, Rousseau, Voltaire, Gibbon,
Hannibal; great events, Waterloo, Cannae; great cities,
Venice, Florence, above all, Rome—they all tell the same
tale, *Vanitas Vanitatum*.  Only Nature, only beauty
endures,—the Alps, the Rhine, Thrasimene as it is now:

> Her lake a sheet of silver, and her plain
> Rent by no ravage save the gentle plow,

and the everlasting sea:

> Dark-heaving, boundless, endless, and sublime,
> The image of Eternity.

Byron's was not the only mind that felt the Dionysiac
mood which is the theme of his turbid, passionate, splendid
rhapsody.  But the deepest personal note in it all is that

which I have indicated, the sense of sin, and a proud passionate conflict with the doctrine impressed on his mind in childhood—Evangelical, Calvinist, Augustinian, of predestined sin and predestined guilt; a passionate denial of the justice of the decree which makes man the victim of inherited passions and untoward circumstances and then condemns him as solely and entirely responsible. Childe Harold flees society because his passions make him the victim of society:

> To fly from, need not be to hate, mankind:
> All are not fit with them to stir and toil,
> Nor is it discontent to keep the mind
> Deep in its fountain, lest it overboil
> In the hot throng, where we become the spoil
> Of our infection, till, too late and long,
> We may deplore and struggle with the coil,
> In wretched interchange of wrong for wrong
> Midst a contentious world, striving where none are strong.

> There, in a moment, we may plunge our years
> In fatal penitence, and in the blight
> Of our own Soul turn all our blood to tears,
> And colour things to come with hues of Night;
> The race of life becomes a hopeless flight
> To those that walk in darkness: on the sea
> The boldest steer but where their ports invite—
> But there are wanderers o'er Eternity,
> Whose bark drives on and on, and anchored ne'er shall be.

Again in the fourth canto, when the Childe has been dismissed, the Grotto of Egeria suggests thoughts of love and its disillusionment, and that with an abrupt transition, only intelligible if one recalls Byron's own experience, to the thought of sin, of the fatal chain of passion and circumstances which had wrecked his life:

> Our life is a false nature—'tis not in
> The harmony of things,—this hard decree,
> This ineradicable taint of Sin,
> This boundless Upas, this all-blasting tree,
> Whose root is earth—whose leaves and branches be
> The skies which rain their plagues on men like dew—
> Disease, death, bondage—all the woes we see,
> And worse, the woes we see not—which throb through
> The immedicable soul, with heart-aches ever new.
>
> Yet let us ponder boldly—'tis a base
> Abandonment of reason to resign
> Our right of thought—our last and only place
> Of refuge; this, at least, shall still be mine:
> Though from our birth the Faculty divine
> Is chained and tortured—cabined, cribbed, confined,
> And bred in darkness, lest the Truth should shine
> Too brightly on the unprepared mind,
> The beam pours in—for Time and Skill will couch the mind.

In *Childe Harold* this, though the central experience determining the mood of the whole poem, is subordinated to the elaboration of the more general theme of historical world disillusionment. In *Prometheus* and *Manfred* it becomes the principal topic. Each presents in a different form the same fixed, unyielding attitude of mind of one who acknowledges delinquency but rejects with defiance the doctrine which arraigns sin as guilt. In *Prometheus* the individual becomes the symbol of humanity, humanity more sinned against than sinning. In the great speech of Satan with which Milton opens the fourth book of

*Paradise Lost* the poet drives home, with stroke after stroke, the responsibility of Satan for his own wrongdoing:

> Had'st thou the same free will and power to stand?
> Thou had'st: whom hast thou then or what to accuse
> But Heaven's free-will dealt equally to all?
> Be then his love accurst since, love or hate,
> To me alike it deals eternal woe.
> Nay curst be thou; since against his thy will
> Chose freely what it now so justly rues.
> Me miserable! which way shall I fly?
> Infinite wrath and infinite despair.

That is, I take it, the orthodox, essentially religious view. Man has no rights; but he has freedom and therefore complete responsibility. Paul, Augustine, Calvin, had doubts about the freedom, none about the responsibility. Byron and the sceptical mind find it difficult to accept either position. To call a conscious being into existence seems to him to involve moral obligations for a righteous creator. Man's freewill is not, experience and thought seem to indicate, thus absolute. If Satan rebelled it was in virtue of something in his nature, the nature which he did not himself make, but received. Free, a man's conscience tells him he is, within limits and relatively, relative to other created beings to whom he cannot transfer his individual responsibility. But neither conscience nor reason tells him that this complex being which is his responsible self, is of his own making, is free absolutely, *i.e.* in its relation to the absolute. So much Byron feels, but he is incapable of a philosophical solution of the enigma. The *Prometheus* is a defiant and unshakeable arraignment of the conception of Providence taught him by Orthodox Evangelicalism:

> Thy God-like crime was to be kind,
>   To render with thy precepts less
>   The sum of human wretchedness,
> And strengthen Man with his own mind;
> But baffled as thou wert from high,
> Still in thy patient energy,
> In the endurance, and repulse
>   Of thine impenetrable Spirit,
> Which Earth and Heaven could not convulse,
>   A mighty lesson we inherit:
> Thou art a symbol and a sign
>   To Mortals of their fate and force;
> Like thee, Man is in part divine,
>   A troubled stream from a pure source;
> And Man in portions can foresee
> His own funereal destiny;
> His wretchedness, and his resistance,
> And his sad unallied existence:
> To which his Spirit may oppose
> Itself—an equal to all woes—
>   And a firm will, and a deep sense,
> Which even in torture can descry
>   Its own concentered recompense,
> Triumphant where it dares defy,
>   And making Death a Victory.

In *Manfred* Byron endeavours to give the same theme dramatic form, the lyrical-dramatic form which Goethe's *Faust* had given vogue to, and in the same metaphysical strain. But Byron's genius was not dramatic, nor had he the lyrical soul of Shelley. Shelley lacked solidity;

Byron lacked wings. Yet *Manfred*, read aright, is an impressive and significant poem. Its closest parallel is Marlowe's *Dr. Faustus*, a poem which in its best passages has more of the essential music of poetry than Byron's, for a deficiency in essential music is Byron's greatest defect as a poet. But Byron's thought goes deeper than Marlowe's. Marlowe set two moods over against one another: on the one hand, lust of knowledge and of the power which knowledge brings; on the other, terror of the supernatural; but he failed to link them logically and dramatically. His sympathies, one feels, are with the soaring ambitions of Faustus, yet at the end he hands him over to the devils of superstition in a speech of splendid power. He failed to show, as Shakespeare did in *Macbeth*, that the forbidden fruit brought its *own* curse. Byron's poem is even less many-mooded than Marlowe's; but its logic, so far as it goes, is lucid and convincing. Manfred is the victim of sin and remorse, but the defiant enemy of the orthodox conception of retribution. The punishment of sin is the consciousness of sin, the consciousness above all of wrong to another, to the one who is loved and has been the victim of passion:

> If I had never lived, that which I love
> Had still been living; had I never loved,
> That which I love would still be beautiful,
> Happy and giving happiness.

> Old man! there is no power in holy men,
> Nor charm in prayer, nor purifying form
> Of penitence, nor outward look, nor fast,
> Nor agony—nor, greater than all these,
> The innate tortures of that deep despair

> Which is remorse without the fear of Hell,
> But all in all sufficient to itself
> Would make a Hell of Heaven—can exorcise
> From out the unbounded spirit the quick sense
> Of its own sins—wrongs—sufferance—and revenge
> Upon itself; there is no future pang
> Can deal that justice on the self condemn'd
> He deals on his own soul.

And when the devils appear it is not to carry off Manfred as they had carried off Faustus.   Retribution is not only useless, it is but to add crime to crime:

> Must crimes be punished but by other crimes
> And greater criminals?   Back to thy hell!
> Thou hast no power upon me, *that* I feel;
> Thou never shalt possess me, that I know;
> What I have done is done;  I bear within
> A torture which could nothing gain from thine.

A step more, one feels, might have led Byron to recognise, with Blake and Tolstoi, that the fundamental principle of Christianity and true religion is the doctrine of the eternal forgiveness of sin.

· *Childe Harold*, Canto III., *Manfred* and *Prometheus* were all written in 1816–17, and were only a few of the products of that wonderful year which produced poems of such different moods as *The Prisoner of Chillon*, the verses addressed to Byron's sister, *The Dream*, *Darkness*, and at the end *Beppo*, of which I must speak again.   To the theme of these three poems, the metaphysic of sin and retribution, Byron returned later and in a calmer mood, drawing himself again, his own temperament and weakness and consciousness of sin, and emphasising his arraignment of the orthodox, evangelical theory of sin and retribution in which he had been reared, when he wrote *Cain*, to the horror of Southey and the delight of Shelley. " If you before thought Byron a great poet, what is your opinion now? Space wondered less at the swift and fair creations of God, when He grew weary of vacancy, than I at this spirit of an angel in the mortal paradise of a decaying body." *Sardanapalus* and *Cain* are Byron's most interesting pieces of self-portraiture. *Sardanapalus* is the *apologia* for his life at Venice, his sins of sense. They have not, he seems to say, through the story of Sardanapalus' heroism in the last encounter, they have not robbed him of courage if the call to heroic action should come, as it was soon to come from Greece; and what after all are the sins of sense weighed in the balance against the endless tale of war and bloodshed which the World applauds and the Church condones?

> Oh, thou wouldst doubtless have me set up edicts—
> " Obey the kind—contribute to his treasure—
> Recruit his phalanx—spill your blood at bidding—
> Fall down and worship, or get up and toil."
> Or thus—" Sardanapalus on this spot
> Slew fifty thousand of his enemies.
> These are their sepulchres, and this his trophy."
> I leave such things to conquerors; enough
> For me, if I can make my subjects feel
> The weight of human misery less, and glide
> Ungroaning to the tomb: I take no licence
> Which I deny to them. We all are men.
>
> .    .    .    .    .    .    .
>
> I feel a thousand mortal things about me,
> But nothing god-like,—unless it may be

The thing which you condemn, a disposition
To love and to be merciful, to pardon
The folly of my species, and (that's human)
To be indulgent to my own.

In *Cain* Byron challenged in his own peculiar way
the scriptural orthodoxy of Evangelical Christianity.   To
understand the tremendous disturbance which the poem
created one has to recall—no easy thing now—the state
of mind of those for whom every part of the Bible was of
equal authority as a revelation of the divine.   No Higher
Criticism had appeared to suggest that the Bible must
be seen in perspective, that the primitive myths of the
Book of Genesis, Deuteronomy, and the legendary Book
of Esther were not documents of the same religious value
as the Psalms, the Prophets, and the Gospels.   Byron
was no such critic.   His criticism is again a moral one,
a challenge to the view of man's entire responsibility for
evil, the doctrine which identifies inherited sin and
inherited guilt, the doctrine of retribution.   To Kennedy
Byron declared that he would certainly say to the potter,
" Why do you treat me thus? " and that " if the whole
world were going to hell he would prefer going with
them, than go alone to Heaven ".   That is the spirit in
which *Cain* is composed—" Why do you treat me thus? "

I need not analyse the argument, for Byron's thought
never gets beyond the simple antinomy of the fact of sin
and the injustice of the evangelical doctrine of responsibility and retribution.   The chief interest of the drama
is in the characters of Cain and Lucifer and Ada.   Cain
is Byron himself, not drawn so melodramatically as in
*Childe Harold* and *Manfred*, but with a mournful understanding—a dark soul, the victim of passions which prompt

to " deeds eternity cannot annul "; a dark soul in whom reason rejects the simple solution of orthodoxy, of gentler souls like Adam and Abel. But Lucifer is Byron too, the critical, sceptical intellect which had haunted the child in Aberdeen with troublesome questions, and had never allowed the imagination to create Shelleyan dreams of a regenerate world:

You talk Utopia.

In all this Byron seems to me the child, the defiant and rebellious child, of Evangelical and Calvinistic Protestant-ism, feeling the power of the doctrine he defied, the reality of sin and evil, as Shelley never did. To call him an atheist, whether in Southey's glib fashion or from the more enlightened point of view of Professor Farinelli, seems to me not quite just. Kennedy's statement is not to be waved aside: " He said that he was not an infidel who denied the Scriptures and wished to remain in un-belief—on the contrary, he was very desirous to believe, as he experienced no happiness in having his religious opinions so unsteady and unfixed ". Byron recognised in Shelley the highest of Christian virtues, " charity and benevolence ". But he could not share Shelley's con-fidence in human nature and a man's power to work out his own destiny. His evangelical training had taught him, what his experience confirmed, that human nature is weaker than clay in the hands of the destiny that moulds it; but the character of that Power he could not read and would not belie. He had been taught to fear that power, and his pride would not stoop to acknowledge the authority of what he feared but could not love. The psycho-analyst might discover the explanation of much in Byron's life in the experiences of his troubled childhood.

But the conflict with his own sense of delinquency and the narrow creed by which he had been taught to interpret and judge of that experience was only one of the themes of the later poetry of Byron. The other principal one was his fight with the English aristocracy which, in hypocritical alliance, as he deemed, with evangelical and middle-class sentiment, had joined in denouncing and driving him into exile:

> The cruelty and envy of the people,
> Permitted by our dastard nobles, who
> Have all forsook me, hath devoured the rest;
> And suffered me by the voice of slaves to be
> Whoop'd out of Rome.

Byron was not quite a Coriolanus, yet the quotation describes aptly enough the circumstances under which Byron was driven from his country. Nor is it any part of my thesis to defend Byron. Apart altogether from the evidence which now makes practically certain the circumstance in which Lady Byron found the final justification to her conscience of the step she took, no one can read the letters she wrote immediately after she left him (brought together in Mr. Prothero's *Letters and Journals,* iii., Appendix to Chapter XII.) without recognising that a separation of some kind was inevitable. His marriage, in the circumstances, and with a woman of his wife's character and principles, drove Byron frantic; and his conduct towards her from her marriage day onward had clearly been intolerable. The very fact that each was a person of abnormal power and character made any such

peaceful existence as Byron submitted to later with La
Guiccioli, impossible.   To Lady Byron her husband was
a Lucifer, a creature of " boundless and impious pride ",
to live with whom she must abandon " every moral and
religious principle against which  .  his hatred and
endeavours were uniformly directed "; and to Byron his
wife, whom he could not but respect and was never able
to forget, represented all that he most detested in English
virtue and piety.   I am not concerned to make excuses
for Byron.   The time is past for that.   He was what
he was.   I am only trying to understand him, aware that
every analysis of an historical character must leave an
inexplicable residuum.   The tragedy of the marriage,
as of many another, is that what each saw in the other
was not the whole truth.   There were elements in
Byron which a different upbringing and perhaps another
woman might have educed.

But in any case he was a poet, in his manner and
measure a prophet, who spoke the truth as it presented
itself to him, even if he was moved to do so by imperfect
motives.   There is an element of truth in Byron's
arraignment of the Evangelical, Protestant doctrine of
retribution; there is power in Byron's satire of aristocratic society and aristocratic government in England
and Europe, which is the theme of his great comic epic
*Don Juan*.   In *Beppo* (1817) Byron had found at last
the medium which allowed him to pour into his poetry
all the humour and wit with which his conversation
and letters overflowed; and in 1818 the first cantos of
*Don Juan* were written.

As *Childe Harold* is more than a record of Byron's
conflict with the Evangelical doctrine of sin and retribu-

tion, *Don Juan* is more than merely a satire on life and
politics in aristocratic Europe.   Like the serious poem,
it is a reflection of his varied and shifting moods but more
many-sided, more gay and brilliant.   Of that aspect of
it I have spoken elsewhere and need not repeat myself.
What I wish to insist on here is that the point of view
from which the whole is seen in best perspective is that
which Byron himself always emphasised, a satire on
higher society, and ultimately, like Swift's, on human
nature.   " I take a vicious and unprincipled character,
and lead him through those ranks of society whose high
external accomplishments cover and cloke internal and
secret vices, and I paint the natural effects of such characters; and certainly they are not so highly coloured as
we find them in real life. . . . It is impossible you
can believe the higher classes of society worse than they
are in England, France and Italy, for no language
can sufficiently paint them."   " You have so many
*divine* poems, is it nothing to have written a *human*
one? "

Even Mr. Coleridge in his final edition of Byron's
poems obscures a little the right perspective in which
the poem is to be seen when he declares that " the argument is a vindication of the natural man ", and that
" the *raison d'être* of his song was not only to celebrate
but by the white light of truth to represent and exhibit,
the great things of the world—Love and War, Death by
sea and land, and Man, half-angel and half-demon, the
comedy of his fortunes and the tragedy of his passions
and fate ".   That is at once to claim too much for *Don
Juan* and to fail to do justice to its chief function.   There
is no such full picture of life in *Don Juan* as this suggests,

and that is why it falls short of being an epic of modern
life.  Byron is not concerned to vindicate the natural
man or life.  He is content to describe with a blend
of Fielding's sympathy with youth, Voltaire's mocking
gaiety, and Swift's sombre reflection on human nature,
life in the class that ruled Europe, from Britain to
Turkey.

And the comparison with Swift is the most fundamental.  Like *A Modest Proposal* and *Gulliver's Travels*,
*Don Juan* is primarily a satire on the royal and aristocratic politicians who governed Europe.  " Here they
are," he seems to say (and the poem closed, or broke off,
just as he had begun to describe that English society in
which he had shone like a meteor for a few short and
fatal seasons), "here they are, the brilliant coteries who
govern us, and to whom Southey and others my savage
critics are so profoundly respectful, the same at St. Petersburg as at London, at their eternal game of war and
diplomacy for which the price is paid in ' the blood and
tears of wretched men ', the one great preoccupation of
their idle moments what they call love.  Some day surely
humanity will rouse itself and put an end to the whole
business."  But Byron's hopes are not as ardent as
Shelley's for he has not Shelley's faith in human nature:

> They accuse me—*Me*—the present writer of
>   The present poem—of—I know not what—
> A tendence to under-rate and scoff
>   At human power and virtue and all that;
> And this they say in language rather rough.
>   Good God! I wonder what they would be at!
> I say no more than hath been said in Dante's
> Verse, and by Solomon and by Cervantes;

By Swift, by Machiavel, by Rochefoucauld,
  By Fénelon, by Luther, and by Plato;
By Tillotson, and Wesley, and Rousseau,
  Who knew this life was not worth a potato.
'Tis not their fault, nor mine, if this be so,—
  For my part I pretend not to be Cato,
Nor even Diogenes.—We live and die,
But which is best, *you* know no more than I.


Socrates said, our only knowledge was
  " To know that nothing could be known "; a pleasant
Science enough, which levels to an ass
  Each man of wisdom, future, past, or present.
Newton (that proverb of the mind) alas,
  Declared with all his grand discoveries recent,
That he himself felt only " like a youth
Picking up shells by the great ocean—Truth ".


Ecclesiastes said, " that all is vanity "—
  Most modern preachers say the same, or show it
By their examples of true Christianity:
  In short all know or very soon may know it;
And in this scene of all-confessed inanity,
  By Saint, by Sage, by Preacher and by Poet,
Must I restrain me, through the fear of strife,
From holding up the nothingness of life.


Dogs, or men—for I flatter you in saying
  That ye are dogs—your betters far—ye may
Read, or read not, what I am now essaying
  To show you what ye are in every way.
As little as the moon stops for the baying
  Of wolves will the bright Muse withdraw one ray
From out her skies—then howl your idle wrath!
While she still silvers o'er your gloomy path.

If, despite such passages, Byron failed to convince his first readers and may still fail to convince us, of the serious satirical purpose of his poem, "the most moral of poems", it is because of the vein of irresponsible fun and flippancy which runs through it as through his conversation and letters, and secondly, because of the indulgence, or sympathy, with which he treats one element in the life he is satirising, the game of love.   There is nothing in *Don Juan* resembling the morbid and revolting treatment of sexual life in Swift's poems and *Gulliver's Travels*.  "There is no indelicacy", Byron writes to Murray; "if Hobhouse wants that let him read Swift, his great idol."   Here Byron draws nearer to Fielding. Young men will love, and young love is probably the best thing life has to give.   In the episode of Haidee, and again in *The Island*, Byron writes in a way to suggest that for his temperament a simpler, more primitive civilisation, less set around with inhibitions and reproving critics, would have cooled the fever of nerves that the complexities of civilisation excited to madness.

Byron's conflict at once with aristocratic society, its politics and morals, and with the one religious force which, like himself, judged and condemned that society, the Evangelical Christianity of Wilberforce, Newton, Cowper, a conflict from which he found no issue, recalls that other and greater aristocrat who declared war against aristocratic society as he knew it from within also, and was driven out of the Faith and Church in which he had hoped to find an ally in his fight.   "I honestly desired to make myself a good and virtuous man; but I was young, I had passions, and stood alone, altogether alone in my search after virtue.   Every time I tried to express

o

the longing of my heart for a truly virtuous life I was
met with contempt and derisive laughter; but directly
I gave way to the lowest of my passions I was praised
and encouraged.   I found ambition, love of gain, lechery,
pride, anger, vengeance, held in high esteem.   I gave
way to these passions and becoming like unto my elders
I felt that the place which I filled satisfied those around
me. . .   My kind-hearted aunt, a really good woman,
used to say to me that the one thing above all others
which she wished for me was an intrigue with a married
woman. . . . Another of her wishes for my happiness
was that I should become, if possible, an adjutant to the
Emperor; the greatest happiness of all she thought for
me would be that I should find a wealthy bride who
would bring me an enormous number of serfs."

When Tolstoi came to realise the vanity and cruelty
of aristocratic life, he sought escape and guidance in the
creed of his upbringing, the Orthodox Church, and for
a time found it in submission and acceptance.   There
was more in that ancient creed and ritual to appeal to
the imagination than in English Evangelicalism and
Methodism.   But in Tolstoi, as in Byron, the sceptical
intellect was too strong for acquiescence.   In the end
Tolstoi found, or believed he had found, an escape when
he realised that despite all the stress which the Church
had laid on the literal inspiration of the Bible there was
one part which every Church had agreed to ignore or
explain away, and that was the Sermon on the Mount.
He turned from creed and sacraments to follow the *way*
of Christ.   It was, as events proved, an imperfect victory.

Byron had not Tolstoi's greatness of soul, nor the
Asiatic, ascetic mystical impulses.   His pride was more

deeply alloyed with vanity. He might satirise; he could not easily break with the tone and traditions of his order. To his critical intellect, too, Tolstoi's solution, which was no solution but an abnegation of life, would have seemed wanting in common sense. A Catholic Byron might, as Scott told him, have become, never a Tolstoian Christian, a Dukhobor. Yet to look back on Byron's life and poetry through the larger soul and experience of Tolstoi is a help to one who would understand the forces as I have tried to describe them, which were at work in his troubled mind and are reflected in his poetry—pride, passion, aristocratic tradition, a religious sense that would not be stifled, a creed the intellect could not accept; and such solution as Byron found had in it the essential elements of Tolstoi's teaching—work and self-sacrifice. Against all his shortcomings as a man it is only fair to set the service he strove to render to the cause of freedom and justice in Italy and in Greece, the fact that he did after all lay down his life for his fellow-men. The spirit in which he undertook his last task is well expressed in two speeches:

"I am come here not in search of adventures, but to assist the regeneration of a nation whose very debasement makes it more honourable to become their friend."

"Poverty is wretchedness; but it is perhaps to be preferred to the heartless unmeaning dissipation of the higher orders. I am thankful I am now clear of that, and my resolution to remain clear of it for the rest of my life is immutable."

# BLAKE & GRAY

THE chance that has brought to light, after nearly one hundred years, the copy of Gray's poems illustrated by William Blake will raise varied feelings in the reader of to-day looking back from the twentieth century on these so striking representatives of two clearly and deeply cut periods in the ever-changing history of English imaginative art in poetry and painting. It would be difficult to think of two more strongly contrasted men and poets— Gray the finest flower of our Augustan culture, shy, sensitive, studious elaborator of a few exquisite poems, the filed and finished art of which disguises as well as reveals the emotion they express; Blake, poet, painter, and prophet, the sansculottist of the Romantic Revival, a wonderful poet and a wonderful artist, in whose multifarious work the greatest want is the virtues in which Gray excels, moderation and correctness. What would Gray, one wonders, have thought of Blake as an illustrator of his polished if fitfully inspired poems? What could Blake, on the other hand, find in Gray's poems to stimulate his restless and powerful imagination, his genius that rode confident and sublime

> upon the seraph wings of Ecstasy
> The secrets of the abyss to spy,

if too often it seems to the uncomprehending reader that his experience is that of Satan voyaging through Chaos:

> All unawares
> Fluttring his pennons vain plumb down he drops
> Ten thousand fadom deep?

Looking back through all the romantic and imaginative poetry of which in 1800—when these drawings were in all probability executed—only Blake's own *Songs of Innocence* (1789) and *Songs of Experience* (1794) and the *Lyrical Ballads* of Wordsworth and Coleridge (1798) had given any clear premonition, we should hardly feel surprised if Blake had ranked Gray with Pope or with the pictures of Rubens and Le Brun. " I was once looking over the prints from Raphael and Michael Angelo in the Library of the Royal Academy. Moser came to me and said: ' You should not study these old, hard, stiff and dry, unfinished works of art: stay a little and *I* will show you what you should study.' He then went and took down Le Brun and Rubens' *Galleries*. How did I secretly rage! I also spoke my mind. I said to Moser: ' These things that you call finished are not even begun: how then can they be finished? ' " That is just what Blake felt about Pope as compared with Shakespeare and the Elizabethans. " Sir, a thousand years may elapse," said Dr. Johnson, " before there shall appear another man with a power of versification equal to that of Pope." Blake's comment would have been that Pope had never begun to versify:

> Wondrous the Gods, more wondrous are the Men,
> More Wondrous, Wondrous still, the Cock and Hen,
> More wondrous still the Table, Stool and Chair;
> But ah! more wondrous still the Charming Fair!

which, of course, is not the whole truth about Pope's verse. But that Gray was not classed with Pope, and that Blake thought it worth his while to illustrate the poems—even if he grew weary of the task before he had

finished—is due in part to the presence of a spirit of
poetry in Gray's slender volume of verse of which, grant-
ing to the full the brilliance of Pope's own peculiar
achievement, there is very little in his poetry, though
there is far more of it—as Gray knew—in Pope's master
John Dryden.  It is also due to the fact that to Blake
and others, who had no Blake and Coleridge and Scott
and Keats to compare or contrast him with, Gray was
far more of a romantic than he appears to us.  What
Blake has done, in the best of his unequal illustrations,
is to emphasise, to exaggerate the romantic element in
Gray's poems.  Gray, said Johnson, " was dull, but dull
in a new sort of way ".  But the " new sort of way "
which Johnson found " dull " was what Blake found
most exciting in Gray's work.

Gray's poetry is, in truth, an endless source of interest
to the curious student of poetry; and, if we care to take
it along with Blake's poetry and art, an instructive text for
the consideration of art and inspiration in " high poetry ".
For Gray had poetic inspiration.  He wrote because he felt
impelled to write: " I will be candid and avow to you that
till fourscore and upward, whenever the humour takes me,
I will write; because I like it and because I like myself
better when I do it."   " I like myself better when I do
it "—that is, he felt the relief of self-expression, and the
joy of artistic expression.  But Gray's was no over-
powering impulse.  He does not write as one who fed

> on thoughts that voluntary move
> Harmonious numbers;

never pours himself out as Christopher Smart in the *Song
of David*, or Blake in the *Songs of Innocence*, or Shelley

Singing hymns unbidden
In the light of thought.

" My vein is .   . of so delicate a constitution, and has
such weak nerves as not to stir out of its chamber above
three days in a year." And one of the inhibitory impulses,
perhaps the chief, was a critical and exquisite sense of
what good poetry should be.

Later critics have found it temptingly easy to decry
and ridicule Arnold's characteristic essay on Gray as a
poet who " never spoke out " because he, a true poet,
fell upon an age of prose. And of course if it is any
use to take a critic's metaphors and hyperboles, whether
Wordsworth's or Arnold's, literally, and tie him to them
like a witness in a law-court, it is easy enough to convict
and hang him. Critical writing is in great measure an
attempt to capture the intangible, to define the undefin-
able. Arnold's suggestion that Gray would have been
a happier man and a more prolific poet if he had lived
in the age of Milton or the age of Burns is just a rhetorical
way of saying—what is obvious enough—that Gray's
taste was not satisfied with the poetry of his own day,
that his poetic instinct led him to cast both behind and
before, while yet he had not the strength of inspiration
or courage of temperament to be a rebel in more than a
very tentative fashion; and so Gray's poetry is at once
the perfect flower of our Augustan age and carries within
it the seeds of the romantic revival.

He wrote Latin before he wrote English verses and
is one of the few English poets whose work bears the
unmistakable imprint of their training in an exacting
language and prosody. Sir Henry Wotton—the Wotton
of " How happy is he born and taught " and " You

meaner beauties of the night "—is the first to show the blend of qualities, moderated feeling, clear and just thought, condensation, perfection of style, to which such a training conduces. Milton is the greatest, but for that very reason perhaps not the most representative. His thought is too individual, his feeling too prophetic, his style with all its grandeur and beauty a little too classical in one sense to be perfectly classical in a better sense, too Latinised to have what Quintilian reckoned the first of all virtues, perfect purity. "Our language sunk under him . . . he was desirous to use English words with a foreign idiom." Gray is the third and the most exquisite; Landor and the present Poet Laureate probably complete the group.

Of such poets the thought that rises to the mind is that for them poetry is an art, first and last. "What led me to poetry ", Mr. Bridges tells us, " was the inexhaustible satisfaction of form, the magic of speech lying as it seemed to me in the masterly control of the material: it was an art which I hoped to learn. I did not suppose that the poet's emotions were in any way better than mine nor mine than another's." That describes admirably Pope's and the Augustan ideal in poetry. Time, indeed, and the history of English poetry have made Mr. Bridges' poetry more personal, more subtle and elusive of mood than Gray's, for another article of the Augustan faith was that the mood which the poet expresses ought to be one that he shares with the generality of civilised men, and of such the chief are those which the eighteenth century described as " the moral sentiments ". " The *Churchyard* abounds with images which find a mirror in every mind, and with sentiments to which every bosom returns an echo "; and the *Ode to Adversity*, in the same captious critic's judgement, excels the original " by the variety of the sentiments and by their moral application. Of this piece at once poetical and rational I will not by slight objections violate the dignity." Yet the delicate *Ode on the Return of Spring* and that *On a Distant Prospect of Eton College* are condemned because of the former " the thoughts have nothing new " and in the latter the prospect " suggests nothing to Gray which every beholder does not equally think and feel ", which seems a rather strange way of condemning what Johnson praises in the *Elegy*, " images which find a mirror in every mind and sentiments to which every bosom returns an echo ".

But Johnson's criticism of poems that are so quint-essentially Augustan is both intelligible and instructive. When the thoughts are of sufficient weight, and effective oratorical appeal, he will praise Gray's poems, not when the sentiment is of slighter texture—of the great *Odes* I shall speak later—because in neither case has he a word of praise for Gray's style, which he frankly dislikes. And though Johnson touches some undeniable weaknesses in Gray's diction—if the charge of " cumbrous splendour " comes strangely from the author of

> Let Observation, with extensive view,
> Survey mankind from China to Peru—

a really close study of his detailed animadversions reveals clearly enough that what he disliked was just the higher poetical quality of Gray's work. The " new way " in which Gray was dull was the old way in which *Lycidas* was " harsh and unpleasing ".

For if Gray was an Augustan, he was not quite a contented Augustan, not altogether at ease in Zion, in the peace of the Augustans or rather of the Georgians, of which his leisured, cultured life, his poetry in which a sweeter, more pensive spirit has taken the place of the combative satiric temper of Pope and his age, is so complete an expression. His own instinct and his profound knowledge of great poetry, Classical and Gothic, Homer and Virgil, Dante and Spenser, Shakespeare and Milton, alike taught him that the poetry of his age was not great poetry. He is a curious and critical reader of his contemporaries, and in his detailed review of Dodsley's Collection, in a letter to Walpole, is both discriminating and fair—much fairer to Johnson than Johnson is to him (" *London* is to me one of those few imitations that have all the ease and all the spirit of an original ")—but what he thinks of the general level is clear enough: " If I say Messieurs! this is not the thing; write prose, write sermons, write nothing at all; they will disdain me and my advice." When, to West, who had found the language of his tragedy *Agrippina* too antiquated and Shakespearian, Gray replies " that the language of the age is never the language of poetry " he is not, I venture to think, affirming so indisputable doctrine as Mr. Saintsbury would have us believe, for the language of poetry may be as pure as it is beautiful, and some of the very best of Gray's prose is, to my ear, almost more poetic than anything he has written in verse because it is more pure and natural. " In the evening walk'd alone to the Lake by the side of Crow-Park after sunset and saw the solemn colouring of night draw on, the last gleam of sunshine fading away on the hill-tops, the deep serene of the waters, and the long shadows of the mountains thrown across them, till they nearly touched the hithermost shore. At distance heard the murmur of many waterfalls not audible in the day-time. Wished for the Moon, but she was 'dark to me and silent, hid in her vacant interlunar cave'." I do not know any passage in Gray's poems so sensitive in word and rhythm as that, and, except for the quotation, it is written in the language of the age.

What Gray was in quest of in his " poetic diction ", and the high adventure of the Pindaric Odes, was what his cultured poetic taste felt the want of in the poetry of his age, inspiration:

> But not to one in this benighted age
>   Is that diviner inspiration given,
> That burns in Shakespeare's or in Milton's page,
>   The pomp and prodigality of Heav'n.

But Gray knew that, if the language of the age be not the language of poetry, there can be no real revival of the language of the past. One may cull phrases with which to decorate; it is impossible to recapture an older idiom as William Morris and Mr. Doughty have in different ways tried to do. For his immediate master Gray, therefore, turned to John Dryden: " Remember Dryden and be blind to all his faults", he wrote to Beattie, whom he also told " that if there were any excellence in his own numbers he had learned it wholly from that great poet ". The letter to West on poetic diction reveals the minute study he had made of Dryden's language in *The Fables*; and he was following Dryden rather than Pope, while drawing on his wider reading of English and

classical literature, when he created his own poetic
diction, of which the general effect is doubtless artificial
and verges on the pompous, yet in detail is frequently so
felicitous and at times beautiful.   It was doubtless with his
eye on Dryden, too, that Gray essayed his most adventur-
ous flight in *The Progress of Poesy* and *The Bard*, Dryden
corrected by Gray's better knowledge and finer appreciation of Pindar and Greek tragedy and Milton.   And if
the *Elegy* is, despite occasional depreciation, likely to
remain Gray's classic, it is in the Odes that Gray is most
a poet, in them that one may mark most clearly the
genuineness of his inspiration and its limitations, appreciate
his achievement and recognise his failure.   And to do
so is to realise wherein Gray made appeal to Blake and
where they necessarily part company, Blake going his
way to write some poems which Gray could never have
attained to, if also to write many that Gray would have
regarded with wonder or contempt.

Johnson's criticism of the Odes, the "wonderful
Wonder of Wonders", does not entirely miss the mark,
but in its detailed condemnation of the style betrays, as
in what he finds fault with in the earlier poems, that
his root objection is to a poetry which transcends his own
comprehension, that he has no feeling for what is most
imaginative, no ear for what is most musical.   "*A stream
of music* may be allowed; but where does *music*, however
*smooth and strong*, after having visited the *verdant vales*,
*roll down the steep amain*, so as that *rocks and nodding
groves rebellow to the roar*?   If this be said of *music*,
it is nonsense; if it be said of *water*, it is nothing
to the purpose."   To criticism of this kind the
only answer can be that for it the greatest poetry is

"nothing to the purpose". It would forbid a poet to sing

> O, my luve is like a red, red rose
> That's newly sprung in June,

unless her cheeks were of that colour. For it overlooks the primary truth that the most imaginative comparisons do not rest on any objective, sensible likeness in the things compared, but on a common element in the feelings they evoke. Perhaps the finest, because the most spontaneous, sincerest stanza in *The Progress of Poesy* is that which describes the joy of poetry:

> Man's feeble race what Ills await,
> Labour, and Penury, the racks of Pain,
> Disease, and Sorrow's weeping train,
> And Death, sad refuge from the storms of Fate!
> The fond complaint, my Song, disprove,
> And justify the laws of Jove.
> Say, has he given in vain the heav'nly Muse?
> Night, and all her sickly dews,
> Her Spectres wan, and Birds of boding cry,
> He gives to range the dreary sky:
> Till down the eastern cliffs afar
> Hyperion's march they spy, and glitt'ring shafts of war.

Johnson's comment upon this is that "the stanza endeavours to tell something, and would have told it had it not been crossed by Hyperion", which, if seriously meant, is a confession that he has failed to realise that what Gray has to say is contained in the simile, that poetry is the sun of life. It was not a mood or an image likely to escape the apprehension of Blake's temper and imagination, and is the subject of the most glowing of his sketches (No. 6).

But to criticism of this kind, and much of what Johnson has to say on *The Bard*—" I do not see that *The Bard* promotes any truth, moral or political "— there can be no end and no answer. Where Johnson comes nearer to the truth is in his complaint that " the mind of the writer seems to work with unnatural violence. *Double, double, toil and trouble* " and (although he does not connect the two criticisms) in his condemnation of the radical want of truth in the thought, in the intellectual framework which supports the splendid and often genuinely poetic texture of phrase and varying rhythm. The fatal want, to which is ultimately traceable the sense which haunts even an appreciative reader of something mechanical—this is not Johnson's charge; to him the diction is unintelligible—in Gray's style and cadences, is the want of truth and depth of inspiration. The progress of poesy in company with liberty is a mere rhetorical " topic " and a false one at that. " His position is at last false: in the time of Dante and Petrarch . . . Italy was overrun by *tyrant power* and *coward vice*, nor was our state much better when we first borrowed Italian arts "— and the prophecy of the bard loses dramatic and convincing power by the neatness and accuracy of its historic detail.

But this brings us precisely to the parting of the ways between Gray and Blake, the divergence between the poetry of Gray's century and the poetry of which Blake's is so strange and complete a microcosm. Gray's genuine poetic inspiration, his sense of something wanting in the poetry of his day compared with the great poetry of the Greeks, and Dante, and the Elizabethans, had induced him to make an effort for which, with all his brilliant technique, he was not quite strong enough, for which his age wanted the right temper and convictions—that is the measure of truth in Arnold's somewhat fanciful criticism.

It is easy to do injustice to the poetry of the eighteenth century—some of which retains its place in the best anthologies with a security which may in the end fail a great deal of romantic poetry—unless one sees quite clearly what was its defect, its limitation. It is not as text-books and confused examination papers declare or imply, that it dealt with the wrong subjects, the town instead of nature, and turned its back on mediæval romance —the revival of romance proved in great measure a glittering, misleading will-o'-the-wisp—nor that it was cold and wanting in feeling, as though Pope and Johnson and Goldsmith and Gray and Collins lacked intensity of feeling.   It is sufficient to recall Johnson's

> There mark what ills the scholar's life assail,
> Toil, envy, want, the patron, and the jail;

or Goldsmith's

> In all my wand'rings round this world of care,
> In all my griefs—and God has given my share—
> I still had hopes my latest hours to crown,
> Amidst these humble bowers to lay me down;
> To husband out life's taper at the close,
> And keep the flame from wasting by repose.
>
> .    .    .    .    .    .    .    .
>
> And as a hare, whom hounds and horns pursue,
> Pants to the place from whence at first she flew,
> I still had hopes, my long vexations pass'd,
> Here to return—and die at home at last ;

or Cowper's

> My mother, when I learn'd that thou wast dead,
> Say, wast thou conscious of the tears I shed?
> Hover'd thy spirit o'er thy sorrowing son,
> Wretch even then, life's journey just begun?
>
> .    .    .    .    .    .    .    .
>
> But me, scarce hoping to attain that rest,
> Always from port withheld, always distress'd—
> Me howling winds drive devious, tempest-toss'd,
> Sails ript, seams op'ning wide, and compass lost.

"Of high poetry", Maeterlinck says, in words which I have quoted in an earlier essay, "the constituents are threefold: beauty of language; the passionate portrayal of what is real around and in us, nature and our own feelings; and, enveloping the whole, creating its peculiar atmosphere, the idea that the poet forms to himself of the unknown, in which floats the being he invokes, the mystery which dominates and judges them, which presides over and assigns their destinies." In neither of the first two of these constituents was the poetry of the century, from Dryden and Pope to Cowper and Crabbe, greatly wanting. For their own purposes they made of the English language a more flexible and uniform, dignified, musical, and elegant medium. There is an element of truth in Johnson's boast that Dryden found English poetry brick and left it marble. There was no such impoverishment of our speech as a medium for poetry as the French language in the same period underwent, admitting that Coleridge and Keats and Shelley were to revive older beauties and engraft fresh ones. Nor is there in Wordsworth and Scott and Keats any more faithful portrayal of objective nature than in Thomson

and Dyer and Gray and Collins and Cowper and Crabbe;
nor can the century of the essay and the novel, of biography and history and letters, be accused of want of
interest in human nature.   It is not here the real difference lies, but in the third of Maeterlinck's constituents
and its reaction on the other two.   What Blake and
Wordsworth brought into poetry was a new vision.   The
eighteenth century did not achieve "high poetry";
Gray's attempt to rise on the wings of Pindar failed,
despite the brilliance of his technique, because his poetry,
and the poetry of his age, lacked the inspiration of an
imaginative and impassioned "idea of the unknown", a
poetic interpretation of life such as that to which, whatever shape it took, the world owes the poetry of Homer,
of Pindar, of the Greek tragedians, of Dante, and all that
is greatest in mediæval poetry.   The century looked at life
and nature in a clear prosaic spirit, and called upon poetry
to unite pleasure with truth "by calling imagination to
the help of reason".   Such a temper may produce some
excellent poetry, satirical, reflective, sentimental; it cannot produce high poetry, and no embellishment of the
diction, even when guided by the fine sensibility and
critical taste and wide knowledge of poetry of Gray, will
make high poetry of commonplace ideas, rhetorical
"topics" begotten in the wits not in the imagination, for
diction and verse are the expression not the embellishment of the passionate, imaginative thinking of the poet.
Of high poetry the idea as well as the dress must be poetic
even if it be simple.   The idea may be fanciful, so that it
is a *genuine* sport of fancy, as Herrick's

> Sweet daffodils, we weep to see
> You haste away so soon;

P

or romantic, pleasantly romantic, as with Chaucer and
Malory and Spenser, or tremendously romantic as in
Dante, or it may be tragic, but it must take its rise in
the impassioned imagination, not in the cool, discursive
intellect.

The eighteenth century was not indeed devoid of
great shaping ideas, but they were not of a kind to inspire
high poetry. To a generation which had escaped from
the outworn and fantastic ideals of the later Middle Ages,
and from the fierce conflict of religious ideals, reason
itself, common sense, *was* an ideal. To solve problems,
not by the clash of swords nor the recital of rival creeds,
but by " sitting down in a cool hour " to think it out, was
a luxury that men would not readily forgo, and enthusiasm
was identified with fanaticism. But high poetry is born
of noble enthusiasms; and the romantic revival was in
its essence a passionate, and perhaps but partially successful, effort to recover ideals and enthusiasms—the worship
and not alone the description of nature; or the loyalties
of an older feudalism, " the pleasing illusions which made
power gentle and obedience liberal. . . . All the super-
added ideas, furnished from the wardrobe of a moral
imagination, which the heart owns and the understanding
ratifies as necessary to cover the defects of our naked,
shivering nature "; or the tenuous dreams of a golden
age, of human society reconstructed by the rule of love:

Years after years,
Through blood, and tears,
And a thick hell of hatreds, and hopes, and fears;
We waded and flew,
And the islets were few
Where the bud-blighted flowers of happiness grew.

Our feet now, every palm,
Are sandalled with calm,
And the dew of our wings is a rain of balm;
And beyond our eyes,
The human love lies
Which makes all it gazes on Paradise.

Of this new spirit, this reawakening of passionate thinking, contemptuous of the "cool hour" and its formulated deductions, Blake's art and poetry is only not a typical because it is an extreme, or complete expression. If there is in our literature an inspired poet and painter it is Blake, and alike the greatness and the failure of his achievement compel one to ponder the nature and the value of inspiration in poetry and art.

For there is a sense in which Gray and Blake and every one who is, in any measure, a true poet is inspired. "All good poets", says Socrates in the *Ion*, "epic as well as lyric, compose their beautiful poems not as works of art but because they are inspired and possessed. And as the Corybantian revellers when they dance are not in their right mind, so the lyric poets are not in their right mind when they are composing their beautiful strains: but when falling under the power of music and metre they are inspired and possessed; like Bacchic maidens who draw milk and honey from the rivers, when they are under the influence of Dionysus, but not when they are in their right mind. And the soul of the lyric poet does the same, as they themselves tell us; for they tell us that they gather their strains from honeyed fountains and dells of the Muses; thither, like the bees, they wing their way. And this is true. For the poet is a light and winged and holy thing, and there is no invention in him until he has been inspired and is out of his senses, and the mind is no longer in him: when he has not attained to this state he is powerless and unable to utter his oracles." "Art is inspiration", says Blake. "When Michael Angelo or Raphael or Mr. Flaxman does any of his fine things he does them in the spirit."

But there would seem to be two kinds or measures of inspiration suggested by Plato's words; and these may co-operate but may also occasionally conflict  Plato's lyric poets fell " under the power of music " and so became inspired.  Well, the gift of musical utterance is itself an inspiration, and so much inspiration every poet must have, Pope and Gray as well as Milton and Blake, the poet whose ideal is to put into verse

> What oft was thought, but ne'er so well express'd,

and not only the poet to whom the Muse dictates oracles. The poet is born subject to the spell of rhythmical words, as the born artist is one who has from the beginning the native aptitude and the strong propensity to reproduce and express himself in forms suggested by those he sees around him in nature:

> Why did I write?   What sin to me unknown
> Dipped me in ink?   My parents', or my own?
> As yet a child, nor yet a fool to fame,
> I lisped in numbers, for the numbers came.

Inspiration in one sense of the word is simply an inborn aptitude and propensity to do certain things comparatively easily and well which others do only under compulsion, painfully and imperfectly; and it is not only poets and artists but, shall we say, mathematicians, physicists, and philosophers who may be so inspired. Pascal working out the proposition regarding the squares on the sides of a right-angled triangle; Clerk-Maxwell worrying his infant mind as to how the wheels go round, these are following the "strong propension" of their nature as certainly as Milton or Pope.   "This problem", says Mr. Sturge Moore, "comes first in æsthetics: Is a poet more essentially one to whom a loved language suggests thoughts worthy of it, or one whom beautiful thoughts compel to find harmonious words?   Is the fundamental artist enabled, by minute capacity for controlling lines and spaces, to give them significance as patterns or as representation, or is he such a lover of what he sees that he must draw it, though he has to begin without any skill?"   This comes dangerously near asking whether the hen or the egg comes first, for feeling and the capacity to express act and react upon one another, and the perception of beautiful form, in the muscular adjustments and rhythms which that perception requires, is already in the nature of a creative act.   "We are all poets", says Carlyle, "when we read a poem well.   The ' imagination that shudders at the Hell of Dante '—is not that the same faculty, weaker in degree, as Dante's own? "

Yet Mr. Sturge Moore's question does help us to distinguish between poet and poet, artist and artist.   It is the difference between his own conception of a poet and that of his friend Dolben which the Poet Laureate refers to in words quoted above.   For himself poetry "was an art which I hoped to learn. . . . I did not suppose that the poet's emotions were in any way better than mine nor mine than another's.   I think that Dolben imagined poetic form to be the naïve outcome of peculiar

personal emotion." That was Blake's conviction alike
as poet and painter. The inspiration of some poets is,
as Carlyle would have it always be, not merely a capacity
to express their feeling in beautiful and musical form, to
tell us

What oft was thought, but ne'er so well express'd,

but a message, a burden, a new insight, at least a greater
depth of feeling. The poet may also be the Vates, the
prophet. It may be that Herrick when he wrote " Sweet
daffodils " was not inspired by any deeper appreciation of
the beauty of the flower than has been felt by many
another who has never written a line of verse; what
inspired him was the discovery of a new and bewitching
rhythm. It may be that when Dante says " I am one
who when love inspires me mark it well, and according
as it dictates to my heart, set it forth to the world ":

Che ditta dentro vo significando;

it may be that he is distinguishing his art, the " dolce stil
nuovo ", from that of more conventional followers of
the Provençal ritual, not claiming that he is a truer lover
than many another who never spake his love:

As though a tongueless nightingale should swell
Her throat in vain, and die, heart-stifled, in her dell.

But there are other poets who write under the burning
conviction that they have a new revelation to make, of
the message of nature, of the significance of love, of the
being and character of God, of the destiny of men.

Are then all prophets poets? Not certainly if we
understand by poetry the expression of our thoughts in
a definite form, according to some accepted convention

of form, metre as we understand it, or in all the different fashions which usage has fixed in China, or Japan, or Burma, or in Hebrew poetry.   The greatest of the Hebrew prophets were poets as well as prophets; Ezekiel, whose visions are as imaginative and vivid as, if more comprehensible than, Blake's, wrote mainly in prose.   If ever man was prophetically inspired, it was St. Paul, and his style, in its greatest passages, on Charity or the Resurrection, has all the qualities of poetry but the pattern, yet it is prose, and the prose of one who reasons. For the prophet the first thing is the idea, not the form, the thought which has suddenly for him illuminated the problem of life and reconciled its painful contradictions. Whatever supernatural incidents may have attended Paul's conversion one thing is certain, he had discovered in the death and resurrection of Christ a new and illuminating reading of the riddle of human history: " As in Adam all died, so in Christ shall all be made alive ".   But Mahomet had a similar inspiration; and Rousseau passed through an experience not unlike Paul's.   " If ever anything resembled a sudden inspiration it was the movement which began in me as I read this.   All at once I felt myself dazzled by a thousand sparkling lights; crowds of vivid ideas thronged into my mind with a force and confusion that threw me into unspeakable agitation;   I felt my head whirling in a giddiness like that of intoxication.   A violent palpitation oppressed me;   unable to walk for difficulty of breathing I sank under one of the trees of the avenue, and passed half an hour there in such a condition of excitement that when I arose I saw that the front of my waistcoat was all wet with my tears, though I was wholly unconscious of shedding them.

Ah, if ever I could have written the quarter of what I saw and felt under that tree, with what clearness should I have brought out all the contradictions of our social system; with what simplicity I should have demonstrated that man is good naturally and that it is by institutions only he is made bad." So Rousseau became a prophet:

> For then he was inspired and from him came,
> As from the Pythian's mystic cave of yore,
> Those oracles which set the world in flame,
> Nor ceased to burn till kingdoms were no more.

It was a like spirit that descended upon William Blake.

That Blake was an inspired poet and artist in the first sense of the word is as obvious, from the best of his poems and pictures, as is the same inspiration in the work of Milton and Gray and Keats and, say, Reynolds or Gainsborough, though each of these attained to a higher level and wider range of virtuosity than Blake's impatient spirit permitted to him. For on Blake fell this weight of a prophetic inspiration, of the same kind as that which came on Isaiah and Paul, on Mahomet and Rousseau, and the study of Blake's work alike as poet and painter is a consideration of the mutual actions and reactions of his inspiration and training as an artist and his inspiration as a prophet burning with a message he desires to communicate. It will make clear what were the great qualities that a passionate inspiration gave that work but also its power to shatter and disperse.

He had the inspiration which is at once a natural aptitude and an aspiration after perfection of craftsmanship. It is the born artist who knows how bad his first work is, who is willing to learn from others,

and in the pursuit of an adequate form to take infinite
pains:

> For how severely with themselves proceed
> The men, who write such verse as we can read!

> I said: It's certain there is no fine thing
> Since Adam's fall but needs much labouring.

And Blake studied his art, and found the models that
appealed to his own genius, as poet and designer, in the
same quarter—in the art of the Middle Ages as he contemplated that art in the Gothic tombs of Westminster
Abbey and in mediæval poetry as represented by the
poetry of the Elizabethans—for the art of the Renaissance was a splendid afterglow of the age of romance and
allegory—or as he discerned the faint ghosts of that
poetry evoked by Chatterton and Macpherson and Gray.

The *Poetic Sketches* of 1783 is a poet's sketch-book
in which we can note his early experiments and detect
his models.  Of some of the forms he essays his control
is uncertain.  He hesitates and even oscillates between
blank verse and cadenced, rhythmical prose such as that
of Macpherson or the poetical books of the Bible.  Some
of the pieces, indeed, which are printed as verse are purely
rhythmical prose.  The opening addresses, for example,
Spring, Summer, Winter, Autumn, are not in blank verse,
" with enjambment, studiously varied pause, epanaphora "
and all the other things of which Mr. Saintsbury tells us,
but Blake knew nothing.  They are pieces of rhythmical
prose, like others in this book and some of the later
Prophetic Books, disguised by being printed in lines
They read best when this arbitrary division is ignored:

O holy virgin! clad in purest white, unlock heav'n s
golden gates, and issue forth; awake the dawn that sleeps in
heaven; let light rise from the chambers of the east, and bring
the honied dew that cometh on waking day. O radiant
morning, salute the sun rous'd like a huntsman to the chase,
and with thy buskin'd feet appear upon our hills.

Much of the verse of *Edward III.* is of the same kind,
though here there is more effort to secure, occasionally
successfully, the pattern of varied but authentic verse.

Where Blake secures instant and complete success is
in song. There is something almost miraculous in the
manner in which Blake achieved alone and unaided the
purification of poetic diction and emancipation of rhythm
which Wordsworth, and even Coleridge, attained to by
prayer and fasting. Gray's effort to attain to " high
poetry " by taking thought for the diction had intensified
rather than weakened the hold of a poetic jargon on his
contemporaries and followers, the fondness for pompous
phraseology, " storied urn and animated bust ", " the
vernal year ",

> The captive linnet which enthrall?
> What idle progeny succeed
> To chase the rolling circle's speed,
> Or urge the flying ball?

Almost the only remnant of such jargon to be found
in Blake's early songs is the second line in

> With sweet May dews my wings were wet,
> And Phœbus fired my vocal rage.

Otherwise the diction of these poems is as pure as it is
musical. For none of the English poets of the century,

before Blake, could sing.    Even Collins's best ode, " How sleep the brave ", has nothing of the soar and sweetness of " My silks and fine array ", " I love the jocund dance ",

> Memory, hither come
> And tune your merry notes;

or the wonderful

> The wild winds weep
> And the night is a-cold;
> Come hither, Sleep,
> And my griefs unfold:
> But lo! the morning peeps
> . Over the eastern steeps,
> And the rustling birds of dawn
> The earth do scorn.

Even when Blake uses less Elizabethan, less winged lyrical measures, when he accepts the iambic movement of contemporary verse, the effect is different:

> How sweet I roam'd from field to field
> And tasted all the summer's pride,
> 'Till I the prince of love beheld
> Who in the sunny beams did glide!

or

> Whether on Ida's shady brow,
> Or in the chambers of the East,
> The chambers of the sun, that now
> From antient melody have ceas'd.

And all Gray's *arioso* and *bravura* effects sound strangely metallic beside

> Prepare, prepare the iron helm of war,
> Bring forth the lots, cast in the spacious orb;

> The Angel of Fate turns them with mighty hands,
> And casts them out upon the darken'd earth!
>                                    Prepare, prepare.

Here then was the young artist tuning his pipe, blowing not a few false notes, uttering some obscure and
ominous accents, but at his best evoking a clearer, sweeter
music than had been heard in English poetry for a century
past. And then on the poet, not yet fully master of his
art, inheriting no authentic tradition of high poetry,
descended the breath of another inspiration, the inspiration of the prophet; and the first effect was to give to
his songs a new and piercing sweetness, a more sonorous
splendour:

> Sweet, sweet, sweet, O Pan!
> Piercing sweet upon the river.
> Blinding sweet, O great God Pan!
> The sun on the hill forgot to die,
> And the lilies revived, and the dragon-fly
> Came back to dream on the river.

It would be hard indeed to imagine any poetry to which
that description applies more aptly than to the *Songs of
Innocence*. For these namby-pamby verses, songs in
which one hears a faint echo of Watts's hymns, this
"glorified nursery-babble", as Sir William Watson calls
it, are "high poetry", have at least one essential of high
poetry which Gray's brilliant odes lack. They are the
perfect expression of passionate feeling and passionate
thinking. These apparently simple songs blend in subtle
fashion the innocent joy of childhood on which has
fallen no shadow of distrust and inhibition, the echo of
that joy in the heart of those who have children and

remember their own childhood, the passionate reflection
of the seer on the significance of this early innocence
and joy and the fate that is in store for it.   The fate
that is in store for it, for the experience from which was
brewed the storm that awoke and transfigured Blake's
vision of life is not completed, though already foreshadowed,
in the *Songs of Innocence* taken by themselves.   Their
complement is the *Songs of Experience*.   *Songs of Innocence
and of Experience.   Shewing the Two Contrary States of
the Human Soul* is the full title which the poet gives to
the record of the fundamental experience from which
issued the Prophetic Books in a furious quest of a reading
of life and death, Heaven and Hell, that should harmonise
the painful antinomies of life, the contrast between the
innocence, joy, and confidence, seen in the child, and the
irrational sense of guilt, the haunting sorrow, the cramping
inhibitions of adolescence and maturity.   " God is all-
powerful, God is all-loving—and the world is what it
is!   How are you going to explain that? "   So said Lord
Salisbury, and so Blake felt, and the two volumes of
songs are his statement of the agitating problem which
in the Prophetic Books he undertook to solve.   Each song
of joy in the *Songs of Innocence* has its complement, its
painful corrective, in the later poems.   In poem after poem
Blake sets over against the mood which he has expressed
in the first its disillusioning counterpart, or weaves both
into the same poem.   The Nurse's song in the first
volume is full of sympathetic innocence and joy;  in the
second it is weighted with remorseful memories, a sense
of the bitterness and the illusion of life.   The first *Holy
Thursday* overflows with the joy of innocence and sublime
pity:

O what a multitude they seem'd, these flowers of London town!
Seated in companies they sit with radiance all their own.
The hum of multitudes was there, but multitudes of lambs,
Thousands of little boys and girls raising their innocent hands.

The second is filled with shame that such charity should
be needful·

> Is this a holy thing to see
> In a rich and fruitful land,
> Babes reduc'd to misery,
> Fed with cold and usurous hand?

As Wordsworth says in a similar mood:

> I've heard of hearts unkind, kind deeds
> With coldness still returning;
> Alas! the gratitude of men
> Hath oftener left me mourning.

In the first *Chimney Sweeper* Blake has tried to look at
life through the eyes of childhood with all its power of
illusion and hope:

> Tho' the morning was cold, Tom was happy and warm;
> So if all do their duty they need not fear harm.

In *London* he voices the sterner truth:

> I wander thro' each charter'd street,
> Near where the charter'd Thames does flow,
> And mark in every face I meet
> Marks of weakness, marks of woe.
>
> How the Chimney-sweeper's cry
> Every black'ning Church appalls;
> And the hapless Soldier's sigh
> Runs in blood down Palace walls.

Even Christian forbearance and forgiveness—in which
Blake was to find the deepest, indeed the only principle
of spiritual life—is perverted into a law from which flow
hypocrisy and hate.  Anger, what Bishop Butler calls
" righteous resentment ", is a just and natural emotion,
the proper precursor of forgiveness:

> I was angry with my friend:
> I told my wrath, my wrath did end.
> I was angry with my foe:
> I told it not, my wrath did grow.
>
> And I water'd it in fears,
> Night and morning with my tears;
> And I sunnèd it with smiles,
> And with soft deceitful wiles.
>
> And it grew both day and night,
> Till it bore an apple bright;
> And my foe beheld it shine,
> And he knew that it was mine,
>
> And into my garden stole
> When the night had veil'd the pole:
> In the morning glad I see
> My foe outstretch'd beneath the tree.

And nowhere is the canker of contradiction so deep-
seated, this conflict of passion and law, of pure and innocent
impulse with harsh and jealous inhibition, so cruelly
evident as in the garden of young love:

> I went to the Garden of Love,
> And saw what I never had seen:
> A Chapel was built in the midst,
> Where I used to play on the green.

And the gates of the Chapel were shut,
And " Thou shalt not " writ over the door;
So I turn'd to the Garden of Love
That so many sweet flowers bore;

And I saw it was fillèd with graves,
And tombstones where flowers should be;
And Priests in black gowns were walking their rounds,
And binding with briars my joys and desires.

Blake was not the first, nor is he the only poet, who has found the great enigma of life in the contrast between the innocent joy and confident trust in life and love of childhood and the disillusionment which experience brings—guilt, sorrow, disappointment, the discovery that there is apparently no purpose in life. It is one of the chief burdens of the verse and prose of Vaughan and Traherne in the seventeenth century:

Happy those early days when I
Shin'd in my Angel-Infancy.

It is the experience which troubled Wordsworth after the first glamour of the Revolution had passed, and before he too found "enlightenment". But Vaughan and Traherne had acquiesced, if they found no intellectual solution, in the orthodox interpretation of the enigma— Sin, the Fall of Man. "The desire satisfied is a Tree of Life", says Traherne; and this is Blake's doctrine too: "he who desires but acts not breeds pestilence". But Traherne's reading of the experience which has beset our desires with inhibitions of law and shame is not Blake's. "Being to lead this life within I was placed in Paradise with some advantages which the angels have

not. And being designed to Immortality . . . I was
to abide with God from everlasting to everlasting in all
His ways. But I was deceived by my appetite. Un-
gratefully I despised Him that gave my being. I offended
in an apple against Him that gave me the whole world:
But Thou, O Saviour, art here upon the Cross suffering
for my sins." Blake was not of the century of Calvin
but of Rousseau. His problem was Rousseau's, " Man
is born free and everywhere he is in chains ", interpreted
with a closer personal reference and in a more religious
spirit. He too believed in the Fall of Man and in Christ
the Saviour of Men. But it was not after the orthodox
fashion of Traherne that he conceived of the Fall and
its consequences. To desire, and therefore to eat, an
apple could hardly have been counted a sin by Blake; and
the God who condemned Adam and pardoned him only
in virtue of the sacrifice of another was not the God
revealed in Christ, the God of the Imagination and the
Heart. He was Jehovah the Leprous, the God of
Materialism and Jealous Laws. The Fall, to Blake
whose mind had been nourished on Swedenborg, his
imagination on Milton, was something greater than the
eating of an apple. It was the fall of Satan, not of Adam
and Eve, the revolt of the reason against the God who
is revealed in the imagination and the heart; and the
fruit of that revolt was this world of space and time,
this bondage within the five senses of which reason is
the ratio, this world of individuals at war with one another
and seeking protection from each other in jealous codes
of morality. Christ did not die, in our sense of the
word, to deliver us, but became alive, descended into this
world of the senses, in space and time, to teach us the

Q

new law which is the old law of freedom, love, and the mutual forgiveness of sins.   In Blake's picture Christ is nailed not to a dead but a living tree, the tree of vegetative life;  in Milton's words, he suffers

this earthy load
Of Death, called Life;  which us from Life doth sever.

And the message of Christ, the new life he gives, is not self-restraint and self-denial, it is love which is freedom and forgiveness:

> Love to faults is always blind;
> Always is to joy inclin'd,
> Lawless, wing'd and unconfin'd,
> And breaks all chains from every mind.

Men are admitted into heaven, not because they have curbed and governed their passions, or have no passions, but because they have cultivated their understandings.   The treasures of heaven are not negations of passion, but realities of intellect, from which the passions emanate, uncurbed in their eternal glory.   The fool shall not enter into heaven let him be ever so holy:  holiness is not the price of entrance into heaven.   Those who are cast out are all those who, having no passions of their own, because no intellect, have spent their lives in curbing and governing other people's by the various arts of poverty and cruelty of all kinds.   The modern church crucifies Christ with the head downwards.

But our immediate concern is not with Blake's Gnostic and mystical philosophy of life, but with its effect upon his art, and first as a poet.   For to read the *Songs of Innocence* and the *Songs of Experience* with Gray's Odes is to realise what Gray, with all his command of a magnificent technique, yet wanted to be able to write " high poetry ". " Out of the mouths of babes and sucklings thou hast perfected praise." These simple lyrics of the *Songs of Innocence* have one essential quality of " high poetry " which *The Progress of Poesy* lacks, a profound and passionate inspiration, an imaginative vision; and the form is adequate, at once sweet and prevailing. And as the inspiration deepens, as the feeling and thought gain in compass, the style and verse promise to become more sonorous and elaborate:

> O Earth, O Earth return!
> Arise from out the dewy grass;
>  Night is worn,
>  And the morn
> Rises from the slumberous mass.
>
> Turn away no more;
> Why wilt thou turn away?
>  The starry floor,
>  The wat'ry shore,
> Is giv'n thee till the break of day.

" I think ", says Mr. Saintsbury, " I would rather have written these lines than anything in English poetry outside of Shakespeare "; and Swinburne is eloquent in their praise: " No possible effect of verse can be finer in a great, brief way. . . . It recalls within one's ear the long relapse of recoiling water and wash of the refluent wave, in the third and fourth lines sinking and suppressed as with equal pulses of soft sobbing music of ebb, to climb again in the fifth line with a rapid clamour of ripples and strong ensuing strain of weightier sound, lifted with the lift of the ringing and running sea."

There may be a touch of exaggeration in this; at any

rate, Blake was not to fulfil the promise of attaining to
a richer and ampler measure in which to utter his high
thoughts.   His achievement as a metrist was not to
extend beyond the compass of his delicate and exquisite
lyrics, and even these, alas!  were to grow ever fewer and
more fragmentary.    It is clear enough why.   The indignation of the prophet, his exalted and even arrogant
confidence in the message of which he believes himself
to be the bearer, is making the poet indifferent to form.
At moments the singer and the prophet become one and
the old charm returns as in:

> Ah, Sunflower! weary of time,
> Who countest the steps of the Sun;
> Seeking after that sweet golden clime,
> Where the traveller's journey is done;
>
> Where the Youth pined away with desire,
> And the pale Virgin shrouded in snow,
> Arise from their graves, and aspire
> Where my Sunflower wishes to go.

But the prophet is too impatient for the artist.   A lyric
will open perfectly:

> Silent, Silent Night,
> Quench the holy light
> Of thy torches bright;

and will end almost hideously.   These measures are not
for these moods; the lyric form will not bear the strong,
fiercely fermenting wine that is poured into them.   But
Blake had not mastered a more adequate form.   If
Gray's poetry wants the *inspiration*, the passionate thinking, of "high poetry", Blake failed in the end to attain

to the *form*, the art, the music, of "high poetry". But both are essential. The Greek choral ode, the odes of Pindar, the Italian canzone, the paragraphs of *Lycidas*, the blank verse of Shakespeare's tragedies and Milton's epics are the historic witness to the need of great forms for great themes: "excellentissima excellentissimis digna sunt", as Dante says in selecting the *canzone* as the fittest form for poetry inspired by the greatest subjects. You cannot make the great forms stand alone, like an empty crinoline, as eighteenth-century writers of blank verse and Pindaric odes came near to thinking; but Gray's was a just instinct, and the beauty and dignity of his workmanship almost disguise the insufficiency of the inspiration—but not quite, and hence Johnson's complaint of a certain strain on the part of the poet, "an unnatural violence.

> Double, double, toil and trouble."

Blake's poetic instinct indeed told him that his deepening inspiration, his fuller message, demanded a more adequate form, measures of richer and ampler compass in which to communicate itself. *The Everlasting Gospel* is the nearest approach to a poem great in compass as in content; and the fervour and beauty of thought raises ever and again the language to a piercing felicity, but only for a line or two. The reeds are shattered by the prevailing breath, the stormy gusts of the prophetic spirit; and the poem remains a series of fragments, of fresh starts that at once break down:

> Dissiluere tamen rupta compage, nec ultra
> Ferre graves potuere sonos.

And Blake turned to his early love, rhythmical prose, or rather, as Professor Saintsbury admits, "what is neither

pure verse nor pure though rhythmical prose, but a
hybrid between them "; but that is to admit Blake's
failure to achieve definiteness and sureness of form.   He
achieves, indeed, occasional success in both directions, in
what is essentially metrical, and in rhythmical prose.   In
the tender and delicate *Book of Thel* Blake at least almost
achieves a *vers libre* that is satisfying throughout.   Now
and again in the wilder Prophetic Books he writes beautiful
rhythmical prose:

Thou hearest the Nightingale begin the Song of Spring:
The Lark sitting upon his earthly bed, just as the morn
Appears, listens silent, then, springing from the waving Corn-
     field! loud
He leads the Choir of Day: trill, trill, trill, trill,
Mounting upon the wings of Light into the Great Expanse,
Re-echoing against the lovely blue and shining heavenly Shell,
His little throat labours with inspiration; every feather
On throat and breast and wings vibrates with the effluence
     Divine:
All Nature listens silent to him, and the awful Sun
Stands still upon the Mountain looking on this little Bird'
With eyes of soft humility and wonder, love and awe.
Then loud from their green covert all the Birds begin their Song:
The Thrush, the Linnet, and the Goldfinch, Robin and the Wren
Awake the Sun from his sweet reverie upon the Mountain:
The Nightingale again assays his song and thro' the day
And thro' the night warbles luxuriant: every Bird of Song
Attending his loud harmony with admiration and love.

Such a passage loses far more than it gains by the
division into lines, and the eccentricities of Blake's
punctuation.   But it is an oasis in pages of writing too
vehement and impetuous to attain to form and rhythm.

Much has been and much will be written on the interpretation and appreciation of the Prophetic Books. One
suspects that little will come of it. The final impression
on a candid mind is of certain great central ideas, ideas of
profound significance, which I shall analyse later, stated
with force in the abrupt prose of *The Marriage of Heaven
and Hell*, and then repeated and repeated in declamatory
or symbolic form. If Blake failed to achieve " high
poetry " on a greater scale than the lyrics—lyrics unique
in their combination of spiritual and rhythmical beauty—
it was perhaps because his message was revealed to himself in fleeting visions. His worth as a prophet would
have been greater had his lyrics been supplemented not
by the chaotic Prophetic Books but by—if not a reasoned,
yet a coherent statement of the content of his message—
a drama like that of the Book of Job, a Gospel like that
of St. John.

The history of Blake's art as a designer and illustrator
is not unlike the history of his poetical career; with this
great difference that in this field Blake's latest work was
his greatest, and this too is not without significance for
such a study of the elements, the factors in high poetry
and high art as the juxtaposition of Gray and Blake,
of Blake and Reynolds, forces upon the mind. The
inspiration of the artist as well as that of the poet Blake
undoubtedly possessed, the native aptitude and the strong
propensity to express himself in form and colour; and
the artist's training is a better understood, more settled,
less self-imposed thing than that of the poet. Of the
technique of engraving he became under Basire's teaching
a careful and accomplished master; and Mr. Basil de

Sélincourt, a severe and not too sympathetic critic, believes that this training " was the means of preserving . . . the citadel of his material imagination ". " But for his regular employment as an engraver the lyric spontaneity of his early designs would have followed the same course as that of the text which they accompanied; instead of reaching the climax of his power in the illustrations to *Jerusalem* and the *Book of Job* he would probably have come to lose himself more and more in wild and vague symbolical complexities."

For Blake was as impatient a student of drawing and colouring as of the technique of poetry. " Practice and opportunity ", he declared, " very soon teach the language of art. Its spirit and poetry, centred in the imagination alone, never can be taught; and these make the artist." It is not thus that the greatest of imaginative artists have regarded the technical side of their work, the mastery over the stubborn material which alone will make it possible to communicate their imaginative inspiration to others or to themselves—to themselves also, for it is only in its realisation in material form that the imagination discovers the whole content and significance of its inspiration. It is in no slavish spirit of imitation that the great painters and great sculptors, Michael Angelo or Rodin, have toiled unweariedly to reproduce the multiform appearances of Nature; it is to learn from her the secrets of expressive form that they might the better express their own visions. Even a great genius must learn the grammar of his art. " The words of the poet are not merely symbols "—and the same is true of the artist's design, and forms and colours—" of what he wishes to say, they *are* what he wishes to say." And Blake himself is aware of this truth: " Invention depends altogether upon execution or organisations ", " Execution is the Chariot of Genius ", " grandeur of ideas is founded on precision of ideas ". But his temperament was too impatient to submit to the discipline of which freedom is born; he distrusted too much (even while he unconsciously succumbed to it) the inspiration of " Dame Memory and her Siren daughters "; he was too ready to attribute to his own works the qualities he knew good work should have, " precision ", " clear colours ", " determinate lineaments ". The result is seen in his actual achievement as judged by a sympathetic and understanding critic. " Between Blake and Michael Angelo ", says Mr. Arthur Symons, " is the difference between the artist in whom imagination overpowers technique, as awe overpowers the senses, and the artist in whom imagination gives new life to technique."

To do justice to Blake's earlier work, his illustrations to Gray and Young, one must recognise that his faults are not due only to failure in command of his instrument. He is endeavouring after something new in technique, an endeavour the final outcome of which was the illustrations to *Jerusalem*, and Dante, and the *Book of Job*. Blake's inaccurate drawing of the human form is not due entirely to incapacity or incomplete training. He is not trying to be accurate. He is trying to use the forms of " vegetative nature ", to express thoughts that transcend nature. Like the poet he transfigures his representations to make them the vehicle of his emotions. Blake is the first of modern artists, the first rebel against the Renaissance imitation of nature. Unfortunately his temperament is impatient, the pressure of his prophetic burden is too

insistent, and he has no tradition to guide him.    Yet in
his greatest work he succeeded, fitfully, but splendidly.

The Hogarth tradition of satiric realism made no
appeal to Blake; and the graces and grandeurs of Reynolds
aroused his fury.    Reynolds's pictures, still more his
artistic doctrines, affected him as one thinks Gray's Odes
might have done had he considered them as carefully, or
had Gray lectured upon poetry in the spirit in which he
worked.    "Burke's Treatise on the Sublime and Beautiful", he wrote, "is founded on the opinions of Newton
and Locke.    On this Treatise Reynolds has grounded
many of his assertions in all his Discourses.    I read
Burke's Treatise when very young, at the same time I
read Locke on Human Understanding and Bacon's
Advancement of Learning.    On Everyone of these Books
I wrote my Opinions, and on looking them over find that
my Notes on Reynolds in this Book are exactly similar.
I felt the same Contempt and Abhorrence then that I
do now.    They mock Inspiration and Vision.    Inspiration and Vision was then and now is and I hope always
will remain my Element, my Eternall Dwelling-Place—
how can I then hear it Contemned without returning
Scorn for Scorn? "

Reynolds and Gray, in their art, have much in common.
" Reynolds' talent ", says a French critic, " is a magnificent victory of the will;    that of Gainsborough the
spontaneous unfolding of a flower."    Reynolds's pictures
were the outcome of native genius disciplined by the
analysis and study of the great painters.    " Even when
painting the most graceful lady, the most English—in
other words, the brightest and freshest—of boys, Reynolds
never became so lost in his models as to forget the old

masters." How like Gray's relation to Horace and
Pindar, Shakespeare and Milton! And, like Gray,
Reynolds was unwearied in his pursuit of perfection of
technique. His experiments, many of them so disastrous,
in pigments and vehicles and methods were all the result
of his pursuit of finer effects in colour and light and shade.
" My frequent alterations arose from a fine taste, which
could not acquiesce in anything short of a high degree
of excellence." And Reynolds, like Gray, has had the
reward that will always attend infinite labour guided by
a strong native aptitude and genuine artistic inspiration.
But, like Gray, Reynolds hankered after a higher and
diviner art than that in which his happiest work was
done. " The Grand Style " of which he had so much
to say in his *Addresses* and of which the historic pieces
(Is not Gray's *Bard* an historic piece in the grand style?)
were his own examples, " Ugolino ", the " Nativity ",
" Cardinal Beaufort ", the " Infant Jupiter ". Contemporary critics spoke of " the visionary and awful
effect " of his Macbeth, " the pathos and force of expression " of Ugolino, the " gravity and simplicity " of his
Nativity. But of the authentically sublime, of the power,
not only to delight, but to move and to beget thought,
Reynolds was, it may be, even less a master than Gray.
His Ugolino and Gray's lines on Richard's death, which
Blake has illustrated:

> Close by the regal chair
> Fell Thirst and Famine scowl
> A baleful smile upon their baffled Guest,

these need only to be put beside Dante's own great lines
to reveal what it was Blake felt the want of in Reynolds

as in the poetry of his contemporaries. Gray's Odes
with all their indubitable excellences are not "high
poetry" of the same kind as Dante's, and Milton's, and
the Book of Job; and Reynolds's "grand style" is not
the grand style of Michael Angelo. Reynolds's example
and precepts led to the dull work of Blake's contemporaries,
"the absurd and monstrous Italianism which soon
enveloped English art and suffocated it". So Gray is
responsible for Mason and the rest,—all the terrible
Pindaric odes and much of the poetical jargon that none
of the romantics except Blake escaped from altogether
at setting out. What he felt the want, the total want,
of in the art as in the poetry of his contemporaries was the
quality of which he was himself possessed in the fullest
measure, Imagination. And if he achieved little that
was perfect, he brought back that priceless and essential
quality into both poetry and art, and the little that is best
is beyond all praise. The best of Blake's lyrics are not
surpassed even by those of Shelley in perfect union of
soul and form—a more human soul, a simpler and equally
spontaneous and exquisite form—and the imaginative
quality in the best of Blake's designs silences criticism of
their technical defects.

Blake's art is the art of the illustrator. It is impossible
to separate his designs from the idea they are intended to ·
communicate, and he brought two things into illustration
that no English illustration had yet revealed an inkling
of—decorative quality and imaginative interpretation. In
the illuminated printing of the *Songs of Innocence*, *Songs
of Experience*, *Heaven and Hell*, *Jerusalem*, the illustrated
page became again, what it had been in the beautiful
Missals of the Middle Ages, a decorative whole of which

text and design are alike parts, and this wholeness of
design and charm of intricate detail are the characteristics of all his best illustrative pages.  And the other
quality of his illustrations is their imaginative rendering
in another medium of the passionate significance of the
poem or Biblical text that in illustrating he is interpreting.
His designs stand to the poem, the thought and feeling
of the poem, in the same relation as the poet's own imagery,
the metaphors with which he makes vivid or transfigures,
by transmission through his own heated imagination, the
thought he would communicate in all its intense significance.  Some of Blake's designs are metaphors made visible
by another art than the poet's—the design to Psalm xviii.
16: " He sent from above, he took me, he drew me out
of many waters ", or that to Shakespeare's *Macbeth* i. vii.
21-25:

> And Pity, like a naked new-born babe,
> Striding the blast, or heaven's cherubin, hors'd
> Upon the sightless couriers of the air,
> Shall blow the horrid deed in every eye,
> That tears shall drown the wind,

or, perhaps the most magnificent of them all, that to Job,
" When the morning stars sang together, and all the sons
of God shouted for joy ".  In this volume he is happiest
when rendering Gray's most fanciful images, those that
gave most offence to Johnson.  In the engraved designs to
the *Book of Job* and the illustrations to Dante, Blake's
power as a great imaginative illustrator reached its height;
and this progress in his power of design, while he ceased
early to be a poet submitting to the conditions of poetic expression, enlarging and enriching the medium to suit his
growing sublimity of conception, is due, I suppose, to the

dominance in his nature of the eye, the visual capacity, and
to the early training and discipline he had received in the
art of engraving; and not least to the fact that in Job and
Dante he found many of his own deepest feelings about God
and Man, and Life and Death expressed in a more coherent
and intelligible and a more splendid poetry than his own.

The illustrations to Gray's poems, here for the first
time reproduced, have not all the interest of those to
Dante or the great series illustrating the *Book of Job*.
They belong to an earlier period, were executed about
the same time as the illustrations to Young's *Night
Thoughts*; and they were never engraved or Blake might
have corrected and improved much of the detail.    The
poem to Mrs. Flaxman with which the volume closes
indicates pretty clearly that they were executed as an
expression of his gratitude to Flaxman for the introduction to Hayley.    The lines are in the spirit of the letter
to Flaxman of September 12, 1800: "My dearest
Friend,—It is to you I owe all my present happiness.
It is to you I owe perhaps the principal happiness of my
life.    I . . . hope, now everything is nearly completed
for our removal to Felpham, that I shall see you on Sunday,
as we have appointed Sunday afternoon to call on Mrs.
Flaxman at Hampstead.    I send you a few lines, which
I hope you will excuse.    And as the time is arrived when
men shall again converse in Heaven and walk with angels,
I know you will be pleased with the intention, and hope
you will forgive the poetry.

*To My Dearest Friend, John Flaxman, These Lines:*

I bless thee, O Father of Heaven and Earth, that ever I saw
Flaxman's face.

Angels stand round my Spirit in Heaven, the blessed of Heaven
are my friends upon earth.
When Flaxman was taken to Italy, Fuseli was given to me for a
season,
And now Flaxman hath given me Hayley his friend to be mine,
such my lot upon Earth.
Now my lot in the Heavens is this, Milton lov'd me in childhood and shew'd me his face.
Ezra came with Isaah the Prophet, but Shakespeare in riper
years gave me his hand,
Paracelsus and Behmen appeared to me, terrors appeared in
the Heavens above,
And in Hell beneath, and a mighty and awful change threatened
the Earth.
The American war began.  All its dark horrors passed before
my face
Across the Atlantic to France.  Then the French Revolution
commenc'd in thick clouds,
And my Angels have told me that seeing such visions I could
not subsist on the Earth,
But by my conjunction with Flaxman, who knows to forgive
nervous fear."

This is an interesting testimony to Blake's friendship
for Flaxman, a friendship which by 1808 was suspended,
and to the reading and experiences that had shaped his
thought and coloured his imagination—Milton, the Bible,
Shakespeare, Paracelsus, and Böhme, the American War
and the French Revolution.  A book that impressed
Blake became for him a personality who appeared to him
in visions.  And in Flaxman he had a friend, not in his
art alone, but to some extent in his deeper thoughts and
feelings, for Flaxman was a Swedenborgian.  Among the
beautiful drawings of Flaxman which Sir Sidney Colvin

has reproduced are a few which, as he notes, are suggestive of Blake's prophetic designs.  A careful study
of them suggests that, if Blake was a much less exact
draughtsman than his friend, the power of his designs
is not altogether unconnected with the bold and irregular
handling.

What suggested to Blake to try his hand at Gray's
poems we cannot say definitely, but it is not hard to con-
jecture.  Two qualities of Gray's poetry were of a kind
to appeal to Blake's imagination—Gray's imaginative and
finished personifications and his feeling for the romantic
element in older English history, and yet more in the
primitive imaginings of Celtic and Scandinavian myth
and poetry.  Personification was a favourite figure with
the poets of the eighteenth century, owing in large measure
to their admiration of Milton.  But their personifications
were so often conventional and frigid that Wordsworth
was tempted to condemn the figure altogether, though he
never did so either in theory or practice.  He did not,
however, except Gray's from his too sweeping condemnation of the poets against whom he was in revolt.  But
the whole bent of Blake's imagination was to personify.
For him every poignant experience became a spiritual
person.  Blake's imagination communicates an intenser
life to Gray's half-conventional personifications, " fair
Venus' train ", the " antic sports and blue-eyed pleasures ",
Hyperion's march and " glittering shafts of war "; a
horror which is excessive, spook-like, to " the vultures
of the mind " and " the painful family of death ".

The other interest in Gray's poems for Blake is the
romantic history in *The Bard*.  As early as 1785 Blake
had exhibited at the Royal Academy water-colour exhibi-

tion a tempera painting of "The Bard" along with subjects from the story of Joseph. To Blake, it is clear, the romantic interest in early history, which Percy and Macpherson, Mallet and Chatterton and Gray had awakened, was more than a quickened sense of the strange and the picturesque. He read the ancient history of Albion as he had read the stories in the Bible. All history, ancient and modern, had for Blake a mythical cast, and the figures of the bard and the prophet were the most majestic in history. He was one of the last persons for whom the old mythical and legendary, Geoffrey of Monmouth history, with which he was familiar, perhaps, from Milton's version of it, had at least a mysterious truth and significance, and there are glimmerings in his works of the lost tribes of Israel dream. His early dramatic fragment, *Edward III.*, closes with a Minstrel's song:

O sons of Trojan Brutus, cloath'd in war,
Whose voices are the thunders of the field,
Rolling dark clouds o'er France . . .

Your ancestors came from the fires of Troy,
(Like lions rous'd by lightning from their dens,
Whose eyes do glare against the stormy fires),
Heated with war, fill'd with the blood of Greeks,
With helmets hewn, and shields covered with gore,
In navies black, broken with wind and tide:

They landed in firm array upon the rocks
Of Albion: they kiss'd the rocky shore;
" Be thou our mother and our nurse," they said;
" Our children's mother, and thou shalt be our grave,
The sepulchre of ancient Troy, from whence
Shall rise cities, and thrones, and arms, and awful powers

R

Our fathers swarm from the ships. Giant voices
Are heard from the hills, the enormous sons
Of Ocean run from rocks and caves; wild men
Naked and roaring like lions, hurling rocks,
And wielding knotty clubs, like oaks entangled
Thick as a forest, ready for the axe.

.    .    .    .    .    .    .

Liberty shall stand on cliffs of Albion,
Casting her blue eyes over the green ocean;
Or tow'ring upon the roaring waves,
Stretching her mighty spear o'er distant lands;
While, with her eagle wings, she covereth
Fair Albion's shore and all her families.

But Blake's patriotism is a mystical and spiritual
patriotism. The Emanation, the finer spirit, the Imagination of Albion is Jerusalem, a city not builded with hands:

Jerusalem the emanation of the Giant Albion! Can it
be? Is it a Truth that the Learned have explored? Was
Britain the primitive sect of the patriarchal religion? . . . It
is true, and cannot be controverted. Ye are united, O ye
Inhabitants of the Earth, in One Religion—the Religion of
Jesus: the most Ancient, the Eternal, and the Everlasting
Gospel. The Wicked will turn it to Wickedness, the
Righteous to Righteousness. Amen! Hurra! Selah! All
things begin and end in Albion's Ancient Druid Rocky Shore.

Of these deeper feelings there is little trace in the
drawings to Gray's poem, for there was little in Gray's
eloquent text-book history to elicit them, and Blake is a
faithful illustrator. If Gray's poem had touched a deeper
chord, Blake's imagination and art would have responded.
Yet there is a touch of sincerer faith in Blake's bard and
prophetic oak and slumbering hurricane than in Gray's,

and careless as the drawing may be, Blake's pictures catch
perhaps more of the spirit of Scandinavian Edda-poetry
than Gray's polished renderings which called forth so
many banal imitations. The picture of Grief among
the roots of Trees which precedes the Ode to Adversity
strikes a mystical note which is not in Gray.

And what were these "deepest feelings about God
and Man and Life and Death", what were the ideas which
so agitated the soul of Blake and burdened his mind,
that all his work as an artist and poet became a passionate attempt to give them utterance, so that his poems
and his designs alike give the impression of a confused
and uncertain blend of tremendous imaginative power and
an almost puerile inefficiency; and the Prophetic Books
present the appearance of a furious welter of unintelligible
figures engaged in endless and bewildering conflicts,
embracements, and parturitions, that one is tempted at
every moment to say this is the voice of madness and
checked in doing so by the emergence of passages of
amazing beauty and wisdom and yet more by the
growing awareness of a method, if an indiscoverable
method, in this madness, a certain texture of thought
and vision, controlling and directing the furious chaos
through which Blake is borne in the bark of his
inspiration and conviction like the poet in Shelley's
*Alastor*:

> A whirlwind swept it on,
> With fierce gusts and precipitating force,
> Through the white ridges of the chafèd sea.
> The waves arose.   Higher and higher still
> Their fierce necks writhed beneath the tempest's scourge
> Like serpents struggling in a vulture's grasp?

Of the exponents of Blake's thought the wisest have
been content to be incomplete, to sketch the main out-
lines without attempting to find the explanation of every
detail in his symbolism, to supply an answer to every
enigma; and the reader who is not himself a mystic
will find his safest guide in M. Berger, who combines a
delicate sympathy with all that is best in Blake with the
loyalty of a Frenchman to good sense and lucidity that
is altogether delightful. In reading the expositions of
other critics and editors—even Mr. S. Foster Damon—
one is too often reminded of Byron's comment on
Coleridge:

> Explaining Metaphysics to the nation—
> I wish he would explain his Explanation.

They are themselves mystics and intelligible only to
each other or to themselves. And yet there is much
in Blake that even the plain man may understand. He
has emphasised certain essential truths whether we can
apprehend or accept the deductions which he draws from
them or not. Two main thoughts run through Blake's
agitated, visionary comment on life, of which one is a
corollary from a particular aspect of the other. The
enigma of life, the fundamental contradiction in which
life is involved, the two sides of which Blake has set
forth in *The Songs of Innocence* and *The Songs of Experience*, consists in the fact that the spirit of man is profoundly divided against itself. The soul of man has
many sides or states or faculties (as the old psychologists
termed them), and these, which should be in harmony,
are at war with one another. What seems to one a true
law of life is to the other false or inadequate. Reason,

which is at least a great disinfectant, has cleared the world of man's consciousness of devils and dreams and ghosts, has ordered and organised his experience, yet seems at times to leave the heart and the imagination without a home:

> Le silence éternel de ces espaces infinis m'effraie;

Freedom is won, and what does Freedom bring us to? It brings us face to face with atheistic science. The faith in God and immortality which we had been striving to clear from superstition suddenly seems to be in the air; and in seeking for a firm basis for faith we find ourselves in the midst of the fight with death.

But the imagination may find itself at war with the heart too, when the devotion to a larger, a more all-embracing vision is inhibited by obligations to, and affection for, narrower circles:

> But he answered and said unto him that told him, Who is my mother? and who are my brethren? And he stretched forth his hand toward his disciples, and said, Behold my mother and my brethren! For whosoever shall do the will of my Father which is in heaven, the same is my brother, and sister, and mother.

Beauty at once awakens and is itself revealed by love; and yet beauty can apparently become divorced from love and inspire lust, which is desire without love:

> The expense of spirit in a waste of shame;

and in consequence love, the intensest, the freest, the most self-transcending of our passions, finds itself beset with shame and ascetic inhibitions and controlled in its working by laws and customs. Inspiration is the soul of poetry and art, yet poetry and art have often become the slaves of tradition and convention and derided inspiration:

> Whether on crystal rocks ye rove,
>     Beneath the bosom of the sea,
> Wandering in many a coral grove,
>     Fair Nine, forsaking Poetry:
>
> How have you left the ancient love
>     That bards of old enjoyed in you!
> The languid strings do scarcely move!
>     The sound is forced, the notes are few!

But the fundamental cleavage is that between imagination and reason, for the state of mind in which the contradictions of the human spirit are most completely transcended is the vision of the poet and prophet and artist. The fall of man has its source in the tyranny of reason, which has set itself above the other faculties, reason or the calculating faculty, whether as revealed in modern, materialistic science or a materialised, moralised religion with its jealous codes and threatened penalties. Hence the world of illusion in which we live, the vegetative world of separate personalities, each crying, like the daughters of the horse-leech, " Give, Give ", and so for ever at war with one another, whether on the battlefield or in the law courts, or in church councils and formulated creeds crying anathema. Satan is the abstract limit of opaque individuality turning for ever on himself. To Adam, the earthly man, God in mercy has set a limit of contraction, left to him a spark of the imagination which transcends self; and Christ, perfect God because perfect Man, has saved men not by dying but by living for them, by coming into this vegetative world of illusion to teach

us the law of life and of immortality, to live by imagination, which transcends self and makes inevitable the
mutual forgiveness of sins; to live by faith, knowing that
this world is a world of illusion, behind which lies a great
reality:

> The Door of Death is made of gold
> That mortal eyes cannot behold,
> But when the Mortal Eyes are closed,
> And cold and pale the limbs reposed,
> The Soul awakes and wondering sees
> In her mild hand the golden Keys:
> The Grave is Heaven's golden Gate.

But Christ is within us, the source of the eternal protest
which the imagination—and imagination, unlike reason
and sense, is not a "state", a faculty, it is the whole
spirit of man—sustains against reason, both the abstrac-
tions of science and the inhibitions of morality. "The
Eternal Body of Man is the Imagination. That is God
Himself, the Divine Body, Jesus. We are his members."
Los, the Imagination as it lives and moves in poets and
artists and prophets, is ever building the City of Gol-
gonooza, which is the never-perfected counterpart of
that New Jerusalem which lies behind the veil of illusion,
the city of the Perfect Man in whom the warfare is over,
reason and passion and sense have surrendered their
abstract claims, absorbed into the full life of the spirit,
restored to the innocent joy of childhood. Urizen,
repentant, acknowledges his error in that he has been

Through chaos seeking for delight and in spaces remote
Seeking the eternal which is always present to the wise,
Seeking for pleasure which unsought falls around the infant's path
And on the fleeces of mild flocks who neither care nor labour.

Such seems to me, putting it as simply as I can, the essence of Blake's thought disentangled from the welter of the Prophetic Books, and I have made no effort to follow up the endless conflicts of Los and Enitharmon, Luvah and Vala, Urizen and Ahania, Tharmas and Enion. Two thoughts, among many, suggest themselves that there is no room to develop fully. The first thought is that of Blake's relation to Milton, the degree to which his imagination is penetrated by that great, strange poem *Paradise Lost*, that perhaps we are only beginning to understand. He saw clearly enough, and he states it emphatically in *The Marriage of Heaven and Hell*, of what Milton had unintentionally made Satan a symbol, man's free spirit in revolt against the tyranny of a jealous omnipotence. But he saw the other side too, what Milton meant to make Satan, the type of perfect selfishness, boundless pride. The second thought which suggests itself is how entirely Blake's poetry is a microcosm of the romantic movement, how much it has in common with the deepest thought of the greater poets of the period, all of them in a measure prophets, as Blake defines the word, "a prophet is a seer, not an arbitrary dictator". For Wordsworth and Shelley and Keats imagination was the soul of man:

> Imagination, which in truth
> Is but another name for absolute power
> And clearest insight, amplitude of power,
> And Reason in her most exalted mood.

Whatever else it was, and however many forms it took, the romantic revival was a movement of the heart and imagination, a passionate quest for a more adequate and satisfying conception of life, something that had been lost with the disappearance of the great Catholic Faith and Philosophy of the Middle Ages and the disintegrating progress of physical science, the displacement of St. Thomas and Dante by Locke and Newton. They all, it may be, failed in the quest; the prophets have always failed. None of them, not Wordsworth, not Shelley, made a more passionate effort than Blake to understand what was amiss, to recover the lost truth. Through the agitations of the American War and the French Revolution, through the personal experiences of love and disappointment and recovered peace of mind, Blake came to a solution that gave him inward peace and joy in a new and personal revaluation of that Christianity on which Shelley turned his back. It was perhaps a wild and heretical reading of Christianity, savouring of gnosticism and antinomianism. It had its root in what was, in part, an illusion, Blake's belief in the innocence of children. St. Augustine saw the evidence of man's fallen nature in the passionate crying of an infant; and one may observe the working of the malevolent passions in a nursery and an infant school as well as in the world of men and women. If Blake was inspired, a philosopher and student of St. Thomas and Bonaventura has said to me, it was perhaps by the Devil. Perhaps; Blake thought charitably of the Devil. A wise Catholic would, I think, allow Blake a considerable degree of licence under the head of "invincible ignorance", for he has stated many truths that were worth restating, and he loved the Divine Christ and had in him no small measure of the spirit of Christ—the Christ who cast out those who bought and sold in the Temple, the Christ who let no " duty " stand between Him and doing the will of the Father:

> No Earthly Parents I confess:
> I am doing my Father's business;

the Christ who

> from the Adulterers turned away
> God's righteous Law that lost its Prey.

" I never," said his friend Linnell, " in all my conversations with him, could, for a moment, feel there was the least justice in calling him insane; he could always explain his paradoxes satisfactorily when he pleased, but to many he spoke so that ' hearing they might not hear '. He was more like the ancient patterns of virtue than I ever expected to see in this world; he feared nothing so much as being rich, lest he should lose his spiritual riches. He was at the same time the most sublime in his expressions, with the simplicity and gentleness of a child, though never wanting in energy when called for." The prophet was too much for the poet, and his work is fragmentary and imperfect. His attempt to write the history of the human spirit, its warfare and redemption, is chaotic and in great measure unintelligible. Yet he was an inspired poet, and his fault is that of the other great romantics, Wordsworth and Shelley. They had more to say than they would always be patient enough to shape perfectly. " Curb your imagination and load every rift with ore " were the wise words of the artist Keats to the prophet Shelley. But if a poet may be too much a prophet, may he not be too purely and cunningly an artist? Gray's inspiration was made sterile by his too learned regard for art. The pre-Raphaelites had all the art which Wordsworth and Byron and Shelley and Blake were too careless of. Their mediæval and Greek reproductions, their sonnets and sestine and canzoni are wonderful exotics. " I like exotics," Oscar Wilde said to the present writer on the one occasion on which he met him, and we spoke of Rossetti and Wordsworth; and who will deny their charm. But there is a fragrance of the wild flower which the exotic wants, and in poetry the source of that fragrance is love and sympathy:

Non satis est pulchra esse poemata, dulcia sunto.

1922.

# CLASSICAL
# AND ROMANTIC:

## A POINT OF VIEW

"CLASSICAL" and "Romantic", not meaning simply Greek and Roman art and literature on the one hand, Mediæval on the other, but used, as they have been since the so-called Romantic Revival, to indicate certain qualities which distinguish, not only periods of art and literature, but individual pictures and poems of the same epoch, it may be of to-day—these are terms no attempts to define which ever seem entirely convincing to oneself or others. "Thought-confounding words" Professor Elton calls them in a recently published lecture on the poetic romancers of the late nineteenth century—nor should I have been tempted to consider them afresh, in such an august environment and holding a lectureship bearing the name of one who was an enemy of the vague and the meaningless, did I not believe that the use of the terms has sprung from the effort to fix by the help of words certain real and recognisable—if elusive and difficult to define—aspects of art and literature which have at least an historical significance. It may prove on careful scrutiny that the words are not the best which could be used, that "romantic" at any rate is either too definite or too indefinite to indicate all I shall propose to bring under it, and yet we may agree that some words were needed to indicate what is a recurrent—or if that beg the question as to the future—has been a recurring sequence of tendencies in the actual history of thought and art and literature. My effort is in this essay—and I would stress the word, and ask you to remember that if I speak dogmatically it is to save time, and that my whole thesis is exploratory—my endeavour is to see the history of Western European literature in a perspective which seems to me valuable and has not, so far as I know, been attempted in so broad a fashion.

The *locus classicus* for the expression of the difficulty which every one has felt, as regards "romantic", since Goethe and Schiller, Hugo and Gautier, is probably that in De Musset's *Lettres de Dupuis et Cotonet*, in which, after various attempts to discover any consistency in the use of a word which at one moment is applied to a drama that neglects the Unities, or blends tragedy and comedy, or imitates English and German plays, at the next to a sunset seen across a river, they are instructed by M. Ducoudray, a magistrate of liberal tendencies, that Romanticism is a reactionary movement dating from the Restoration of the Bourbons, a sentimental revival of Mediæval Catholicism. De Musset has, of course, French romanticism in view; and Heine, speaking of the German movement, comes to the same conclusion: "What was the Romantic School in Germany? It was nothing other than the reawakening of the poetry of the Middle Ages as that manifested itself in songs and pictures and buildings, in Art and Life. But this poetry had its origin in Christianity; it was a passion-flower which sprung from the blood of Christ." And Heine proceeds firstly, to define the essence of Christianity as he understood it, "in whose primary doctrine is contained a condemnation of all flesh; which not only gives to the spirit the control over the flesh but will destroy the flesh in order to exalt the spirit "; secondly, to describe the historical importance of this spirit of asceticism; and thirdly, to deduce from it all the characteristics of Mediæval art and poetry. Now that Mediævalism was a strand in the Romantic Revival, in the full sense of the term, in English as well as in French and German romanticism, no one will deny. Sir Walter Scott has been claimed as a source of the Oxford Movement and all that has followed from it. But it was certainly not the only strand, not the whole of that complex phenomenon. What is there of Mediævalism in the nature-poetry of Wordsworth, in the lyrical raptures with which Shelley sings, not of the past but of the future, or in Byron's poetry, who in the preface to *Childe Harold* is frankly contemptuous of the Middle Ages: " So much for chivalry. Burke need not have regretted that its days are over, though Marie Antoinette was quite as chaste as most of those in whose honour lances were shivered and knights unhorsed." Yet Byron, too, felt the power and sweetness of Dante. " Why, there is a gentleness in Dante beyond all gentleness when he is tender. Who *but* Dante could have introduced any ' gentleness ' at all into Hell? Is there any in Milton's? No—and Dante's heaven is all love and glory and majesty." Whether he realised it or not, Byron indicates here what was the deepest attraction of the Catholic Middle Ages, the wonderful tenderness which redeems its barbarities and austerities. But Byron is not a romantic in Heine's sense, yet when we speak of the Romantic Revival we think of Wordsworth and Byron and Shelley as well as of Scott and Coleridge. In the fuller sense of the word Goethe, Schiller, and Heine himself are romantics as well

as Tieck and the Schlegels; Rousseau as well as Chateau-
briand. Moreover, is it just to describe Mediæval
romance and lyric as essentially or entirely Christian, in
Heine's words "a passion-flower sprung from the blood
of Christ", in Sir Walter Raleigh's words "a Christian
literature, finding its background and inspiration in the
ideas to which the Christian Church gave currency"?
In a measure that is true, but in an equally large measure
it is not. What of the barbarous superstitions and warlike
spirit which seemed to Hurd the essence of Romance?
Is the cult of woman and love essentially Christian—are
*Aucassin and Nicolette, Tristram and Iseult, Lancelot* passion-
flowers which have sprung from the blood of Christ?

But if "romantic" be difficult to define, so is
"classical". If the former carry us back to the Middle
Ages, the latter points us to the Greeks and Romans, the
age of Pericles, the age of Augustus. Classical poetry, we
say, has some of the qualities we admire in the poetry of
Sophocles and of Virgil. And modern poets who have felt
the power of the ancients, and whose own bent of mind has
been towards definiteness of form, and a certain balance of
thought and feeling, have been tempted to choose themes
from ancient myth and legend and to essay antique forms—
Walter Savage Landor, Goethe after his first period of
*Sturm und Drang* was over, in *Iphigenie* and *Hermann und
Dorothea* and the *Roman Elegies*. But are such poems really
classical? The late Professor Vaughan, an enthusiastic
worshipper of Goethe, finds it " hard not to bear a grudge
against Goethe for giving a false direction to powers so
original as those of Schiller and, in our own literature, of
Arnold". Brandes, in like manner, contrasting both
Racine and Goethe with the Greeks, writes, " And yet

when in comparing the two Iphigenias I ask myself the
question: Which of the two, the Frenchman's or the
German's, more resembles the Greek? the answer I gave
myself was—The Frenchman's ".   In another sense than
Brandes has here in view I hope to suggest that Racine
*was* more truly classical than Goethe.   But again, are
the Greek and Latin poets all equally classical in the sense
in which I am using the word (trying to define it) to
describe poetry of a certain quality?   Homer, who so
delighted the Romantics, is, we feel, in some ways less
classical than Sophocles and Virgil.   "In Homer", says
Mr. Mackail in a recent essay, "this deep human sympathy is present as an inner life, but only, so to say, in
the germ.   In Greek poetry of the central and classical
period—the poetry which was concentrated in its utmost
brilliance at Athens—it was kept under severe control;
it was subordinated to an incomparably luminous but,
as those who have since resought the springs of Helicon
have often been inclined to think, a somewhat hard intelligence."   I quote this to emphasise that the "classical"
literature of Greece has a character that is not quite that
of the Homeric poems, and because the phrase "hard
intelligence" is worth bearing in mind when I come to
consider what are the qualities of a classical literature.
There is no greater romance in certain essential qualities
of romance than the *Odyssey*; and yet again Virgil in the
fourth book of the *Aeneid* is more romantic in another
way than Homer.   Dido is one of the saints of Mediæval
romance.   Euripides is more romantic than Sophocles.
I feel that, like Adeimantus and Glaucon, I am stating
the problem in so extreme a fashion that, in the part of
Socrates, I shall find it difficult to resolve.

Indeed one is tempted at times to cut the knot by resolving the problem into one of form alone; and thinking of poets like Goethe and Landor, Arnold and Heredia, to say that, in calling a modern poem classical, we mean that it has something of the definiteness and perfection of form which we admire in the work of Sophocles and Virgil and the great Greek sculptors (even when the work is not imitative of ancient forms), whereas the essence of Romantic art is that in it the spirit counts for more than the form, or rather gives to the form its peculiar indefinite charm and undeniable inequality, its tendency to be lyrical and rhapsodical. In the work of a romantic poet, like Wordsworth and Shelley, the poet's art is good or less good as the inspiration flags or is full, whereas a more classical poet, like Milton or Sir William Watson, can often disguise the failure of his inspiration. The manner goes on writing when the man, the poet is nodding.

Well, we *do* thus use the word " classical ", but I think we are quite conscious that this is a very relative use of the term. It is not entirely just to ancient poetry which often has the elusive, delicate charm—in Euripides, for example, in Virgil—we call romantic; and the romantic movement brought new beauties of form into poetry English and French. Moreover, we feel that, in calling the best ancient poetry, Sophocles' *Oedipus Tyrannus*, Virgil's *Aeneid*; the best tragedies of Corneille and Racine, *Cinna*, *Bérénice*, the comedies of Molière; I would add the essays of Addison and even the *Vanity of Human Wishes*, classical, we have more in view than beauty of form alone. It is quite certain that a mere regard for form does not make poetry classical. There is no clearer sign of literary decadence than a too curious attention to

S

form for its own sake, as with the Italian scholars of the fifteenth century " who ", Bacon tells us, " began to hunt more after words than matter, and more after the choiceness of the phrase, and the round and clear composition of the sentence, and the sweet falling of the clauses and the varying and illustration of their works with tropes and figures than after the weight of matter, worth of subject, soundness of argument, life of invention, and depth of judgement ". Weight of matter, worth of subject—this is the solidity which Goethe has in view when he contemplates classical art in Rome: " Wer sich mit Ernst hier umsieht und Augen hat zu sehen, muss solid werden, er muss einen Begriff von Solidität fassen, der ihm nie so lebendig war ". An essential condition of classical art and literature is, we feel, a balance of matter and form, a certain high degree of worth in both.

But what the history of literature and art seems to suggest is that this balance, this " Solidität ", this worth of matter and form has been attained at certain periods in a nation's life to a higher degree than at others; that it is not entirely a product of individual genius, but partly of social and intellectual conditions. This, as you are aware, is Brunetière's view, and in what I have to say I may seem to you to be repeating that great critic, but, if you will be patient with me, I hope to show that I am suggesting some modifications of his definition of " classical " literature and more particularly of his condemnation of romantic. In his chapter on *La Nationalisation de la Littérature* Brunetière traces the steps by which French literature became truly classical. Shaking off the remains of barbarism and coarseness, of pedantry, of preciosity, French literature finally, in the works of Pascal, Bossuet,

Boileau, Racine, Molière, became in form and content
*natural*. These founded and edified *l'école du naturel*.
In their work the essential of art is the *imitation of nature*.
What they admired in the ancients was the fidelity of this
imitation.   But art does not alone imitate, it perfects
nature;  and the means to this end is *a perpetual preoccupation with form or style*.   Moreover, the nature which
a classical artist imitates is not nature in all her aspects, her
aberrations and eccentricities, and minute details, the streaks
upon the tulip, but what nature reveals in herself " *de plus
général et de plus permanent* "   The classical artist
delights in

> What oft was thought but ne'er so well expressed.

The works of the great French writers are, Brunetière
claims, valid for all times and places,—are true, *i.e.* in what
they reveal, of men *universally*, not of Frenchmen only.
Yet, though thus universal classical literature is also
*national*. French literature in this age shows no longer
the influence of Spain and Italy; it is so national that it
cannot be fully appreciated by a foreigner.   Finally it is
*didactic, moral*.   " No great writer of this period separates
the idea of art from the idea of a definite social function or
purpose."   Natural, beautiful in form, national, edifying
—these according to Brunetière are the qualities that make
a literature *classical*.   It is little wonder that the romantic
literature which succeeded later to the decline of the
classical seems to him a deformation, even though he may
and does admit that among the romantic poets there may
have arisen more gifted individual singers.

Now I am not concerned to vindicate or dispute the
justice of the French critic's claim for the literature of

this period.  I rather suspect that the terms " natural ",
" human ", " beautiful ", " edifying " are more relative
than he suspects.  However it be with physical science,
in the region of human nature, which is the sphere of
literature and art, things may appear natural, human,
beautiful, wise, to one generation and civilisation which
do not appear equally so to another.  Not every French
critic is so sure of the permanent worth, the entire
" Solidität " of French literature of the seventeenth
century as Brunetière was.  Listen to Rénan.  " One
cannot refuse to the seventeenth century the specific
quality which makes a literature classical.  I mean
thereby a certain combination of perfection of form with
measure (I was going to say mediocrity) in the thought,
in virtue of which a literature becomes an ornament in the
memory of all and the perquisite of the schools; but the
limits proper to schools ought not to be imposed upon
the human spirit.  The fact that such a literature is the
obligatory instrument of education, and that there is no
one who must not say of it: *Puero mihi profuit olim*, is no
reason why we should attribute, to it exclusively, excellence
and beauty.  This exclusive character I cannot assign to
the writings of the seventeenth century in particular,
however durable and solid its qualities may be."  Having
pointed out, what Brunetière admits, that the literature of
this period has never appealed to other people so strongly
as to the French, he continues: " That literature is too
exclusively French; it will suffer, I fear, from the advent
of a criticism whose native country is the domain of man,
whose peculiarity is to have no exclusive preferences.
Its title of classical will not be disputed. . . . But that it
will remain in its entirety the exclusive reading of men of

taste, that the great minds of all times will continue to resort to it to console themselves, to obtain light upon their destiny, of that I doubt. We have passed beyond the condition of mind in which that literature was produced; we descry a thousand things that the most penetrating minds of the seventeenth century did not perceive; the supply of accurate knowledge on which they lived is to our eyes insufficient and inexact. It is difficult to believe that the favour of the reading public, the public which reads, not at the bidding of conscience, but from an intimate sense of need, will attach itself indefinitely to books in which there is little to learn on the problems that engage us, in which our moral and religious feelings are often wounded, and where we encounter at every step errors even while we admire the genius of those who commit them."

Nor am I entirely at one with Brunetière when, in another place, he affirms that a classical period can come but once in a nation's literature, at the moment when its language attains perfection and before the inevitable process of decay has set in. Brunetière was too much dominated by the organic conceptions of his century. After a certain stage of development has been reached, a language may change without necessarily improving or decaying. For certain purposes the English prose of the sixteenth century—or even late fifteenth,—" the splendid prose of Malory and Berners ", the prose of the English Bible, has never been surpassed. It is not true that Dryden " found English poetry brick and left it marble "; and if, as Sir George Trevelyan says, " the most agreeable English that has ever been written " is " the English of the middle-classes in the generation before the French

Revolution, which Johnson spoke always and wrote when
he was old ", we must not be robbed of our enjoyment of
the prose of Lamb and De Quincey and Newman and,
I will add, Carlyle.   Things are good in different ways.

Allowing all this, I would still maintain that Brunetière
does describe the main conditions under which a classical
literature has at different times appeared, and what are
its chief qualities.   It is the product of a nation and
a generation which has consciously achieved a definite
advance, moral, political, intellectual; and is filled with
the belief that its view of life is more natural, human,
universal, and wise than that from which it has escaped.
It has effected a synthesis which enables it to look round
on life with a sense of its wholeness, its unity in variety;
and the work of the artist is to give expression to that
consciousness, hence the solidity of his work and hence
too its definiteness, and in the hands of great artists its
beauty.   Literature at such a period is not personal—at
least in quite the same sense or to the same degree as it is,
say, in Rousseau or Byron or Carlyle or Ibsen, because
there is, as it were, a common consciousness throbbing in
the mind and heart of each individual representative of
the age, or member of the circle for which he writes, for
one must admit, and this is significant, that a classical
literature has generally been the product of a relatively
small society—Athens, Rome, Paris, London.   The work
of the classical artist is to give individual expression, the
beauty of form, to a body of common sentiments and
thoughts which he shares with his audience, thoughts and
views which have for his generation the validity of universal
truths.   His preoccupation with form is not, as with those
whom Bacon describes, due to disregard of weight of

matter and worth of subject, but to the fact that the matter is given to him by his age, has for him the weight and worth it possesses for his audience; and so we find critics stressing opposite things in classical literature. Matthew Arnold, trying to wean his countrymen from the luxuries of romance, dwells on " the all-importance of the subject matter, the necessity of accurate construction, the subordinate character of expression ", whereas Brunetière, in the same spirit, declares that substance is nothing, " c'est la forme qui est tout ". And they mean much the same thing.

A classical age, again, is an age of reason—good sense —not of rationalism which is reason dogmatising beyond the limits that its premises, the experience on which it rests, will sanction—but there is nothing of which such an age is so acutely conscious as that it has escaped from the weight of tradition into the free life of intelligence. But the individual is still controlled by the social consciousness which checks eccentricity, compels a regard for the mean, and so literature and art approximate at any rate to that balance of qualities which Brunetière describes: " A classic is a classic because in his work all the faculties find their legitimate function—without imagination overstepping reason, without logic impeding the flight of imagination, without sentiment encroaching on the rights of good sense, without good sense killing the warmth of sentiment, without the matter allowing itself to be despoiled of the persuasive authority it should borrow from the charm of form, and without the form ever usurping an interest which should belong only to the matter ".

I have not time now to justify this by an examination of the classical literature of a period, but must just point to three such epochs—the age of Pericles, when the defeat of the Persians had given Athens confidence, prestige, and hegemony, while at the same time she was absorbing and making her own the philosophical culture of Ionia, the rhetoric of the West.   Its great product was the Attic drama; and that Aeschylus and Sophocles reflected in different ways the best convictions of their age is at any rate suggested by Aristophanes' indignation with the disintegrating spirit of Euripides.   In Rome the classic age, I would suggest, extends through the later republic and reign of Augustus, from Cicero and Lucretius to Virgil and Horace,—writers conscious of having mastered and made their own the literary inheritance of Greece, but who are using these forms to express a spirit that is not Greek but Roman, inspired by the greatness and mission of Imperial Rome.   The third such age was the age of Louis XIV. in France, and that which was inaugurated by Dryden in this country, running closely parallel to one another and yet interestingly divergent, the idea of authority, for example, having for the French of the classical period a universal validity that it had not for Englishmen, to whom constitutional liberty and religious toleration were rather the achievements which gave them a right to look back on the past with a complacent sense of their own advance; with this difference also that our classical writers were conscious that there had been giants in the age which preceded their own.   No French critic— Malherbe, Boileau, or Bouhours—ever spoke of Ronsard and his generation with the respect which Dryden, sweeping Rymer aside, taught his age and successors to feel for Shakespeare and Jonson and Milton.

But I cannot attempt this afternoon to justify my

view of these ages as classical in the sense in which I have tried to define. Probably the Roman age was not classical in quite so full a measure as the Periclean age of reason and imagination, poetry and philosophy at Athens, or as " the age of reason " in Western Europe at the end of the seventeenth century, when the human mind recovering again the freedom of the Greeks, modern science was beginning its long march and—before the disillusionment which science had in store for human pride and hopes was yet revealed—men's minds were aware of nothing so much as the sense of liberation, the relief of escaping from a necessity of proving their

> Doctrine Orthodox,
> By Apostolick blows and knocks,—

the joy of sitting down in a cool hour to think the matter out.

Nor must I let myself be tempted into a digression on the subject of classical comedy which illustrates with shining clearness the character of a classical age. It is a classical comedy which Bergson has in view when he describes comedy as using ridicule to protect the common ideals of society; it is the classical artist who, as Mr. Belloc says, " takes for granted many data, common to himself and his hearers, both with regard to the material in which he works and with regard to the moral standard which he and they are equally supposed to accept ". Classical comedy finds its source of amusement in the weaknesses or eccentricities of individuals which make them unable to live up to the standards whose validity they do not deny, the hypocrisy by which they accommodate practice to sincere profession. The work of the romantic dramatist—Euripides, Ibsen, Shaw—is rather different. His aim is, seriously or by means of ridicule, to make his hearers aware that they no longer accept the standards to which they still proffer lip-service; the object of their criticism is not the frailty of human flesh and blood which will not let men live up to the standards they acknowledge, or at least do not seriously dispute, the eccentricities which make them push justifiable principles to extremes—Tartuffe, Alceste; it is rather the tendency of the human spirit to go on living in outworn formulæ, dealing solemnly with musical banks whose values it no longer really accepts.

Achievement, then, I suggest, is the note of a living, healthy, classical literature and art. It reflects the spirit of a self-confident society seeking in art and literature the expression of its ideals and convictions, and requiring of art the same attention to form, to correctness, which it seeks in manners and all the gestures of life. A weakness, indeed, of classical art is that its work may be controlled by a spirit of etiquette rather than the requirements of essentially artistic form. The enforcement of the Unities by the French Academy, the proscription of words which have been "sullied by passing through the mouth of the vulgar" are examples of what I mean. But the great defect of a classical period and art is, what the criticism of Rénan suggests, that it cannot endure. It represents a synthesis, a balance; and a synthesis effected by the human mind involves exclusions, sacrifices, which will sooner or later be realised; all balances in human affairs are precarious. A classical literature perishes in different ways. It gradually dries up. The forms which have established themselves are reproduced mechanically;

convictions become conventions.   Greek literature lived on in a remarkable way after the great age was over, and threw out some charming shoots, Middle-Comedy and the pastorals of Theocritus.   In the later epics of Apollonius it threw out a romantic shoot, for love is a perennially romantic motive; and Apollonius was to inspire Virgil— but that was not an immediately important development. No new and profound spirit quickened Greek poetry. The old forms became conventional and academic.

Again the classical synthesis may disintegrate, the fine balance of intellect and feeling, of form and matter, may give way to exaggeration of one or other.   So Brunetière describes " la déformation de l'idéal classique " in French literature of the eighteenth century.   Feeling was over-stressed, at the expense of good sense, by the sentimentalists, " c'est ici, dans les romans de Prévost que la sensibilité se déborde ".   Reason became dogmatic, ignoring the in-completeness of its premises, the experience on which it built, in the work of the Encyclopædists.   And, as regards form, the purification of the vocabulary became an im-poverishment, Voltaire condemning the extravagances of Corneille (as Dryden had in a mood of spleen criticised Shakespeare), Condorcet condemning Pascal's use of familiar and proverbial phrases.

But something may happen as this process of desiccation or disintegration goes on.   Disintegration may become violent disruption, because a fresh sap is beginning to rise in the veins of the human spirit, a wave of fresh thought and emotion is pouring over the nation or the world of which this or that nation is a conscious part. The minds of men become aware of what has been left out in the synthesis, the balance of which a classical art is the reflection.   The *spiritual*, or it may be the *secular*, side of man's nature has been repressed or ignored.   A new vision dawns on the imagination.   In some of its manifestations the new movement, and the literature which expresses it, will be sentimental and fanciful, a literature of *Sturm und Drang*; to some minds it will come, at some period at any rate, as almost entirely an artistic movement, a rejection of old forms, a delight in new experiments in vocabulary and metres ; but for its greatest minds it is a spiritual and philosophical movement also. At all times " Le romantisme " has been " tout traversé de frissons métaphysiques ".   But this spiritual quickening reacts on the form of literature, hence the qualities which distinguish the literature of such a movement from classical literature.   It lacks the confident clarity, the balanced humanism, the well-proportioned form, the finished correctness of the literature of a period which knows its own mind.   But it is shot through and through with new and strange beauties of thought and vision, of phrase and rhythm.   Language grows richer, for words become symbols, not labels, full of colour and suggestion as well as clear, definable meaning; and the rhythms of verse and prose grow more varied and subtle to express subtler if vaguer currents of thought and feeling.

That is the character of a romantic movement, and I think we can point to three such movements in the history of Western European literature.   The first is felt to some extent, but mainly as a disintegrating force in the tragedies of Euripides, more certainly, distinctly, positively, I think, in the dialogues of Plato.   I feel disposed, despite the diffidence with which I must speak before an audience in Cambridge, to claim Plato as the

first great Romantic; and if I feel like Socrates encounter-
ing a mighty wave, let me take shelter for a moment under
the undeniable fact that it is to Plato the greatest Romantics
have always turned to find philosophical expression for
their mood—Spenser, Wordsworth, Shelley, the German
romantic philosophers Schelling and Fichte.   Nor does
it invalidate my contention to urge that if ever there was
a classical prose it is the perfect prose of Plato, for it would
not be the first time in which a romantic movement was
generated in the very heart of a classical literature.   To
take a much lesser instance, Addison's classical essays on
the ballad of " Chevy Chase "—and he criticises from a
classical point of view, finds in the ballads qualities of
classical masterpieces—awakened a geni which was to
quicken the dormant spirit of romance.   It was Plato
who, despite his condemnation of the poets, effected that
interrelation of philosophy and poetry which has charac-
terised every great romantic movement.   Is there anything
that gives more of the romantic thrill than the myths of
the Cave, of Er, of the chariot of the soul in the *Phaedrus*?
Plato was the first great romantic because his thought,
his romantic conception of an ideal world behind the
visible, his " city laid up in heaven ", his daring deduction of all being and knowledge from the Idea of
Good, was the ferment which disintegrated the ancient
view of life, of man and his relation to the divine; and
working through the Stoics and the Neo-Platonics, helped
to beget the great romantic movement which we know as
the Christian religion, for the next great Romantic after
Plato is St. Paul.

Wilamowitz-Moellendorf's description of St. Paul's
irruption into Greek religious thought and Greek prose

seems to me a complete, at least an essential, description
of what I mean by a romantic movement, its spirit, and
the reaction of that spirit on the form, the vehicle,—an
effect at once disintegrating and revivifying.  I wish I
could quote it in full, but I must content myself with a
few sentences: " At last, at last some one speaks in Greek
from a fresh, inner experience of life; that is Paul's faith;
he is sure of the hope within him, and his ardent love
embraces humanity—a fresh life of the soul bubbles up
wherever he sets his foot. . . . For him all literature is a
plaything, he has no artistic vein, but all the higher must
we estimate the artistic effects which he all the same
achieves. . . . In the Hellenic world of conventional
form, smooth beauty, this absence of form in a style which
is yet quite adequate to the thoughts and feelings expressed,
has a quickening force.  What stylistic effect could
heighten the intimate charm of the Epistle to the Philip-
pians? . . . The whole of Greek classicist literature
stands hereby condemned that the imitation of the classics
was productive of new classics only in Latin,—in Cicero,
Horace, Virgil.  The Greek language, when it came
straight from the heart, had to be devoid of art, as it is
in Paul, in Epictetus, in Plotinus.  ' Dann ist auch das
vorbei.' "  There is much in these words relevant to my
theme.  Let me for the moment insist only on this that
they describe exactly, allowing for such reduction of the
scale as individually you may wish to make, the spirit in
which William Blake turned away from the technique of
art, in painting and poetry, when his " message " came
upon him, in which Wordsworth called upon poetry to
cast away " the bracelets and snuff-boxes and adulterous
trinkets " of poetic diction and return to her legitimate

home in the heart of men and the language which is
uttered by men under the actual pressure of passion, or at
least of passion recollected in tranquillity; for " poetry is
the image of man and nature, the breath and finer spirit
of all knowledge, the impassioned expression which is in
the countenance of all science ".

The effect of Christianity, this new romantic ferment,
on the subsequent history of literature is, of course, beyond
my scope, but I would just remind you of this.   The
new spirit would not adjust itself, despite the efforts of Pru-
dentius and others, to the traditional classical forms.   The
Christian temper found adequate poetic expression in the
Greek and Latin hymns of the Eastern and Western
Churches; and, ever since, the hymn has been the special
vehicle of Christian sentiment, accompanying every
spiritual revival.   Remember the great hymns in which
the troubled spirit of Germany found utterance in the
seventeenth century, the hymns which accompanied the
Wesleyan and Evangelical movements, and every subsequent revival.   I am not concerned for the moment
with the quality of the hymns.   Such a mood as we have
described, the romantic mood, tends to rhapsody, and a
hymn is rather a rhapsody of love or penitence or praise
or doctrinal confession than, like a lyric proper, the full
expression of an, perhaps complex, individual mood.
Religious lyrics, like those of Donne, Herbert, Crashaw,
and Vaughan, are not hymns.

The *third* great romantic movement, for I wish to
keep the *second* in reserve for a moment, is that from which
I started, the flame which Rousseau kindled and which
spread to Germany and England.   Dr. Johnson's attitude
illustrates admirably the spirit and the grounds of classical

resistance to such a movement.    Johnson's reading of the
history of English poetry is clear and definite.    After an age
of experiment beginning in the sixteenth century, which
produced great men but faulty artists, *e.g.* Shakespeare and
Milton, Dryden at last " found English poetry brick and
left it marble ", he gave us a poetic diction and a harmonious verse, which latter Pope perfected :—" Sir, a thousand
years may elapse before there shall appear another man
with a power of versification equal to that of Pope ".    To
Johnson accordingly efforts to revive the ballad were an
attempt to return to a mood of childhood;  " ' Chevy
Chase ' pleased the vulgar but did not satisfy the learned;
it did not fill a mind capable of thinking strongly " ;
Gray's imitation of the Greek ode issued in obscurity
and bombast;  and devout though Johnson was, the poetic
manipulation of religious or popular marvels and superstitions seemed to him unworthy of a reasonable age.
" Incredulus odi!    What I cannot for a moment believe
I cannot for a moment behold with interest or anxiety."
But the subject is at once too large and too familiar for me
to dwell upon, except just to point out this, that if less intense and fruitful than that described, it was more complex
and manysided.    It had its spiritual, its religious aspect in
the poetry of Blake and Wordsworth, perhaps of Shelley,
in the philosophy of Schelling and Fichte and Schleier-
macher, in the revival of mediæval Catholic feeling of
which I spoke at the outset.    It had the Antinomian
aspect, the note of rebellion, of expansion, of surrender
to impulse and passion on which Mr. Paul Elmer More
and Professor Babbitt have dwelt, in some phases of the
work of Blake and Shelley, and in what Goethe calls the
" dreadful negativity " of Byron.    It has its purely artistic

aspect, as in Keats's delight in new beauties of language
and harmony, though as you are aware he was not quite
content with this.   Its themes are as numerous as its
spirit is manifold—the worship of nature, the revival of
mediævalism, dreams of a golden age, a new Hellenism.

But instead of dwelling on this, I wish, if you will bear
with me a very little longer, because it is essential to my
argument, to turn back to my starting-point and ask what
was the significance of the mediæval element in the
romantic revival, or rather to ask what was the *differentia*
of mediæval romance?   Am I justified in claiming the
romantic literature of the twelfth and thirteenth centuries
as the *second* of the movements, as romantic not in virtue
of its themes Germanic, Celtic, Oriental, but because
of its spirit of revolt, of joyous emancipation?   Heine's
view, as I said, was inadequate as a description of the
Romantic Revival, apart from the German school which
gave so much trouble to Schiller and Goethe and evoked
the brief and final statement of the latter: " Classisch ist
das Gesunde, Romantisch das Kranke ".   The romantic
cult of Mediæval Catholicism was, after all, only a phase
of the spiritual element in the revolt, its reaction from the
temper of the *Aufklärung*, the bondage of the *secular*,
which led others to the worship of Humanity and Liberty
and Nature.   But Heine is equally or more misleading in
his description of Mediæval Romance, of the spirit of
mediæval poetry.   Are *Launcelot and Guinivere, Tristram
and Iseult, Aucassin and Nicolette* really passion-flowers
which have sprung from the blood of Christ?   " In Paradise
what have I to win? " cries Aucassin, " therein I seek
not to enter but only to have Nicolette, my sweet lady that
I love so well.   For into Paradise go none but such folk

T

as I shall tell thee now. Thither go these same old priests, and halt old men and marred, who all day and night cower continually before the altars and in the crypts; and such folk as wear old arrices and clouted frocks, and naked folk and shoeless, and covered with sores, perishing of hunger and of thirst, and of cold, and of little ease. These be they that go into Paradise, with them have I naught to make. But into Hell would I fain go; for into Hell fare the goodly clerks, and goodly knights that fall in tourneys and great wars, and stout men at arms, and all men noble. With these am I lief to go. And thither pass the sweet ladies and courteous that have two lovers, or three, and their lords also thereto. Thither goes the gold, and the silver, and the cloth of vair, and cloth of gris, and harpers, and poets, and the princes of this world. With these I would gladly go, let me but have with me Nicolette my sweetest lady." That is a strange flower to blossom from the blood of the cross, or from the pure worship of the Virgin. Heine, indeed, recognises that there are romances, or elements in romance, which are not Christian but pagan: "in them still rules the whole pre-Christian mode of thought and feeling, the raw power not yet softened into knighthood; there they stand like stone figures, the stubborn champions of the North, and the soft light and moral atmosphere of Christianity has not yet penetrated their iron mail". This is true enough, but it is not the whole truth or the most important one. That is this,—that the spirit of chivalry as it took shape in the love-lyrics of the Provençals and the Arthurian and other romances was itself a spirit of revolt, the revolt of the secular spirit of man against the long preoccupation with theological and ascetic ideals.

The important thing is not that the ideals of romance may be traceable to pagan sources, Teutonic, Celtic and Classical; the important thing is the new value, the new treatment they received. In romantic poetry the spirit of man found an outlet for feelings that Christianity condemned and strove to repress, for ideals which the Church might and did strive to annex and to modify, but which are essentially anti-Christian, the ideal of personal prowess and honour, the ideal of passionate love and devoted service, not of God, but of a woman. Romance was not, of course, heretical, it was not concerned with dogma—though one must not forget the connection of the Troubadours with the Albigensians, the part they took in ridiculing clerical teaching about Hell and Purgatory (of which there is perhaps an echo in *Aucassin and Nicolette*) —but the spirit of romance, the glorification of personal honour and passionate love, was not in truth compatible with Christian ethics. The Church had no place in its scheme of life for secular literature.[1] When Boccaccio

[1] " The literature of the first three centuries of the Church differs in this respect from all other literatures, that it is wholly theological and religious. The remark may be applied with almost equal accuracy to the centuries that immediately follow. And if to these we add the entire mediæval period, with all its complex life, we shall find the same statement substantially true. No doubt, in this latter period, some forms of secular thought emerge and find a more or less articulate utterance. But, speaking broadly and popularly, we may assert that the long succession of ages from the time of the New Testament to the Revival of Letters, if not absolutely restricted to theological modes of expression, is dominated throughout by a theological spirit. This is surely a very striking phenomenon Theological ideas are not so easily grasped as to form the natural clothing of man's thought, nor so comprehensive as to cover its entire field. Nor, if we survey the history of those other literatures

and Chaucer are afflicted with a fit of remorse their first thought is to burn *all* their secular writings. *Troilus and Criseyde* seems to us immoral in its whole treatment of love. To Chaucer as a romantic the only sin was Criseide's want of fidelity in love; as a Christian, *all* earthly love was a vanity:

---

which have most powerfully influenced mankind, shall we find any adequate parallel. The literatures of India, of Persia, of Islam, though springing from a religious source, and long confined within a religious sphere, include many other elements. Even the Scriptures of the Old Testament and Apocrypha display numerous features that are not wholly spiritual. They embrace history, law, politics, poetry, legend. How comes it, then, that for so immense a period Christian literature was so predominantly theological? " so Cruttwell in his *Literary History of Early Christianity*; and his answer is that it was due to " the transcendent power of the central Christian truth " and to " the inevitable reaction from the long and exclusive dominion of the secular intelligence ". Well, Romance, in the twelfth century, I suggest, despite its Christian assumptions and atmosphere, was a reaction from " the long and exclusive dominion " of the spiritual, a reaction which culminated in the Renaissance of the fifteenth century. But the spirit of the Renaissance was Italian, not French and Celtic; and the Renaissance found in ancient philosophy a rational justification of its secular interests. See Lecky, too, *History of European Morals*, where, after describing the anarchy and barbarism of the dark ages, he adds: " And yet this age was, in a certain sense, eminently religious. All literature had become sacred. Heresy of every kind was rapidly expiring. . . . The seventh century which, together with the eighth, forms the darkest period of the dark ages, is famous as having produced more saints than any other century except that of the martyrs." Romance was a symptom of the emancipation of the human spirit from barbarism to the cultivation of more refined ideals, from asceticism to the cultivation of more human ideals. Yet it may be—I do not have full enough knowledge to speak with confidence—that the romantic revolt of the twelfth and thirteenth centuries had, like that of the late eighteenth,

O yonge, freshe folkes, he or she,
In which that love up groweth with your age,
Repeyreth hoom from worldly vanitee,
And of your herte up casteth the visage
To thilke god that after his image
You made, and thinketh al nis but a fayre
This world that passeth, sone as floures fayre.

The Church, as I have said, made great efforts to conciliate
and control the spirit which it could not exorcise,—to
consecrate chivalry, to direct the spirit of love into devout
channels, hence the romance of the Grail, the idealisation
of Galahad over against the chivalrous knight *par excellence*,
Lancelot; hence also the transcendental love-poetry of
Guinicelli and Dante. But the other mood was the
stronger and the result is the dualism, apparent in the

---

its religious aspect also, the great emotional disturbance that we
associate with the name of St. Francis, the mysticism which, though
to some extent it penetrated Scholasticism, was more essentially a
revolt against the classical tendency of Scholasticism, its effort to
attain definition, ratiocination, " Solidität ". " Mysticism in the
West has always been a spirit of reform, generally of revolt " (Inge,
*Christian Mysticism*). The joyousness which, despite self-abnegation
and ascetic discipline, we associate with the life of St. Francis, is the
romantic mood, for " romantic melancholy ", on which stress is so
often laid, is but the shadow which waits on all high-wrought feeling,
whether as a sense of the fleetingness of joy, disillusionment, or the
sense of expectations and ideals unfulfilled.

" Joy was it in that dawn to be alive ", etc.

If I understand Mr. Chesterton aright, he does connect St. Francis
with the awakening of romance, " the romantic fairyland of the
Troubadours ", and does see in this a reaction of the spirit against
asceticism; but he claims that the secular spirit awoke purified as a
result of the disciplinary experience of Christian asceticism through
which it had passed.—*St. Francis of Assisi*, pp. 38-9.

verses I have read from Chaucer, which is so remarkable
in Petrarch.    For him Laura is, on the one hand, " the
flower of all perfection herself and the awakener of every
virtue in her lover.    Yet his love for Laura is a long and
weary aberration of the soul from her true goal which
is the Love of God."    As Sidney cries:

> Leave me, O Love, which reachest but to dust;
> And thou my mind, aspire to higher things; ·
> Grow rich in that which never taketh rust;
> Whatever fades, but fading pleasure brings.

It is common to assert that the mediæval ideal of love
owed much to the cult of the Virgin.    It has always
seemed to me at least a statement needing definition and
qualification.    The Church endeavoured (as the doctrine
of the Immaculate Conception ultimately proves) to
*distinguish* the Virgin from other women;  and there are
no coarser critics of women than some of the Fathers and
the clergy.    Read the prologue to the *Wife's of Bath's Tale*
and study the sources from which Chaucer draws.    The
influence, I suspect, was as much or more the other way.
The chivalrous love-poetry affected the tone of hymns to
the Virgin.    The mediæval cult of Woman owes less to
her who " came pale and a maiden and sister to sorrow ",
" a slave among slaves and rejected " than it owed,
through Ovid, to her who was:

> a blossom of flowering seas
> Clothed round with the world's desire as with raiment, and fair
>     as the foam,
> And fleeter than kindled fire, and a goddess, and mother of Rome.

The secular spirit of man reawoke in poetry not in the
fifteenth century, as Heine and others insist, but in the

twelfth.   Under the influence of the Classical Renaissance
it was further quickened, but the same tones are audible:

> Was this the face that launched a thousand ships
> And burned the topless towers of Ilium?

But, and this is the other side of the picture, the centuries
of romance, the twelfth and thirteenth, were just those
in which the Church built up for herself a complete, well-
articulated body of reasoned dogma in the work of the
schoolmen, of Thomas Aquinas; presented mankind with,
not only the claims of authority, and an appeal to the
heart and imagination, as a romantic, lyrical impulse and
ferment, but with a reasoned, comprehensive conception
of life.   The Church, as Signor Papini says, " represented
throughout the Middle Ages the classical spirit ".   But
for that spirit to create a classical literature there was
needed a more living medium than Latin, and none of the
vernaculars was quite ready.   But one was nearly so.
Dante is the classical poet of Catholic Christianity because
he, controlling and transmuting the romantic spirit which
he inherited from his Provençal progenitors, carried so
much of it as might be purified or transmuted into the
poetic expression of the reasoned and comprehensive,
Catholic view of life; and transcending the limits of the
lyric, even the great *canzone*, created one of the larger,
more comprehensive forms in which the classical spirit
delights, his great dramatic epic, the *Divina Commedia*.
Nowhere is the difference between the classical and the
romantic spirit seen more clearly than in Dante's treatment of love.   Aucassin would go to Hell to live with
Nicolette.   Dante meets two lovers, Paolo and Francesca,
who have thus gone to Hell, drawn thither by love, and

he has no illusions about their happiness: " While the one spirit thus spake the other so wept that I fainted with pity:

E caddi, come corpo morto cade.

He knows where all the romantic lovers, the saints of Love's Calendar, are. They are in Hell—Dido, Cleopatra, Helen, Achilles, Paris, Tristan—more than a thousand others:

Che la ragion sommettono al talento.

But the crucial test is Beatrice. Another classical poet before Dante had treated love as a motive in a poem intended to be a comprehensive picture of human virtue and life. " Dido ", says an historian of Latin literature, " blocks the advance of fate. . . . Aeneas's alliance with Dido was wrong. His interests were the interests of Rome. . . . Desertion of Dido becomes a duty: it cannot be judged—or at least understood—by standards of chivalry." In like manner, one might add, Titus is called on to part from Bérénice in Racine's beautiful play. But Virgil's chivalry, his poetic feeling, the romantic in Virgil, defeated his purpose. The world has declared for Dido against Aeneas and Rome. It was not so that Dante dealt with Beatrice. Instead of rejecting her and human love he sublimates them. She remains her whom he had loved in youth, but no word approaching earthly love ever falls from his lips or hers. She is always theology, divine wisdom whose inspiration is love, but love that is the fulfilment of the Law. For the romantic, Love; for the classic, Law—but in the end these are one.

One cannot speak, therefore, of a classical age at the end of the thirteenth century, producing an abundant classical literature, as in the Periclean age in Athens or the age of Louis XIV., but there was a classical mood, a classical spirit, a classical synthesis, of which Dante's poem is the great expression.  He speaks for Italy primarily, but for all Western Christendom also; and this is significant because if a classical age came again it could not, even Brunetière sees this, be confined to one people. It would have to be at least European and American.

But to sum up, what I have tried to bring out is this:

(1) That the word "classical"—like the word "heroic" applied to "heroic poetry"—has its full meaning only historically.  Classical literature is the literature of such a society as I have tried to describe, a generation conscious of achievement, advance, the attainment of a reasonable and comprehensive view of life and the attainment in language and artistic forms of a fitting medium for the expression of its mind.  It is thus quite a distinct thing from a literature which simply imitates the ancients, what one might call a "classicist" literature, following Wilamowitz, who calls the later Greek epic and other poetry "die griechische Literatur des Klassizismus".  The essential difference is this, that such a literature looks back.  The poet is consciously and deliberately endeavouring to revive old modes and old moods—Virgil in as far as he merely imitates Homer, Goethe in *Iphigenie* (though this is not the whole truth), Arnold, Swinburne in *Atalanta* and *Erechtheus*, Landor. These are genuine products of the romantic quest for new refinements.  The *differentia* of the true classic, Sophocles, Virgil in all that is greatest in his poem, Racine, Addison, is that he stands firmly on his own age, is consciously and proudly the mouthpiece of his own age of reason and enlightenment.  Racine's dramas are more truly classical

than Goethe's or Arnold's just because they express so entirely the spirit of the Frenchman of that age; and because their form is no mere imitation of the antique but a living form, the product of a conflict between the need of a living stage tradition for action, story, suspense, and the demand of cultured circles—represented by the Academy—for the beauty and regularity of ancient drama. Corneille and Racine completed a movement which began with Hardy when he realised that the classic plays of Garnier and the *Pléiade* could not live on the stage.

(2) When the word is not used in this historical sense it is applied in a merely relative and rather vague way to literature that seems to the critic to have the qualities of the great writers of such a period; "classical" art is that in which good sense, a comprehensive view of life, a balance of reason and feeling, of matter and form predominate. "Poetry in Goethe's view", says Hume Brown, "should deal with worthy subjects, and should be inspired by reason as well as by imagination. To achieve the highest effects it must be restrained by law; there must be precision of detail and harmony of all the parts and a latent logic even in its wildest flights." We in this country are familiar with that ideal from the criticism of Matthew Arnold—the all-importance of the subject, the necessity for construction, etc.—all very admirable, but not things to be obtained by any poet merely through sitting down in a cool hour to take thought; for a poet is the child of his age, and not every age is sure of itself, is convinced as to what are worthy subjects or what is a reasonable view of life. A classical age believes it knows, is convinced of the reasonableness and naturalness of many things, feels that it has achieved

an equilibrium between faith and reason, sense and feeling, matter and form. Time invariably proves that the balance was imperfect and precarious. But if we are to call the poetry of Goethe and Arnold "classical" it should, I think, not be because they cultivated Greek forms but because, by virtue of worth of substance and beauty of form, their work has in it the promise of endurance, *some* of the elements which every classical synthesis must include. And here perhaps we descry a possible reconciliation of classical and romantic. Some works that are the genuine product of such a period of ferment as I have described may, in virtue of some elements in them, some essential solidity and beauty, outlive the movement that begot them, while others that once sparkled as brightly remain like withered, if richly coloured, weeds, left by a tide that came in like a spring-flood but has receded now out of sight and out of hearing.

With the epithet "romantic" we must proceed even more tentatively though perhaps less relatively. The romantic mood is always with us. We are all romantics at times, even if it be only

When sleep comes to close each difficult day,

or when we are in love; and so there will at all times be more or less romantic poets and artists. But a romantic *movement* is a definite and justifiable phenomenon in the history of thought and literature and art. Classical and romantic—these are the systole and diastole of the human heart in history. They represent on the one hand our need of order, of synthesis, of a comprehensive yet definite, therefore *exclusive* as well as inclusive, ordering of thought and feeling and action; and on the other hand the inevitable finiteness of every human synthesis, the inevitable discovery that, in Carlyle's metaphor, our clothes no longer fit us, that the classical has become the conventional, that our spiritual aspirations are being starved, or that our secular impulses are " cribb'd, cabin'd, and confined "; and the heart and imagination bursts its cerements and reaches out, it may be with Faust after the joys of this world:

> Had I as many souls as there be stars,
> I'd give them all for Mephistophelis;

it may be with Rousseau and Wordsworth and Shelley after a " return to nature ", a freer, juster, kinder world:

> When love is an unerring light
> And joy its own security;

it may be after "a past that never was a present ", " the glory that was Greece ", for

> Greece and her foundations are
> Built below the tide of war,
> Based on the crystalline sea
> Of thought and its eternity;

or it may be the ages of faith, the Gothic Rose:

> The Middle Ages sleep in alabaster.
> A delicate fine sleep.  They never knew
> The irreparable Hell of that disaster,
> That broke with hammers Heaven's fragile blue.
> .    .    .    .    .    .    .    .
> All gone, it was too beautiful to die:
> It was too beautiful to live;  the world
> Ne'er rotted it with her slow-creeping hells:
> Men shall not see the vision crowned and pearled,
> When Jerusalem blossomed in the noon-tide bells.

But it is not the subject matter which in itself, at any time, makes poetry romantic.  It is not the fairies and magicians of Celtic literature, the heroisms of Germanic tradition, the marvels of Oriental tales which make romantic the poems of the Middle Ages, it is the use which was made of them.  To their original authors and audiences, Celtic, Germanic, and Eastern, we do not know how these stories appealed.  Marvellous, doubtless, but perhaps in the main quite credible.  It is the conscious contrast with reason that makes romance in the full sense.  It is not because it reflects the life and serious thought of the age that mediæval romance is interesting, but because it does not, but represents men's dreams. This is, I think, the very essence of the word " romantic " as we apply it to the literature of these great periods and great poets—this conscious contrast of what the heart and the imagination envisage and beckon us to follow, and reason, not the scientific reason which has thought out the matter and attained conviction, but reason in the sense of what the society in which a man lives deems reasonable.  Paul is a romantic Christian because he realises, as possibly few of his fellow-apostles did, the tremendous venture on which he has embarked; he knows that Christ crucified is "unto the Jews a stumbling-block, and unto the Greeks foolishness".  The romantic quality of the Mediæval Christian hymns resides in nothing so much as in the definite, matter-of-fact way in which dogmas are affirmed in sonorous language and the tremendous, reason-transcending character of the content of these dogmas.  To an earlier people the symbols of the Grail —the lance, the plate, the sword, the wounded Fisher-King—had, if I may believe Miss Weston, a definite

enough character in a fertilising ritual.   For the romantic
poets of the Middle Ages they were consciously mysterious,
inexplicable things which they wove into their expression
of ideals transcending all rational limits, ideals secular
and sacred, ideals of honour and love, of humility and
asceticism.    And in like manner at the romantic revival
there is a conscious transcendence of reason in Wordsworth's:

> sense sublime
> Of something far more deeply interfused,
> Whose dwelling is the light of setting suns,
> And the round ocean and the living air
> And the blue sky, and in the mind of man;

the romantic poet who revives mediæval chivalry or
catholicism knows that he is dreaming, though the dream
may have for him elements of perennial value.   If Shelley,
despite the ardour and music of his poetry, yet seems
sometimes hardly a romantic in the sense that Wordsworth and Coleridge and Keats and Morris are, it is not,
as Crabbe, because he is a realist but for the very opposite
reason because he has *no* grasp of reality, no clear definable
consciousness of the contrast between what is and what
he dreams of and desires, or, as far as he has it, can express
it only in musical lament.   The great romantic knows
that he lives by faith and not by reason.

1923.


**THE END**